Sherlock Holmes
and Conan Doyle Locations

Sherlock Holmes and Conan Doyle Locations

A Visitor's Guide

ALLAN FOSTER

McFarland & Company, Inc., Publishers
Jefferson, North Carolina, and London

LIBRARY OF CONGRESS CATALOGUING-IN-PUBLICATION DATA

Foster, Allan, 1950–
Sherlock Holmes and Conan Doyle locations : a visitor's guide /
Allan Foster.
p.   cm.
Includes bibliographical references and index.

ISBN 978-0-7864-4617-9
softcover : 50# alkaline paper ∞

1. Doyle [sic], Arthur Conan, 1859–1930 — Homes and haunts —
Scotland.   2. Doyle [sic], Arthur Conan, 1859–1930 — Homes and
haunts — England.   3. Holmes, Sherlock (Fictitious character)
4. Literary landmarks — Scotland — Guidebooks.   5. Literary
landmarks — England — Guidebooks.   6. Authors, English — Homes
and haunts — Scotland.   7. Authors, English — Homes and haunts —
England.   I. Title.
PR4623.F67   2011   823'.8 — dc22   2011000092

BRITISH LIBRARY CATALOGUING DATA ARE AVAILABLE

On the cover: Edinburgh, Scotland at dusk (Shutterstock);
(inset) Sir Arthur Conan Doyle, 1900 (Photos.com)

Manufactured in the United States of America

*McFarland & Company, Inc., Publishers
Box 611, Jefferson, North Carolina 28640
www.mcfarlandpub.com*

For my mother, Cissie,
granddaughter of a hansom cabbie

Table of Contents

Acknowledgments

There is no doubt in my mind as to whom I owe the greatest debt. As always, it is to my wife Chris. Also the invaluable help of Conan "Doylean" scholars Phillip Bergem and Brian Pugh was crucial to the end result. Others I should like to thank are Harry Winslow, Jason Patient, Geoff Apps, Pinkerton's Detective Agency, Ali Bowden and Edinburgh UNESCO City of Literature, Sarah Pearson and the Hunterian Museum at the Royal College of Surgeons of England, Kent Police Museum, Maidstone Museum, John Cavers, Glasgow's Mitchell Library, Maureen Still, Melissa McDermott, Richard McDermott, Hazel and John Sant, Lucy Foster, Chloe Foster, Jack Foster, Kit Foster, Rob Muskett, Helen Brown, the Edinburgh Room of Edinburgh's Central Library, the University of Edinburgh, Alan Doak and Waverley Excursions, the Spa Valley Railway, Jean Wakeham, Beaulieu Abbey, Brian Tapp, Caroline White and the Hindhead Together Partnership, the Victorian Society, Jenny Macintosh and Dunedin School, Patrick McFall and Napier University, Alan Wilson and Max Inanaga.

He knows from long experience what to expect: the striking young woman will ask him when he is going to write another Sherlock Holmes story, and did he really die at the Reichenbach Falls, and perhaps it would be better if the consulting detective were to marry, and how did he think up such an idea in the first place? And sometimes he answers with the weariness of a man wearing five overcoats, and sometimes he manages a faint smile and replies,

"Your question, young lady, reminds me why I had the good sense to drop him over the Falls in the first place."

from *Arthur & George* (2005) by Julian Barnes

Introduction

"Personally, I'd walk a mile in tight boots just to read his letters to the milkman."

Stephen Fry

My first introduction to the works of Sir Arthur Conan Doyle was, fittingly, through a criminal act. My older cousin (who shall remain nameless) worked as a porter in a well-known Edinburgh bookshop in the early 1960s when I was around thirteen or fourteen years old. Occasionally my cousin purloined the odd book, and most Saturday mornings he would pay a visit to our house. This particular morning he waited until the elders had left the room, slipped his hand inside his trench coat (he was going through a crime-fiction phase), pulled out a pristine paperback, and dropped it into my lap. "Read this, kid," he remarked through a cloud of cigarette smoke. "It'll put hairs on your chest."

The cover, which I remember clearly to this day, had a picture of a dinosaur, its jaws dripping with blood as cowering little men in pith helmets peered at it through tropical undergrowth. *The Lost World*, by Sir Arthur Conan Doyle, had made its illicit entrance into my teenage life. That night I read it voraciously in bed, my pillow drenched in adrenaline. By the end of the last chapter I had become a dedicated fan with faint hair follicles emerging from my chest. So began my boyhood fascination with all things Conan Doyle.

At school I read Shakespeare, Kipling, Stevenson and George Eliot, but Conan Doyle never reached the heights of their reverence.

He never made it into the same league as the giants of English literature, although it was not for the want of trying. What Conan Doyle wrote best was mass-market fiction; this, however, does not diminish his genius; if anything, it elevates him to one of the world's greatest storytellers, creator of the two most famous fictional characters on the planet: Doctor Watson and Sherlock Holmes. He was the master of the short story and one of the main catalysts for what evolved into the Golden Age of detective fiction, becoming father and mentor to those who followed in his mass-market wake, including E. C. Bentley, Agatha Christie, Dorothy L. Sayers, Margery Allingham, Ngaio Marsh, and John Dickson Carr.

"For strange effects and extraordinary combinations," he once wrote, "we must go to life itself, which is always far more daring than any effort of the imagination." Using this maxim I've tried to locate and recapture in this book numerous scenes and incidents from Conan Doyle's and Sherlock Holmes's fascinating lives, using — where possible — Conan Doyle's own words. It is, therefore, a book of signposts, directing you through the highways, byways and crossroads of their lives. The book is arranged geographically by region from the Highlands of Scotland to the southern coast of England, opening up the factual and fictional landscapes of Conan Doyle and Sherlock Holmes in an easy to use and easy to read way, with helpful cross-references, illustrations, further-reading lists and essential information on birth and burial places, childhood and former homes, walks and trails, museum exhibits, archives and specialist libraries, literary inspirations, and sites with a literary connection. The Edinburgh of Conan Doyle's youth has also been explored in considerable depth; in the past it was never given the credit it deserved for nurturing the seeds of his powers of deduction. Appendices provide further information on the life and works of Sir Arthur Conan Doyle, and include a chronology, information on his residences, a genealogy and selected bibliography.

The journey is a spellbinding experience, one I hope you will enjoy as much as I did when researching and writing it. The number of books that have already been written about Conan Doyle and his writings is extraordinarily vast, and there seems no end in sight; they just keep coming. By adding another to that long list, I can only hope that the reader will find in it something that is new and that goes some way towards a better understanding of the man and his literary creations.

EDINBURGH

Greenside

Picardy Place

Site of the Sherlock Holmes statue and site of Conan Doyle's birth

> "I was born on May 22, 1859, at Picardy Place, Edinburgh, so named because in the old days a colony of French Huguenots had settled there..." — Arthur Conan Doyle, *Memories and Adventures* (1924)

All evidence of Conan Doyle's birthplace at 11 Picardy Place was obliterated in 1969, when the entire south side of the street was demolished to make way for a major traffic junction. Take a walk today along what's left of the street, now one of the city's ugliest and noisiest locales, and the hansom cabs, gaslit streets and grubby street urchins of Conan Doyle's era seem as remote as Mars. Born of Irish-Catholic parentage, he was the third of ten children of Mary Foley and Charles Doyle, an assistant surveyor. His sister Annette was also born at Picardy Place in 1856, followed in 1858 by his sister Catherine who died of hydrocephalus (commonly known as "water on the brain") when she was six months old. By 1861 Mary's mother and sister had also moved into Picardy Place. In cramped and impoverished conditions, and with a husband sinking into alcoholism, the family moved a few miles along the coast to the Edinburgh suburb of Portobello in 1862.

A statue to Sherlock Holmes was erected close to Conan Doyle's birth site in Picardy Place in 1991 by the Federation of Master Builders. It was sculpted and cast by Gerald Ogilvie Laing at Kinkell Castle in Sutherland, and funding was raised by a variety of means including an amateur boxing match which took

The Sherlock Holmes statue, Picardy Place (Ali Bowden).

place in a pub. It's ironic that a statue celebrating Conan Doyle's birthplace is of Sherlock Holmes and not the man who brought him into existence; a supreme example of a creation overshadowing its creator.

FURTHER INFORMATION: Picardy Place is so called because it was built on the site of the village of Picardy formed by French Calvinist Protestants (also known as Huguenots) from the province of that name. They came to Edinburgh after the revocation of the Edict of Nantes in 1685, which effectively made Protestantism illegal in France, creating a mass exodus of refugees. Opposite the Sherlock Holmes statue stands The Conan Doyle pub.

SEE ALSO: St. Mary's Cathedral (p. 4).

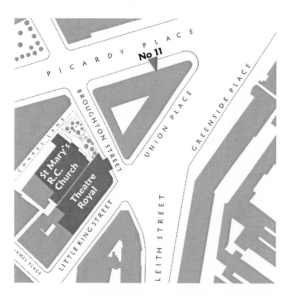

Greenside, around the time of Conan Doyle's birth in the 1850s. The island of buildings where 11 Picardy Place once stood was demolished in 1969 (Geoff Apps).

61 York Place
St. Mary's Cathedral

Where Conan Doyle was baptized and his parents were married

Charles Doyle and Mary Foley were married at St. Mary's on 31 July 1855. Their first child, Annette, born on 22 July 1856, was also baptized here, as was their second daughter, Catherine, born 22 April 1858. Then followed their first son, born on 22 May 1859 and baptized Arthur Ignatius Conan on 24 May 1859. His name signified not only his heritage, but was also suggestive of resilience and spirit. Arthur was from the legendary king, and Ignatius from the Bishop of Antioch, St. Ignatius, and commemorating the saint's day on which his parents were married. Conan was from his paternal grandmother, Marianne Conan. Situated just a few minutes from the site of Conan Doyle's birth at 11 Picardy Place, St. Mary's was the first new Roman Catholic chapel to be consecrated in Edinburgh since the Reformation. Built in 1813 by James Gillespie Graham (1776–1855), it was elevated to cathedral status in 1878. Nothing much remains of the original chapel, its structure having been altered considerably over the years. Inside it has an impressive roof

and above the sanctuary arch can be seen a painting of the *Coronation of the Blessed Virgin Mary as Queen of Heaven* by the Belgian painter, Louis Beyart.

According to Phillip Bergem in his *The Family and Residences of Arthur Conan Doyle* (2007), Conan Doyle was baptized into one more religious organization:

> The Church of Jesus Christ of Latter-day Saints (LDS), commonly known as the Mormons, believes strongly that spiritual life continues after death.... The LDS Church has a central belief that Christian baptism can occur and family unity can be preserved after death when covenants and ordinances are made in temples on behalf of one's ancestors. It is also believed that some deceased, not necessarily ancestors of Church members, can be baptised.... The names extraction program was an activity conducted by the Church that involved completing the LDS ordinances of baptism, endowment and sealing for all people covered by a set of church records (e.g. a church's baptism register). The bulk of the names in the LDS International Genealogical Index were generated in this manner.... In the early 1980s some of the records of St. Mary's Cathedral in Edinburgh were processed through the names extraction programme. As a result, Arthur Conan Doyle became baptised into the Church of Latter-day Saints.

Those in the spirit world are free to reject these offerings, but from the Mormon's point of view, they were at least given the choice. Considering Conan Doyle's inaccurate and hostile treatment of the Mormons in *A Study in Scarlet* (1887), it's ironic he was entered into the names extraction program in the first place; but as he was never high on their list of favorite people, maybe the Mormons were having the last laugh.

SEE ALSO: Picardy Place, Ward, Lock & Company (p. 3, 92).

Liberton
Nether Liberton Lane
Liberton Bank House

Former home of Mary Burton and where Conan Doyle lived from 1866–68

Mary Burton was an educationalist who campaigned rigorously throughout her life for social, educational and political reform. An

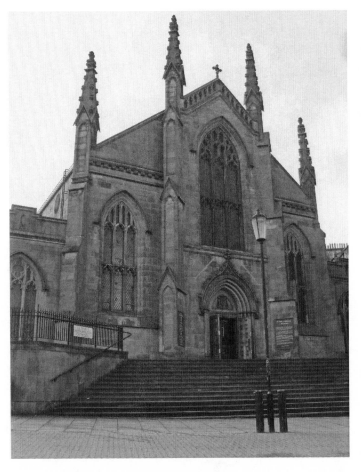

St. Mary's Cathedral.

side, had a large garden, and was the perfect place to heal the scars of parental distress. It was here young Arthur befriended Willie Burton, Mary Burton's nephew, who became a life-long friend. Conan Doyle resided at Liberton Bank from 1866 to 1868, attending school at nearby Newington Academy. Afterwards he returned to the family home which was now in Sciennes Hill Place, about a mile away from Liberton Bank, and back into the arms of his mother.

Up until just a few years ago the fate of Liberton Bank was hanging in the balance and was threatened with demolition to make way for a McDonald's fast-food outlet. A proposal described by Doylean scholar, Owen Dudley Edwards, as "an effort to sell Scotland's cultural past for a hamburger." Fortunately for literary history it was eventually gifted by the owners to a conservation trust who refurbished the building for Dunedin School, a small independent school for children with behavioral problems and learning difficulties who were previously based in a nearby scout hut. The downside to the development deal was that an enormous two-story medical center, named after Conan Doyle, was built over the large front garden of the house. Against the odds, however, Liberton Bank House has survived, and is now a curious and solitary oddity on the edge of a huge shopping mall car park—a compromise it has learned to live with.

FURTHER INFORMATION: Liberton Bank House is located at the western edge of Cameron Toll shopping center car park which is accessed from Lady Road. The house is not open to the public but can be viewed clearly from the shopping center car park. Also in full view is a tree stump sculpted into the image of the Hound of the Baskervilles, the only visible

ardent campaigner for women's rights, she was once described as "a unique example of the Victorian woman on the warpath." In 1844 she left the family home at Craig House and moved into Liberton Bank with her mother. She was a close friend of Mary Doyle, whom she probably met through the Philosophical Institution, an Edinburgh literary and debating society of which they were both members. Such was their friendship that Mary Doyle named her baby daughter—whose birth certificate reveals she was born at Liberton Bank in 1866—Caroline Mary Burton Doyle. When Arthur, her third born, was around seven or eight years old his mother sent him to live with Mary Burton to distance him from the trauma of living with an alcoholic father. Located on the southeast edge of the city, two miles from the center, Liberton Bank was surrounded by open country-

Liberton Bank House —now home to Dunedin School.

reminder of Conan Doyle. The ancient sycamore tree that stood in the garden had to be felled because it was unsafe; but as a tribute to Sherlock Holmes, a violin was made from its wood and it is used to teach music to the school's children. Edinburgh's Heriot-Watt University Management and Museum and Archive buildings (Riccarton Campus) are both named in Mary Burton's honor for her role in persuading its forerunner, the Watt Institution and School of Fine Arts to open its classes to female students.

SEE ALSO: William Burton (p. 6), Newington Academy (p. 9), Sciennes Hill Place (p. 8).

Craiglockhart

Craighouse Road
Craig House

Former Home of William Burton (1856–99),
*   engineer, photographer and childhood friend*
*   of Conan Doyle*

"William Burton's overall contributions to modern Japan are beyond measure but he remains a figure more revered in his adopted homeland than here in Scotland."— Jenny Rees, Napier University, Edinburgh

William Burton was the son of the historian and economist, John Hill Burton (1809–81), who lived at Craig House, a large rambling Victorian mansion in the Craiglockhart district of the city. In 1855 Burton married his second wife, Katherine Innes, daughter of the Scottish antiquary, Cosmo Innes, and after whom Conan Doyle's mother named her second son, Innes, born in 1873. The Burtons had four children, the eldest of whom was William Kinninmond Burton. The young Conan Doyle probably

A tree stump sculpted in the image of the Hound of the Baskervilles in the garden of Liberton Bank House.

met Willie Burton for the first time when he staying at Liberton Bank, the cottage of Willie's aunt Mary. It was here the two boys explored the countryside, fished in the Braid Burn, and cemented a lifelong friendship.

In 1873 Willie became apprenticed to a local engineering company and later moved to London where he went into an engineering partnership with his uncle Cosmo. He became an enthusiastic exponent of photography, an obsession he passed on to his friend Arthur. In 1879 the Burtons moved to Morton House, and a nearby tower

William Burton in kimono

called the Belvedere was converted into a workshop and photographic laboratory. A place Conan Doyle probably came to know well. Willie joined the Edinburgh Photographic Society and began contributing articles to photographic journals. Later he recommended Conan Doyle's writing talents to the British Journal of Photography, a periodical he began contributing essays to regularly.

In 1887 Willie was appointed First Professor of Sanitary Engineering at the Imperial University of Tokyo, and later was influential in developing water and sewage works throughout Japan. Poor quality water and cholera was a constant threat for most Japanese cities as human sewage was used to fertilize the rice fields. Rain then washed it into the rivers where it entered the water supply. Willie Burton effectively modernized a medieval system by improving filtration techniques and building reservoirs to store fresh water, and in doing so saved thousands of lives. His book *The Water Supply of Towns* became essential reading for young engineers in Britain and Japan. He also designed a 12-story brick pagoda in Tokyo called Ryounkaku (cloud surpassing pavilion) that became Japan's tallest building. Unfortunately the building fell victim to an earthquake in 1923

and had to be demolished. An enthusiastic observer of Japanese life, Burton's photography skills not only contributed to his engineering work, but were an important part in documenting its culture and were instrumental in introducing modern photography to Japan.

He married a Japanese girl with whom he had one daughter. He died young, in his early forties, from a liver infection. His tomb in Tokyo's Aoyama Cemetery is still visited annually by devotees who lay floral tributes and sing Scottish folk songs around his grave. His obituary in the British Journal of Photography described him as "a perfect type of painstaking and experimental photographer, with a happy gift of being able to transmit his knowledge to others." Conan Doyle later dedicated *The Firm of Girdlestone* to him; and Willie was no doubt an inspiration for the Sherlock Holmes story "The Adventure of the Engineer's Thumb" and the Anglo-Jap in "Jelland's Voyage," a short story from *Tales of Pirates and Blue Water*.

FURTHER INFORMATION: Shortly after the departure of the Burtons from Craig House in 1879, the house and estate were acquired by the Royal Edinburgh Asylum. It reopened as a Craig House Hospital in 1894. Since 1994 it has been a campus of Napier University. On 9 Sep-

The unveiling ceremony of William Burton's memorial stone bench at Craig House in 2009 commemorating the 110th anniversary of his death. In the foreground William Burton's great-great grandson, Kevin Masayama Kmetz, plays the Tsugaru-Shamisen, a three-stringed Japanese lute (Alan Wilson).

tember 2006 a memorial stone to William Burton was erected beside Craig House commemorating the 150th anniversary of his birth. On 12 September 2009 a stone bench was unveiled in the garden commemorating the 110th anniversary of his death. The latter-day home of the Burtons was Morton House, which lies approximately seven miles south of the center of Edinburgh and one mile north of the Pentlands Hills. Located between Frogston Road West and the City Bypass.

FURTHER READING: W. K. Burton, *The Water Supply of Towns and the Construction of Waterworks* (London, UK: Crosby Lockwood & Son, 1898); *Photographic Optics: A Text Book for the Professional and the Amateur* (Ann Arbor: Uni-

versity of Michigan Library, 2009), *The Processes of Pure Photography* (Whitefish, MT: Kessinger, 2007). J. M. Gibson and R. L. Green, "Trial of Burton's Emulsion Process" in *Essays on Photography* (London, UK: Secker & Warburg, 1982).

SEE ALSO: Liberton Bank House (p. 4), Robert Louis Stevenson (p. 27).

Sciennes

3 Sciennes Hill Place
Former childhood home of Arthur Conan Doyle

"The blows were almost simultaneous — a savage swing which whistled past Montgomery's ear, and a straight drive which took the working man on the chin. Luck was with the assistant. That single whizzing uppercut, and the way in which it was delivered, warned him that he had a formidable man to deal with. But if he had underrated his antagonist, his antagonist had also underrated him, and had laid himself open to a fatal blow... There he lay with his bandy legs drawn up and his hands thrown abroad, the blood trickling over the surgery tiles." — Conan Doyle, "The Croxley Master — A Great Tale of the Prize Ring" (*Strand Magazine*, 1899)

Sciennes Hill Place — a class divided.

In 1864 the Doyle family moved from Tower Bank House, Portobello, to Sciennes Hill Place — a sombre, dead end street on the southern edge of the city. But to a "rough" little boy, eager for a fight, as Conan Doyle described himself, it was one of the early battlefields of life where many a bloody street feud was fought. Sciennes Hill Place was unfortunate in its social division. One side of the street was dreary, working-class tenement flats, while the other side consisted of more elegant villas — a situation adults can live with but to young boys with a chip on their shoulder it was a war zone.

Conan Doyle always fancied himself as a fighter in his youth, never shying away from a fistfight, and "rejoicing in battle." He once fought a memorable fight in the garden of one of the villas with himself representing "the poorer boys" and his opponent representing "the richer boys" — a stalemate contest that resulted in a black eye for each contestant.

FURTHER INFORMATION: Sciennes (pronounced sheens) is a corruption of Sienna, derived from St. Catherine of Sienna, to whom was dedicated a convent erected in the area around 1514. Nearby in Sciennes House Place, once the residence of philosopher and historian Adam Ferguson, a plaque on the restored Sciennes Hill House commemorates the only meeting of Walter Scott and Robert Burns in 1786–7.

Newington

8 Salisbury Place

Site of Newington Academy, former school of Arthur Conan Doyle

"From the age of seven to nine I suffered under [a] pockmarked, one-eyed rascal who might have stepped from the pages of Dickens." — Conan Doyle, recalling his tyrannical schoolmaster, *Memories and Adventures* (1924)

In the fall of 1866 seven-year-old Arthur attended Newington Academy, a short walk from his home at Liberton Bank, where he underwent "a thorough education in the elementary parts of the Classics." During his time there he was taught French by Eugene Chantrelle, a former French medical student turned language teacher, who seduced a fifteen-year-old pupil, one Elizabeth Dryer. She became pregnant and Chantrelle married her, but their relationship was fiery to say the least. He repeatedly beat her, on one occasion putting her jaw out of alignment, and once threatened her with a gun. He also threatened to poison her "so that not even the Edinburgh University faculty [sic] could detect his work." And this is exactly what he did. In October 1877 he insured his wife for £1,000, and a few months later poisoned her with raw opium, a drug that couldn't be detected in the body.

Chantrelle maintained she had died from gas inhalation, and pointed out a defective pipe in the bedroom where she died. The doctor who attended his unconscious wife shortly before her death seemed certain that gas poisoning was the cause. There then arrived on the scene two men Conan Doyle would acquaint himself with in the very near future — forensic experts Dr. Joseph Bell and Sir Henry Littlejohn. They immediately detected brown vomit stains on Elizabeth Chantrelle's pillow and night-gown, the analysis of which found traces of opium, and combined with the fact that Chantrelle had recently purchased numerous doses of opium; from a local chemist, he was brought to trial for murder.

The jury reached their verdict of guilty swiftly, and on 31 May 1878, Chantrelle mounted the scaffold. Z. M. Hamilton, a witness at the execution, recalled Chantrelle's last words: "The morning of the execution Chantrelle appeared on the scaffold beautifully dressed and smoking an expensive cigar. Dr. Littlejohn was there in accordance with his duty. Just before being pinioned, Chantrelle took of his hat, took a last puff on his cigar, and waving his hand to the police physician, cried out, 'Bye-bye, Littlejohn. Don't forget to give my compliments to Joe Bell. You both did a good job in bringing me to the scaffold.'"

SEE ALSO: Joseph Bell, Stonyhurst (pp. 12, 15, 21, 26, 31, 35–6, 63).

34-42 South Clerk Street

Site of Livingston Mission Hall where Conan Doyle campaigned for parliament in 1900

"It is no light matter to change the vote of a Scotsman, and many of them would as soon think of changing their religion." — Arthur Conan Doyle

In 1886 William Gladstone's Liberal Party joined forces with the Irish Nationalists and overturned the minority Conservative government of Lord Salisbury, making Gladstone Prime Minister for the fourth time. His success, however, was short-lived and collapsed after only a few months due to the introduction of his Home Rule Bill for Ireland. The issue split the Liberal Party and a breakaway group formed the Liberal Unionist Party of which Conan Doyle became an enthusiastic supporter. It eventually led to him standing in the 1900 election as their candidate for Central Edinburgh.

Conan Doyle knew that being a famous author and the creator of Sherlock Holmes didn't count for much in the political sparring matches of a heated and often hostile election campaign. He described it as "a vile business," with the art of heckling taken to extremes by the Scottish voter, who was a particularly hard nut to crack. Tough as it was, however, Conan Doyle was never one to run from fight; and although he had been offered safe seats, he chose to go up against the Radical Party's stronghold of Central Edinburgh.

He made speeches on street corners and in crowded meeting halls, any pedestal he could find to get across his policies, often amidst rowdy and often riotous crowds. One such evening meeting took place in the packed hall of the Livingston Mission towards the end of his campaign. Hecklers bellowed and the police stood in readiness on the sidelines. "We want Sherlock Holmes" the crowd roared at Conan Doyle, and out of the crowd his real-life counterpart, Dr. Joseph Bell, mounted the stage. Now in his sixties, Bell commented, "If Conan Doyle does half as well in Parliament as he did in the Royal Edinburgh Infirmary, he will make an unforgettable impression on English politics," to which the crowd roared out more applause.

On the eve of the polls, a bigoted poster campaign was started condemning Conan Doyle's Catholicism (a faith which paradoxically he had rejected in his youth) branding him as "a Papist conspirator, a Jesuit emissary, and a Subverter of the Protestant Faith." But the real issue for the electors, according to Conan Doyle, was not Ireland or papist conspiracies, but the continuation and victory of the Boer War; and this is

what he pressed home to the electorate. Dedicated as he was to this cause, it overshadowed immediate concerns that were happening on the doorstep of the Edinburgh voter, and ultimately lost him the election. He did, however, reduce the Liberal majority by 1,500 votes and lost the election by only 569 votes.

SEE ALSO: Joseph Bell, Hawick (pp. 12, 15, 21, 26, 31, 35–6, 40).

The Southside
Old College
Former location of the University of Edinburgh Medical Faculty where Conan Doyle studied medicine

"I was always one of the ruck, neither lingering nor gaining — a sixty-per-cent man at examinations." — Arthur Conan Doyle, *Memories and Adventures* (1924)

Conan Doyle entered Edinburgh University's Medical Faculty in October 1876, graduating

Conan Doyle in graduation robes, 1881.

in 1881. Although he was born and studied in the city, he never had any great love for its university. In his 1884 novel, *The Firm of Girdlestone*, he commented that "Edinburgh University may call herself, with grim jocoseness, the 'alma mater' of her students, but if she is to be at all, she is one of a very stoic and Spartan cast, who conceals her maternal affection with remarkable success. The only signs of interest she ever deigns to evince towards her alumni are upon those not infrequent occasions when guineas are to be demanded from them." Harsh words, but he did have an axe to grind. After passing the entrance examinations the university awarded him a bursary of £40 — a sum which would have been a great financial boost to him as a struggling student. Unfortunately, the university had awarded the bursary in error as it was only available for arts students, and he had to make do with an apology and £7 compensation.

In the mid 1870s the Faculty of Medicine had around 1,000 students who all began, recorded Conan Doyle, "the long weary grind at botany, chemistry, anatomy, physiology, and a whole list of compulsory subjects, many of which have a very indirect bearing upon the art of curing." Edinburgh, however, was not Oxford or Cambridge. It had none of the collegiate activity of the English university. There were no halls of residence. Students paid fees directly to lecturers and examinations were challenging, requiring much skill and effort, resulting in a pass rate of around 60 percent.

In the *The Firm of Girdlestone* Conan Doyle sums up "the merits and faults" of the "Scotch system" through the eyes of his own personal experience:

> There is symbolism in the very look of her, square and massive, grim and grey, with never a pillar or carving to break the dead monotony of the great stone walls. She is learned, she is practical, and she is useful. There is little sentiment or romance in her composition, however, and in this she does but conform to the instincts of the nation of which she is the youngest but the most flourishing teacher.
>
> A lad coming up to an English University finds himself in an enlarged and enlightened public school. If he has passed through Harrow and Eton there is no very abrupt transition between the life which he has led in the sixth form and that which he finds awaiting him on the banks of the Cam and the Isis. Certain rooms are found for him which have been inhabited by generations of students in the past, and will be by as many in the future. His religion is cared for, and he is expected to put in an appearance at hall and at chapel. He must be within bounds at a fixed time. If he behave indecorously he is liable to be pounced upon and reported by special officials, and a code of punishments is hung perpetually over his head. In return for all this his University takes a keen interest in him. She pats him on the back if he succeeds. Prizes and scholarships, and fine fat fellowships are thrown plentifully in his way if he will gird up his loins and aspire to them.
>
> There is nothing of this in a Scotch University. The young aspirant pays his pound, and finds himself a student. After that he may do absolutely what he will. There are certain classes going on at certain hours, which he may attend if he choose. If not, he may stay away without the slightest remonstrance from the college. As to religion, he may worship the sun, or have a private fetish of his own upon the mantelpiece of his lodgings for all that the University cares. He may live where he likes, he may keep what hours he chooses, and he is at liberty to break every commandment in the decalogue as long as he behaves himself with some approach to decency within the academical precincts. In every way he is absolutely his own master. Examinations are periodically held, at which he may appear or not, as he chooses. The University is a great unsympathetic machine, taking in a stream of raw-boned cartilaginous youths at one end, and turning them out at the other as learned divines, astute lawyers, and skilful medical men. Of every thousand of the raw material about six hundred emerge at the other side. The remainder are broken in the process.
>
> The merits and faults of this Scotch system are alike evident. Left entirely to his own devices in a far from moral city, many a lad falls at the very starting-point of his life's race, never to rise again. Many become idlers or take to drink, while others, after wasting time and money which they could ill afford, leave the college with nothing learned save vice. On the other hand, those whose manliness and good sense keep them straight have gone through a training which lasts them for life. They have been tried, and have not been found wanting. They have learned self-reliance, confidence, and, in a word, have become men of the world while their *confreres* in England are still magnified schoolboys.

In 1878, Conan Doyle's friend and associate, J. M. Barrie entered Old College, and although he never experienced any great financial hard-

Old College viewed from the Quadrangle. The dome was erected in 1887, on top of which stands the "Golden Boy" holding the torch of knowledge.

ships at university, he did recall "three undergraduates who lodged together in a dreary house at the top of a dreary street; two of them used to study until two in the morning, while the third slept. When they shut up their books, they woke number three, who rose, dressed and studied until breakfast time."

The original college of the University of Edinburgh was founded in 1583 by the town council of Edinburgh and for many years it was known as the Tounis College of Edinburgh. It was built in the grounds of the Collegiate Church of St. Mary's in the field known locally as Kirk o' Field. It was here that Mary, Queen of Scot's second husband, Lord Darnley, was murdered in 1567. The new building, now known as Old College, was started in 1789 and took 40 years to complete. The original plan of the building was by Robert Adam, who died in 1792, before it was completed. Work was then interrupted by the Napoleonic Wars. But in 1816 William Playfair was appointed to complete the building, which he finally accomplished in the late 1820s. Much of Adam's design survived in the building, including the huge vaulted entrance on South Bridge.

Other literary alumni who attended Edinburgh University include Charles Darwin, David Hume, Oliver Goldsmith and Robert Louis Stevenson. And Sherlock Holmes himself came face to face with Edinburgh University in 1896 when Conan Doyle was asked, as a distinguished alumni, to contribute to a charitable appeal by the university *Student* magazine. He responded with *The Field Bazaar* in which Holmes delights in explaining the contents of an unopened letter which Watson has just received from Edinburgh University:

"But how —!" exclaims Watson.
"It is as easy as possible," states Holmes, "and I leave its solution to your own ingenuity. In the meantime," he added, raising his paper, "you will excuse me if I return to this very interesting article upon the trees of Cremona, and the exact reasons for the pre-eminence in the manufacture of violins. It is one of those small outlying problems to which I am sometimes tempted to direct my attention."

FURTHER INFORMATION: The interior of Old College is not open to the public, but visitors are welcome to stroll around the old quadrangle.

SEE ALSO: Royal Infirmary (p. 12), Surgical Hospital (p. 15), New Surgical Hospital (p. 17), Joseph Bell (pp. 10, 12, 15, 21, 26, 31, 35–6), Surgeon's Hall Museum (p. 21)

Infirmary Street

Site of the old Royal Infirmary where Conan Doyle was taught the science of deduction and met the man who inspired Sherlock Holmes

"The students were pouring down the sloping street which led to the infirmary — each with his little sheaf of note-books in his hand. There were pale, frightened lads, fresh from the high schools, and callous old chronics, whose generation had passed on and left them. They swept in an unbroken, tumultuous stream from the university gate to the hospital. The figures and gait of the men were young, but there was little youth in most of their faces. Some looked as if they ate too little — a few as if they drank too much. Tall

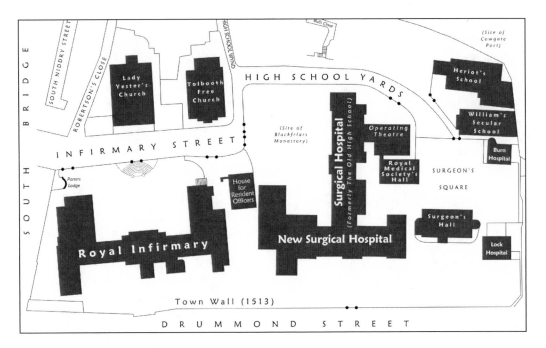

The Infirmary area of Edinburgh shortly after the completion of the New Surgical Hospital in 1853.

and short, tweed-coated and black, round-shouldered, bespectacled, and slim, they crowded with clatter of feet and rattle of sticks through the hospital gate." — Conan Doyle, describing his fellow students attending extra-mural classes at the Royal Infirmary, "His First Operation" *Round the Red Lamp* (1894)

In the late 17th century the study of medicine started in earnest in Europe. Schools of medicine were being established across the continent, and in 1726 a Faculty of Medicine was founded at Edinburgh University. Before it could become a complete medical school, the building of a hospital in which medicine and surgery could be practiced had to be built. In 1729, through money raised by subscription, Edinburgh's first Royal Infirmary was opened in Robertson's Close, just off Infirmary Street. Known as the Little House, it was only a six-bed hospital amid a city with a population of around 30,000, but it was a beginning. In 1741 a new and larger Royal Infirmary was built, again by public subscription, on the south side of Infirmary Street, a site now occupied by buildings which were once part of a Victorian school. The new hospital had 228 beds and was on four floors, with an east wing

for men and a west wing for women; and perched on the top floor was a 200-seat amphitheater and operating theater, complete with glass windows in the roof for maximum light. This was progress, but to say it resembled hospital care as we know it today would be stretching it. Two of its most serious defects were a lack of understanding about hygiene and the dire inefficiency of the nursing system. Nurses were untrained and ignorant of what their proper duties were. They were underpaid, ill-fed and poorly-housed. They were servants rather than nurses. But in the mid–19th century one English woman changed everything. Her name was Florence Nightingale, the founder of modern nursing. Trained Nightingale nurses started to arrive at the Infirmary in the early 1870s, and hospital care began to resemble what we know today, but it still had a long way to go.

Conan Doyle entered the Medical Faculty of Edinburgh University at Old College a few years later in 1876, and began his extra-mural training at the Royal Infirmary, just a short distance away on the other side of South Bridge. Extra-mural meant outside the walls of the faculty in local hospitals and teaching establishments under the auspices of experienced medical men, a method of teaching introduced at Edinburgh in 1855, allowing students to take at least half their classes extra-curricularly. These classes were extremely popular, often outnumbering those within the walls of the Faculty.

"There were no attempts at friendship, or even acquaintance, between professors and students at Edinburgh," wrote Conan Doyle, "It was a strictly business arrangement by which you paid, for example, four guineas for anatomy lectures and received the winter's course in exchange, never seeing your professor save behind his desk and never under any circumstances exchanging a word with him."

His professors may have been businesslike and formal, but they were a group of remarkable men, who made a lasting impression on him, and many of their names, temperaments and idiosyncrasies he accumulated in his memory for future use.

There was Professor Sir Robert Christison who taught materia medica (pharmacology), an expert in toxicology who once swallowed a poisonous calabar bean to register its consequences. Fortunately he survived, but Conan Doyle recalls the incident in *A Study in Scarlet* when Watson describes Holmes as "a little too scientific for my tastes — it approaches to cold-bloodedness. I could imagine his giving a friend a little pinch of the latest vegetable alkaloid, not out of malevolence, you understand, but simply out of a spirit of inquiry in order to have an accurate idea of the effects. To do him justice, I think he would take it himself with the same readiness. He appears to have a passion for definite and exact knowledge."

Conan Doyle would also have attended Sir Henry Littlejohn's lecture's on medical jurisprudence. Littlejohn became Edinburgh and Scotland's first Medical Officer of Health in 1862. As police surgeon to the city he came into contact with many criminal cases and acted as expert medical witness for the Crown. His students would have been privy to many of the forensic details of his cases.

There was also, recalled Conan Doyle, "the squat figure of Professor Rutherford with his Assyrian beard, his prodigious voice, his enormous chest and his singular manner. He fasci-

nated and awed us. I have endeavoured to reproduce some of his peculiarities in the fictitious character of Professor Challenger. He would sometimes start his lecture before he reached the classroom, so that we would hear a booming voice saying: 'There are valves in the veins,' or some other information, when the desk was still empty."

The first Dr. Watson Conan Doyle ever met was probably Dr. Patrick Heron Watson, a forensic expert and an associate of Joseph Bell; but whether he was the inspiration for the fictional Watson is debatable as Doyle also came into contact with a Dr. James Watson when practicing in Southsea.

His inspiration for Sherlock Holmes, however, has never been in doubt. Joseph Bell lectured in clinical surgery at the extra-mural School of Medicine, and in October 1878, Conan Doyle, now a second year medical student with poor grades, paid his fee of 4 guineas and enrolled in Bell's course. That same year Bell appointed him his out patient clerk, an experience he described in his autobiography, *Memories and Adventures*, in 1924:

> On my return to Edinburgh (after Stonyhurst) I met the man who suggested Sherlock Holmes to me — here is a portrait of him as he was in those days.... I was clerk in Mr Bell's Ward.
> I would show them (i.e. the patients) into Dr Bell who would have the students gathered round him. His intuitive powers were simply marvellous. A case would be introduced and Bell says, "A cobbler I see."
> Then he would turn to the students and point out to them that the inside of the knee of the man's trousers was worn. That was where the man rested the lapstone — a peculiarity found only in cobblers. All this impressed me very much. He was continually before me — his sharp piercing gray eyes, eagle nose, and striking features. There he would sit in his chair with fingers together — he was very dextrous with his hands — and just look at the man or woman before him. He was most kind and painstaking with students — a real good friend — and when I took my degree and went to Africa the remarkable individuality and discriminating tact of my old master made a deep and lasting impression on me, though I had not the faintest idea that it would one day lead me to forsake medicine for story writing.

When Bell made Conan Doyle his outpatient clerk, it gave him the opportunity to study Bell's methods at close-quarters. The position of clerk, although a privileged one, was a common post to be given to a student. It was a sharp learning curve, which taught a student to think fast, write fast, and communicate swiftly with patients. Often there would be seventy or eighty patients to assemble and write notes on before Bell began his outpatient clinic, and woe betide Doyle if he didn't have them ready on time. He would then usher them in, one by one, to a large room in which Bell sat surrounded by students, where, "with a face like a Red Indian, [he would] diagnose the people as they came in, before they had even opened their mouths. He would tell them their symptoms. He would give them details of their lives, and he would hardly ever make a mistake."

This was an age before X-rays and scans. What Bell was trying to do was to emphasis to his students the use of the powers of perception. Taste, touch, smell, and what they could hear through their stethoscopes. To do this he had various tricks up his sleeve. One of them was a classic, which to this day is still probably used as an example to medical students.

Bell would hold a vial of bilious looking liquid aloft for all his students to see. "This, gentlemen, contains a most potent drug. It is extremely bitter to taste. Now I wish to see how many of you have developed the powers of observation that God granted you. But sair, ye will say, it can be analysed chemically. Aye, aye, but I want you to taste it — by smell and taste. What! You shrink back? As I don't ask anything of my students which I wouldn't do alone wi' myself, I will taste it before passing it around." Bell would then dip a finger into the obnoxious liquid and place it in his mouth, followed by an expression of disgust. "Now you do likewise," and the students would proceed to pass the vial amongst themselves. When the vile concoction eventually returned to Bell, he would sigh in despair, saying, "Gentlemen, I am deeply grieved to find that not one of you has developed his power of perception, the faculty of observation which I speak so much of, for if you had truly observed me, you would have seen that, while I placed my index finger in the awful brew, it was my middle finger — aye — which somehow found its way into my mouth."

FURTHER READING: A. Logan Turner, *The Story of a Great Hospital, The Royal Infirmary of Edinburgh 1729–1929* (Edinburgh, UK: Oliver and Boyd, 1937).

SEE ALSO: Surgical Hospital (p. 15), New Surgical Hospital (p. 17), Surgeon's Hall Museum (p. 21), Old College (p. 10), St. Andrew's Square (p. 26), Castle Terrace (p. 31), Mauricewood (p. 36), Livingston Mission Hall (p. 9), Robert Louis Stevenson (p. 27).

Infirmary Street
High School Yards

The Surgical Hospital where Joseph Bell studied under Dr. James Syme (1799–1870), "The Napoleon of Surgery"

"Mr. Syme then and there made his diagnosis, which to us young ones seemed magical and intuitional." — Joseph Bell

Joseph Bell may have "made a deep and lasting impression" on the young Conan Doyle, but who introduced Bell to the skills of deductive reasoning? Who were the men who honed his analytical mind and in doing so would have had an indirect influence on Conan Doyle? There were several medical legends on the faculty during Bell's student years, all of whom would have effected his development, including Joseph Lister, surgeon and antiseptic pioneer; James Young Simpson, Professor of Midwifery and anaesthetic pioneer; and surgeons James Miller and James Spence. But the one who rose head and shoulders above them all in Bell's eyes, was his mentor, Dr. James Syme, affectionately known as "The Napoleon of Surgery."

Syme, the son of an Edinburgh lawyer, taught clinical surgery at the Infirmary for thirty-six years, from 1833 to 1869, and had a formidable reputation as a teacher and a surgeon. He was not a showy or elegant surgeon. He had no flourish or dash, but his knowledge and skill saved many lives. One of Syme's assistants commented that "he never wasted a word, a drop of ink, or a drop of blood." Joseph Bell was closer to him than most, as Syme chose Bell as his dresser (assistant). Bell wrote:

Unless it was raining the students attending Syme's wards might, if they chose, run down a

steep flight of stairs, past one or two old houses, across a square of rough gravel surrounding a plot of measly grass, generally decorated by old broken iron bedsteads or decaying mattresses, to a low two-storied building in severely classical style.... In the angle, dark and confined, of the lower floor of the Surgical Hospital admitting to the general surgical waiting rooms ... the large operating theatre, a really finely-proportioned and well-arranged building, with some small wards, house surgeon's rooms — extended beyond the main lines of the old High School, and formed part of a quaint old square, now nearly demolished, called Surgeon's Square.... I saw Dr. Syme daily for the greater part of his last fifteen years. His hospital life was on this wise — two clinical lectures a week, operations two days more (perhaps three), a ward visit when he wished to see any special cases.... Before his select class he examined each new and interesting case that could walk in.... Mr. Syme then and there made his diagnosis, which to us young ones seemed magical and intuitional....

Then if it was a lecture day, a tremendous rush of feet would be heard of the students racing to get the nearest seats in the large operating theatre.... Chairs in the arena were kept for colleagues or distinguished strangers; first row for dressers on duty; operating table in centre; Mr. Syme on a chair in left-centre. House surgeons a little behind, but nearer the door; instrument clerk with his well-stocked table under the big window. The four dressers on duty march in (if possible in step), carrying a rude wicker basket, in which, covered by a rough red blanket, the patient peers up at the great amphitheatre crammed with faces. A brief description ... and then the little, neat, tyro sees at once a master of his craft at work — no show, little elegance, but absolute certainty, ease and determination; rarely a word to an assistant — they should know their business.

In 1859 Joseph Bell graduated. Ten years later, in April 1869, James Syme suffered an apoplectic seizure and was forced to retire from the chair of clinical surgery. He died on 26 June 1870, aged seventy years, and was interred in the family vault at St. John's Episcopal Church, at the West End of Princes Street.

FURTHER INFORMATION: The buildings in High School Yards are now part of Edinburgh University, but the public are free to wander through the grounds. The Surgical Hospital described by Joseph Bell now houses the archaeology faculty and its pillared entrance faces you at the bottom of Infirmary Street. The operating theater referred to by Bell was behind the main

Top: "The Napoleon of Surgery," Dr. James Syme. *Bottom*: Joseph Bell — student of medicine.

building and was part of the wing which projects into the square at the rear. It was originally the old high school building, erected in 1777. In the autumn of 1832, after the high school had moved to new premises on Calton Hill, the building was reopened as the Surgical Hospital. A plaque can be seen to the right of the entrance (behind the pillars) dedicated to Syme and Lister. Surgeon's Square can be seen by walking through the tunnelled passageway to the right of the entrance. Here you will find the "steep flight of stairs" and the "plot of measly grass" described by Joseph Bell. The stairs divide the old 17th century Surgeon's Hall and what became known as the New Surgical Hospital, built in 1853 facing onto Drummond Street (now the university geography faculty). The land which is now High School Yards was once the site of the monastery of the Black Friars, the Dominicans, which was destroyed by the mob during the Reformation in 1538.

The Surgical Hospital.

FURTHER READING: R. Paterson, *Memorials of the Life of James Syme, Professor of Clinical Surgery in the University of Edinburgh, Etc. (1874)* (Whitefish, MT: Kessinger, 2008).

SEE ALSO: Surgeon's Hall Museum (p. 21), Old College (p. 10), Royal Infirmary (p. 12), St. Andrew's Square (p. 26), Castle Terrace (p. 31), Mauricewood (p. 36), Livingston Mission Hall (p. 9), Robert Louis Stevenson (p. 27).

Drummond Street
The New Surgical Hospital

Where W. E. Henley was hospitalized from 1873 to 1875

"I went down and lunched with the redoubtable one legged Henley — the original of John Silver in 'Treasure Island.' He has a most extraordinary menage. He is the editor of the National Observer, the most savage of critics, and to my mind one of our finest living poets..." — Arthur Conan Doyle, extract from a letter to his mother c.1893

The son of a Gloucester bookseller, William Ernest Henley (1849–1903) came to Edinburgh in 1873 to be treated by Professor Joseph Lister for tubercular arthritis, which seven years previously had resulted in the amputation of his left leg below the knee. Lister's skills saved Henley's other leg and probably his life, but the treatment was painful, and he was hospitalized in Edinburgh for almost two years. Henley is chiefly remembered today as a poet, notably for his "Invictus," but Henley was an imperialist and a Tory, and much of his poetry was a platform for his jingoistic patriotism. His "Hospital Sketches," first published in *Cornhill Magazine* in 1875, grimly recalls his distressing time when hospitalized in Edinburgh. He was also a critic and held a series of editorships, including *Pen* (1880) and *Magazine of Art* (1881–86), and in 1889 he returned to Edinburgh to edit the *Scots Observer*. A stinging critic and a fearless editor, Henley published the works of Hardy, Barrie, Kipling, H. G. Wells, Yeats, Henry James, and Robert Louis Stevenson, who immortalized him as Long John Silver in *Treasure Island*. He also published the struggling Joseph Conrad's "The Nigger of Narcissus" in *The New Review*. "Now that I have conquered Henley," wrote Conrad, "I ain't afraid of the divvle himself."

We don't know if Conan Doyle was afraid of Henley, but he certainly admired him as an editor and a poet. In *Through the Magic Door* (1907) he summed up his admiration as follows:

> He was a remarkable man, a man who was very much greater than his work, great as some of his work was. I have seldom known a personality more magnetic and stimulating. You left his presence, as a battery leaves a generating station, charged up and full. He made you feel what a lot of work there was to be done, and how glorious it was to be able to do it, and how needful to get started upon it that very hour. With the frame and the vitality of a giant he was cruelly bereft of all outlet for his strength, and so distilled it off in hot words, in warm sympathy, in strong prejudices, in all manner of human and stimulating emotions. Much of the time and energy which might have built an imperishable name for himself was spent in encouraging others; but it was not waste, for he left his broad thumb-mark upon all that passed beneath it. A dozen second-hand Henleys are fortifying our literature today.
>
> Alas that we have so little of his very best! for that very best was the finest of our time. Few poets ever wrote sixteen consecutive lines ["Invictus," 1875] more noble and more strong than those which begin with the well-known quatrain —
>
> "Out of the night that covers me,
> Black as the pit from pole to pole,
> I thank whatever gods may be
> For my unconquerable soul."
>
> It is grand literature, and it is grand pluck too; for it came from a man who, through no fault of his own, had been pruned, and pruned again, like an ill-grown shrub, by the surgeon's knife. When he said —
>
> "In the fell clutch of circumstance
> I have not winced nor cried aloud.
> Under the bludgeonings of chance
> My head is bloody, but unbowed."
>
> It was not what Lady Byron called "the mimic woe" of the poet, but it was rather the grand defiance of the Indian warrior at the stake, whose proud soul can hold in hand his quivering body.
>
> There were two quite distinct veins of poetry in Henley, each the very extreme from the other. The one was heroic, gigantic, running to large sweeping images and thundering words. Such are the "Song of the Sword" and much more that he has written, like the wild singing of some Northern scald. The other, and to my mind both the more characteristic and the finer side of his work, is delicate, precise, finely etched, with extraordinarily vivid little pictures drawn in carefully phrased and balanced English.

Such are the "Hospital Verses," while the "London Voluntaries" stand midway between the two styles. What! you have not read the "Hospital Verses!" Then get the *Book of Verses* and read them without delay. You will surely find something there which, for good or ill, is unique. You can name — or at least I can name — nothing to compare it with. Goldsmith and Crabbe have written of indoor themes; but their monotonous, if majestic metre, wearies the modern reader. But this is so varied, so flexible, so dramatic. It stands by itself. Confound the weekly journals and all the other lightning conductors which caused such a man to pass away, and to leave a total output of about five booklets behind him!

FURTHER INFORMATION: The New Surgical Hospital, built in 1853, was part of Edinburgh's old Royal Infirmary which stood in nearby Infirmary Street until its closure in the late 1870s. The gateway of the old Infirmary was dismantled during demolition and reassembled at the entrance of the New Surgical Hospital on Drummond Street (now part of Edinburgh University) and can still be seen today.

FURTHER READING: J. M. Flora, *W. E. Henley* (New York: Irvington, 1970); J. H. Buckley,

The New Surgical Hospital.

William Ernest Henley — A Study in the Counter-Decadence of the Nineties (Princeton, NJ: Princeton University Press, 1945).

SEE ALSO: Surgical Hospital (p. 15), Surgeon's Hall Museum (p. 21), Old College (p. 10), Royal Infirmary (p. 12).

53-62 South Bridge
Site of James Thin's Bookshop

Described by Conan Doyle as "The most fascinating bookshop in the world"

"Come through the magic door with me, and sit here on the green settee, where you can see the old oak case with its untidy lines of volumes. Smoking is not forbidden. Would you care to hear me talk of them? Well, I ask nothing better, for there is no volume there which is not a dear, personal friend, and what can a man talk of more pleasantly than that? The other books are over yonder, but these are my own favourites — the ones I care to re-read and to have near my elbow. There is not a tattered cover which does not bring its mellow memories to me.

Some of them represent those little sacrifices which make a possession dearer. You see the line of old, brown volumes at the bottom? Every one of those represents a lunch. They were bought in my student days, when times were not too affluent. Threepence was my modest allowance for my midday sandwich and glass of beer; but, as luck would have it, my way to the classes led past the most fascinating bookshop in the world. Outside the door of it stood a large tub filled with an ever-changing litter of tattered books, with a card above which announced that any volume therein could be purchased for the identical sum which I carried in my pocket. As I approached it a combat ever raged betwixt the hunger of a youthful body and that of an inquiring and omnivorous mind. Five times out of six the animal won. But when the mental prevailed, then there was an entrancing five minutes' digging among out-of-date almanacs, volumes of Scotch theology, and tables of logarithms, until one found something which made it all worth while. If you will look over these titles, you will see that I did not do so very badly. Four volumes of Gordon's 'Tacitus' (life is too short to read originals, so long as there are good translations), Sir William Temple's Essays, Addison's works, Swift's 'Tale of a Tub,' Clarendon's 'History,' 'Gil Blas,' Buckingham's Poems, Churchill's Poems, 'Life of Bacon'— not so bad for the old threepenny tub." — Arthur Conan Doyle, *Through the Magic Door* (1907)

In 2004 Edinburgh was designated the world's first "City of Literature" by UNESCO, confirming and publicizing to the world the city's vast literary heritage. This heritage also includes a city overflowing with bookstores, the oldest, and greatest of which was James Thin. It prospered because it was opposite the university where thousands of students browsed its shelves for over 150 years, including the young Arthur Conan Doyle. Here he would often forgo his lunch and spend the money earmarked for a pie and a pint on a battered second-hand book penned by one of his literary heroes — Scott, Addison, Swift, and of course, Thomas Babington Macaulay, one of his early obsessions. Conan Doyle described James Thin's as "The most fascinating bookshop in the world," and few would have disagreed with him.

In 1863 James Thin (1823–1915) was apprenticed to an Edinburgh bookseller. His starting wage was two shillings and sixpence a week, out of which he had to provide himself with a pen and pencil. His working hours were 9 A.M. to 9 P.M. and meals were eaten in the shop. After 12 years of training, he set himself up in business in 1848, when he bought the stock of a failed bookseller and leased a shop at 14 Infirmary Street. His first day's sales totalled five shillings and sevenpence. Concentrating mainly on academic books and working closely with the University, his business prospered and expanded. He was also a keen hymnologist and had a personal collection of 2,500 hymnbooks. Three generations later, his family were still controlling the business.

In 1891 James Thin, aged 67, was interviewed by *The Publisher's Circular*, who drew from him a delightful insight into Edinburgh's literati and their tastes: "Mr Thin has met most of the famous men who have visited Edinburgh, or been associated with its history during the past half century. He remembers Macaulay well, and speaks with enthusiasm of the historian's oratorical power. De Quincey used to visit Mr Thin's shop in search of books. The author of 'The Confessions of an English Opium Eater' was described by Mr Thin as a meagre, nervous, shrivelled little man, who went skulking about after nightfall as if he could not stand the light of day.... But of all the great men whom he has known, Mr Thin speaks with the greatest cordiality of Carlyle — indeed, he talks of the sage

Blackwell's Bookshop — formerly James Thin's.

of Chelsea with a deep and open reverence....
Mr Thin remembers the sudden rise of 'Pickwick'
and the slower ascent of Thackeray. In those days,
it was all Dickens. Now the better
class of readers are forsaking him for
his once neglected rival — a circum-
stance that strikes Mr Thin rather
favourably."

FURTHER INFORMATION: The
Blackwell family took over James
Thin on South Bridge in 2002. It
stands directly opposite Edinburgh
University Old College on the corner
of South Bridge and Infirmary Street.

FURTHER READING: *James Thin,
150 Years of Bookselling 1848–1998*
(Edinburgh, UK: Mercat, 1998).

SEE ALSO: Sir Walter Scott (p. 38),
Thomas De Quincey (p. 32), Thomas
Babington Macaulay (p. 86), Thomas
Carlyle (p. 101), George Borrow (p.
25), Edgar Allan Poe (p. 98), Ruther-
fords (p. 20).

Drummond Street
Rutherfords

*Former watering hole of Conan Doyle and Edin-
burgh University medical students*

> "It was the first day of the winter session, and
> the third year's man was walking with the first
> year's man. Twelve o'clock was just booming out
> from the Tron Church.
> 'Let me see,' said the third year's man. 'You
> have never seen an operation?'
> 'Never.'
> 'Then this way, please. This is Rutherford's
> historic bar. A glass of sherry, please, for this gen-
> tleman. You are rather sensitive, are you not?'
> 'My nerves are not very strong, I am afraid.'
> 'Hum! Another glass of sherry for this gentle-
> man. We are going to an operation now, you
> know.'
> The novice squared his shoulders and made a
> gallant attempt to look unconcerned." — Arthur
> Conan Doyle, "His First Operation" (1894)

Until its closure and subsequent conversion
into an extension of a nearby Italian restaurant
in the winter of 2007, Rutherfords still retained
the sparse decor and friendly atmosphere of
the traditional Scottish howff (tavern). It first
opened its doors in 1834 and became a popular
watering hole for the students of Edinburgh
University just around the corner in South
Bridge. Electric lights had been installed and
the price of a pint had increased dramatically,

The wooden facade of what was once Rutherford's pub —
now The Hispaniola.

but one got the feeling that Rutherfords hadn't changed very much since the days when Conan Doyle would have sauntered through its doors for lunch and a welcome pint after a tedious morning of note-taking on acute coronary syndromes. Rutherford's fed and watered Edinburgh University students for well over a hundred years, amongst them J. M. Barrie and the velvet-jacketed Robert Louis Stevenson. I was "the companion of seamen, chimney-sweeps and thieves," wrote Stevenson of Ruther-fords. "My circle was being continually changed by the action of the police mag-istrate."

FURTHER INFORMATION: The wooden Victorian facade of Rutherfords is still in-tact and preserved on Drummond Street as its frontage is architecturally listed, but its interior has been completely gutted — a sad loss to literary Edinburgh and lovers of the good old Scottish drinking den.

SEE ALSO: James Thin (p. 19).

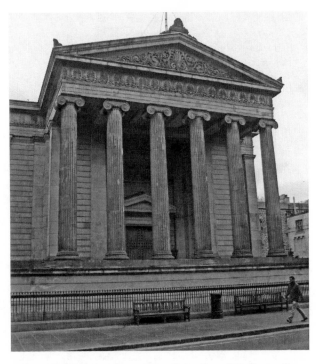

Surgeon's Hall, headquarters of the Royal College of Surgeons, designed by William Playfair in 1832.

Nicolson Street
Surgeon's Hall Museum
Royal College of Surgeons of Edinburgh
"The Real Sherlock Holmes" Exhibition

Come fill up your cups and your glasses again
Like wise philosophical medical men
I'll sing you a snatch of a song if I can
by the Royal College of Surgeons
For there's many a pickle in jar and in pot
The examining fogies there have got
And they want you to know the devil knows what
at the Royal College of Surgeons
    — Extract from a poem in Conan Doyle's student notebook referring to his anatomy ex-aminations, which took place in the Pathology Museum at Surgeon's Hall

Originally developed as a teaching museum for medical students, The Museum of the Royal College of Surgeons of Edinburgh is Scotland's oldest museum and contains the largest collec-tion of surgical pathology objects in the UK. It's exhibitions and collections have been open to the public since 1832. In 2006 a permanent exhibition was launched which concentrates mainly on the relationship between Conan Doyle and Joseph Bell. "The Real Sherlock Holmes" exhibition contains letters, artworks, objects

and even rare film footage of Conan Doyle talk-ing to the camera about his old teacher.

Exhibits include:

- The famous letter from Conan Doyle to Joseph Bell, dated May 4, 1892, confirming the gen-esis of Holmes, which states, "It is most cer-tainly to you that I owe Sherlock Holmes, and although in the stories I have the advantage of being able to place him in all sorts of dramatic positions, I do not think that this analytical work is in the least an exaggeration of some of the effects which I have seen you produce in the out-patient ward."
- Joseph Bell's own copy of *A Study in Scarlet* with an introduction titled, "Mr Sherlock Holmes by Joseph Bell," from an article first published in *The Bookman* in 1892.
- Newspaper cuttings collected by Joseph Bell on the subject of "The Real Sherlock Holmes."
- The first book edition of *A Study in Scarlet* with illustrations by Conan Doyle's father, Charles Altamont Doyle, published in 1888.
- Conan Doyle's hand-written clinical note book (1879–80), detailing lecture notes and notes taken during ward rounds. It also contains his short story "The American's Story," his second

published work which appeared in the *London Society Journal* in 1879, and the comic poem featured above.

- A copy of *A Manual of Surgery*, Joseph Bell's 1866 guide for students and greenhorn doctors, which attempted to simplify many of the basic operations of surgery. His jaunty, no-nonsense approach to surgery is summed up in the final paragraph of his preface: "In excuse of the frequent baldness and brevity of the style, the author must point to the size and price of the work. Its composition would have been easier had its dimensions been greater. Though intended chiefly to guide the studies, on the dead subject, of students and junior practitioners, the author ventures to hope that the Manual may be useful to those who, in the public services, in the colonies, or in lonely country districts, find themselves constrained to attempt the performance of operations which, in the towns, usually fall to the lot of a few Hospital Surgeons."

- Specimens of severed ears, which no doubt Conan Doyle recalled when writing "The Adventure of the Cardboard Box" in 1917: "As a medical man, you are aware, Watson, that there is no part of the body which varies so much as the human ear. Each ear is as a rule quite distinctive and differs from all other ones. In last year's *Anthropological Journal* you will find two short monographs from my pen upon the sub-

ject. I had, therefore, examined the ears in the box with the eyes of an expert and had carefully noted their anatomical peculiarities. Imagine my surprise, then, when on looking at Miss Cushing I perceived that her ear corresponded exactly with the female ear which I had just inspected. The matter was entirely beyond coincidence. There was the same shortening of the pinna, the same broad curve of the upper lobe, the same convolution of the inner cartilage. In all essentials it was the same ear."

- And last, but not least, specimens of Dermoid cysts, caused by the growth of unused stem cells, of which Conan Doyle elaborates on their possibilities in *The Stark Munro Letters* (1895): "Well, if a single cell contains so much perhaps a single molecule and atom has more than we think.... Have you ever had any personal experience of dermoid cysts?... You know that such cases are common enough in surgery, and that no pathological museum is without an example.... But what are we to understand by it? So startling a phenomenon must have a deep meaning. That can only be, I think, that every cell in the body has the power latent in it by which it may reproduce the whole individual."

FURTHER INFORMATION: Surgeon's Hall Museum, Royal College of Surgeons of Edinburgh, Nicolson Street, Edinburgh, UK, EH8 9DW. The museum is located within the campus of the Royal College of Surgeons of Edinburgh. The entrance to the Museum is located at 9 Hill Square, although visitors can enter via the main college entrance on Nicolson Street where they will be directed to Hill Square via the main building. For opening hours consult www.museum.rcsed.ac.uk. Tel: +44(0)131 527 16 49/678.

SEE ALSO: Surgical Hospital (p. 15), New

Joseph Bell's amputation kit (Brian W. Pugh Collection).

Surgical Hospital (p. 17), Joseph Bell (p. 12), Old College (p. 10), Royal Infirmary (p. 12).

23 George Square

Former home of Conan Doyle from 1876 to 1880

> But I must add (the more's the pity)
> that though in fair Dunedin's city
> Scotland's taste is quite delightful,
> the smaller Scottish towns are frightful.
> — Sir Arthur Conan Doyle, "Songs of the Road" (1911)

This is the residence most associated with Conan Doyle in Edinburgh, and compared to his other homes in the city, George Square was by far the most select and well-heeled. The boyhood home of Sir Walter Scott (1771–1832) was at No. 25 and Thomas Carlyle (1795–1881) wooed Jane Welsh at No. 22. George Square was also home to Lord Braxfield (1722–99) and inspiration for Robert Louis Stevenson's *Weir of Hermiston*. The square was designed by the builder and architect James Brown in 1766 and was not named after royalty or a worthy man of letters, but James's brother George. In the 18th century it was a fashionable place to live,

but more importantly it was a healthy place to live being the first new build outside the medieval squalor of the Old Town.

The Doyles moved into No. 23 in the summer of 1877 from their cramped flat at 2 Argyle Park Terrace, just a few minutes walk away on the southern edge of The Meadows Park. The street-level rooms at No. 23 George Square were occupied by the Doyles and their lodger, Bryan Waller, who paid the £85 annual rent. Waller was a consultant pathologist who had recently inherited his family estate, so cash flow did not appear to be one of his immediate problems. From No. 23 Conan Doyle would have walked across the square to the university medical faculty and the Royal Infirmary on South Bridge. In 1881 the family moved to nearby Lonsdale Terrace, and in the summer of 1882, Bryan Waller, together with the Doyles, retired to his estate in Yorkshire.

In the early 1960s much of this beautiful square was demolished to make way for a new university campus, considered by many to be a disgraceful act of architectural vandalism. Fortunately No. 23 survived on the western side of the square, along with a few houses in the north east corner, but the square remains one of Edinburgh's most controversial redevelopments.

SEE ALSO: Salisbury Crags (p. 34), Masongill (p. 57).

Old Town

Chambers Street
Statue of Sir William Chambers (1800–83)

Publisher of The Mystery of Sasassa Valley, *Conan Doyle's first published work*

> "I was groping down the valley, looking for that cow of Madison's, and I had, I suppose, got halfway down, where a black craggy cliff juts into the ravine on the right, when I halted to have a pull at my flask. I had my eye fixed at the time upon the projecting cliff I have mentioned, and noticed nothing unusual about it. I then put up my flask and took a step or two forward, when in a moment there burst, apparently from the base of the rock, about eight feet from the ground and a hundred yards from me, a strange, lurid glare, flickering and oscillating, gradually dying away and then reappearing again. No, no; I've seen many a glow-worm and firefly — nothing of that

23 George Square.

sort. There it was, burning away, and I suppose I gazed at it, trembling in every limb, for fully ten minutes. Then I took a step forward, when instantly it vanished, vanished like a candle blown out. I stepped back again; but it was some time before I could find the exact spot and position from which it was visible. At last, there it was, the weird reddish light, flickering away as before. Then I screwed up my courage, and made for the rock; but the ground was so uneven that it was impossible to steer straight; and though I walked along the whole base of the cliff, I could see nothing..."—Arthur Conan Doyle, *The Mystery of Sasassa Valley* (1879)

From March 1879 until February 1880 Conan Doyle worked as a student assistant to Dr. Reginald Ratcliff Hoare in Birmingham. "I first learned that shillings might be earned in other ways than filling phials," he remarked, and he started to write a story titled *The Mystery of Sasassa Valley*. More skillful than his previous efforts, this mystery adventure story of two fortune-seeking young men was set in South Africa. The manuscript was accepted by *Chambers's Journal*, an Edinburgh weekly magazine, for which he received the sum of three guineas. "After receiving that little cheque," he commented, "I was a beast that had once tasted blood, for I knew that whatever rebuffs I might receive—and God knows I had plenty—I had once proved I could earn gold, and the spirit was in me to do it again."

Like Conan Doyle, Chambers' publishing house had very humble beginnings. The brothers William and Robert Chambers were born into a mill-owning family in the Scottish Borders who hit hard times after their charitable father reputedly issued cloth on credit to French prisoners of war to make themselves clothes during the war with Napoleon. After the war, they returned to France promising to repay their benefactor but never did, and the family was ruined. William became apprenticed to an Edinburgh bookseller, and shortly afterwards his younger brother Robert set up as a bookseller in the city. When William's apprenticeship came to an end, he went into partnership with his brother. They purchased a small hand-press, and in 1832 they began publishing *Chambers's Journal*, a weekly magazine, the circulation of which reached 84,000 copies within a few years. *Chambers's Encyclopaedia* followed

William Chambers' statue was erected in 1891. The plinth is decorated with female figures by Hippolyte Blanc representing Literature, Liberality and Perseverance.

in 1859, published in 520 parts between 1859 and 1868. Educational publishing made both brothers extremely wealthy, and William was twice Lord Provost (Mayor) of Edinburgh and is buried in the city's St. Giles Cathedral.

FURTHER INFORMATION: Chambers was family-owned until 1989 and it is now part of the Vivendi University Publishing group.

George IV Bridge
The National Library of Scotland
The Blackwood Archives

"Ever since the days of John Keats, to be bludgeoned by Blackwood has been the hallmark of an author of ideas."—Thomas Hardy, 1907

The National Library of Scotland (NLS) is Scotland's largest library and is the world center for the study of Scotland and the Scots. It also ranks among the largest libraries in the UK, housing 14,000,000 printed books, 120,000 volumes of manuscripts, 2,000,000 maps and over 25,000 newspaper and magazine titles.

Since 1925, the NLS has also been collecting literary manuscripts, working papers and correspondence of writers such as Robert Burns, Sir Walter Scott, Robert Louis Stevenson, and of course, Sir Arthur Conan Doyle.

The NLS holds various letters of Conan Doyle, including the original manuscript of "The Adventure of the Illustrious Client," bequeathed by the late Dame Jean Conan Doyle, last surviving child of Conan Doyle. It also holds the original manuscript for "The Haunted Grange of Goresthorpe," a 24-page handwritten manuscript which Conan Doyle submitted to *Blackwood's Magazine* in the 1870s.

Many of the literary greats of the 19th and early 20th century were published in *Blackwood's Magazine*, the monthly periodical known affectionately as "The Maga." The witty satirical journalism of its early editors, John Wilson and John Gibson Lockhart, set the tone of "The Maga" as it praised and pilloried leading literary figures of the day. Depending on your point of view, you either rolled about in hysterics or contacted your lawyer. "How I have longed for their utter extinction!" wrote Gerard Manley Hopkins in 1863. They were, however, a platform for many struggling writers in their day, and went on to publish Sir Walter Scott, Anthony Trollope, Joseph Conrad, George Eliot, Thomas De Quincey and many of the stalwarts of 19th-century literature. It was only natural, therefore, that the 18-year-old medical student, Arthur Conan Doyle, should submit a short story in 1877 to this illustrious periodical based in his home city of Edinburgh. Blackwood's failed, however, to detect his talent, and rejected "The Haunted Grange of Goresthorpe." The story was filed by Blackwood's and was never returned to Conan Doyle, perhaps because he failed to supply a stamped addressed envelope. It lay forgotten until the Blackwood's archives were presented to the NLS in 1942, but was not published because the Doyle family thought it was not up to standard. The story, although lacking any great literary merit, does show that the concept of Holmes and Watson was being nurtured within him much earlier than had previously been thought. It was eventually published by the Arthur Conan Doyle Society in December 2000.

FURTHER INFORMATION: The National Library of Scotland, George IV Bridge, Edinburgh. Tel: +44(0)131 226 4531. www.nls.uk

FURTHER READING: F. D. Tredrey, *The House of Blackwood, 1804–1954* (Edinburgh, UK: W. Blackwood & Sons, 1954); M. Oliphant, *Annals of a Publishing House* (Edinburgh, UK: W. Blackwood & Sons, 1897).

SEE ALSO: Sir Walter Scott (p. 38), Robert Louis Stevenson (p. 27), Thomas De Quincey (p. 32), Joseph Conrad (p. 17).

Edinburgh Castle

Childhood home of George Borrow (1803–1881), picaresque writer greatly admired by Conan Doyle

"It is hardly necessary to say much about this Castle, which everybody has seen; on which account, doubtless, nobody has ever yet thought fit to describe it — at least that I am aware. Be this as it may, I have no intention of describing it." — George Borrow, *Lavengro* (1851)

George Borrow was an English author held in high regard by Conan Doyle. He wrote about him, and once lectured on him at his local literary society in Southsea. In 1825 Borrow left his legal work to take up a wandering life, traveling alone and living with gypsies whose life and culture fascinated him. He was an accomplished linguist and acted as agent for the British and Foreign Bible Society writing extensively, although not always accurately, about his travels. Conan Doyle gives us a thumbnail sketch of this strange and enigmatic man in *Through the Magic Door* (1907):

There are some authors from whom I shrink because they are so voluminous that I feel that, do what I may, I can never hope to be well read in their works.... But no one could raise this objection to Borrow. A month's reading — even for a leisurely reader — will master all that he has written. There are *Lavengro*, *The Bible in Spain*, *Romany Rye*, and, finally, if you wish to go further, *Wild Wales*. Only four books — not much to found a great reputation upon — but, then, there are no other four books quite like them in the language.

He was a very strange man, bigoted, prejudiced, obstinate, inclined to be sulky, as wayward as a man could be. So far his catalogue of qualities does not seem to pick him as a winner. But he had one great and rare gift. He preserved through all his days a sense of the great wonder and mystery of life — the child sense which is so quickly dulled. Not only did he retain it himself, but he was word-master enough to make other people hark back to it also. As he writes you cannot help seeing through his eyes, and nothing which his eyes saw or his ear heard was ever dull or commonplace. It was all strange, mystic, with some deeper meaning struggling always to the light.... Borrow's views of literature and of literary men were curious. Publisher and brother author, he hated them with a fine comprehensive hatred. In all his books I cannot recall a word of commendation to any living writer, nor has he posthumous praise for those of the generation immediately preceding.... The reason was, I expect, that his proud soul was bitterly wounded by his own early failures and slow recognition. He knew himself to be a chief in the clan, and when the clan heeded him not he withdrew in haughty disdain. Look at his proud, sensitive face and you hold the key to his life.

In 1813 Borrow's soldier father was posted to Edinburgh Castle and the family lived within its walls. The famous landmark features in Borrow's autobiographical novel *Lavengro*. "To scale the rock was merely child's play for the Edinbro' callants [young boys]," he recalled. Once, he casually remarked to a friend while seated at the rock's summit that the story of William Wallace was "full of lies." To this, his friend retorted, "Ye had better sae naething agin Willie Wallace, Geordie, for if ye do, De'il hae me, if I dinna tumble ye doon the craig."

FURTHER READING: J. Hooper, *Souvenir of the George Borrow Celebration* (Norwich, UK: Jarrold & Sons, 1913); H. J. Jenkins, *The Life of George Borrow* (Boston: Adamant Media Corp., 2001).

New Town

22 St. Andrew Square

Birthplace of Joseph Bell (1837–1911), physician, surgeon, forensic pioneer, and inspiration for Sherlock Holmes

"Sherlock Holmes was the literary embodiment of my memory of a professor of medicine at Edinburgh University." — Arthur Conan Doyle

If Sherlock Holmes had not existed, Joseph Bell would have been long forgotten. A painted portrait, a few hand-written diaries, a surgical

22 St. Andrew Square.

handbook for students and a letter to him from Florence Nightingale would have been the sum total of his existence. Conan Doyle, however, etched his memory in the consciousness of his voracious reading public when he publicly named him as his inspiration for Sherlock Holmes, and in so doing made his memory immortal.

He was born on 2 December 1837, the first of nine children of Cecilia Craigie and Benjamin Bell, and was named Joseph after his grandfather. The Bells trace their roots back to the Scottish Border country where their family seat was at Blackwood Tower (pronounced Blackett) in the parish of Middlebie, Dumfriesshire. The Bell medical dynasty began with Joseph Bell's great grandfather, Benjamin Bell (1749–1806), who became apprentice to a Dumfries surgeon and went on to study surgery at medical schools in Edinburgh, Paris and London. In the 1780s he published the first detailed and extensive textbook of surgery ever written in the English language, a six volume opus titled *A System of Surgery*. This cemented Benjamin's reputation and was one of the early catalysts in establishing Edinburgh as one of the foremost surgical centers in the world of 19th century medicine. Benjamin's two sons, George (1777–1832) and Joseph (1786–1848), also became surgeons; and it was Joseph's son Benjamin (1810–83) who was the father of Joseph Bell.

Benjamin married Cecilia Craigie from Perthshire, and their marriage produced six boys and three girls. A deeply religious man, he specialized in diseases of the eye and much of his services were devoted to the Royal Blind Asylum in Edinburgh, where he acted as medical attendant for over thirty years. His son Joseph was almost six before he started his elementary schooling. From 1847 to 1854 he attended the august Edinburgh Academy, founded in 1824 at Henderson Row on the southern fringe of Edinburgh's New Town. Its notable alumni included the physicist James Clerk Maxwell, children's author R. M. Ballantyne, and Robert Louis Stevenson. It was a sink or swim environment. Some pupils flourished. Others sank like a stone. Fortunately for Sherlock Holmes fans, Joseph Bell was a model student, winning prizes in everything from biblical scholarship to mathematics. Next on the horizon was medicine, and at the tender age of sixteen he entered the hallowed walls of Edinburgh University's medical school.

FURTHER READING: E. Liebow, Dr. Joe Bell, *Model for Sherlock Holmes* (OH: Bowling Green University Popular Press, 1982); J. Saxby, *Joseph Bell, An Appreciation by an Old Friend* (Edinburgh, UK: Oliphant, Anderson and Ferrier, 1914); M. Magnusson, *The Clacken and the Slate, Story of the Edinburgh Academy 1824–1974* (London, UK: Collins, 1974).

SEE ALSO: Old College (p. 10), Royal Infirmary (p. 12), Surgical Hospital (p. 15), Surgeon's Hall Museum (p. 21), Mauricewood (p. 36), Castle Terrace (p. 31), Livingston Mission Hall (p. 9), Robert Louis Stevenson (p. 27), Dean Cemetery (p. 35).

17 Heriot Row

Former home of Robert Louis Stevenson (1850–94), literary hero of Conan Doyle

Vailima, Apia, Samoa, April 5th, 1893.

Dear sir,

You have taken many occasions to make yourself very agreeable to me, for which I might in de-

cency have thanked you earlier. It is now my turn; and I hope you will allow me to offer you my compliments on your very ingenious and very interesting adventures of Sherlock Holmes. That is the class of literature that I like when I have the toothache. As a matter of fact, it was a pleurisy I was enjoying when I took the volume up; and it will interest you as a medical man to know that the cure was for the moment effectual. Only the one thing troubles me: can this be my old friend Joe Bell?

I am, yours very truly,

Robert Louis Stevenson

P.S.—And lo, here is your address supplied me here in Samoa! But do not take mine, O frolic fellow Spookist, from the same source; mine is wrong.

R. L. S.

Conan Doyle and Robert Louis Stevenson were both born in Edinburgh, and were both students at Edinburgh University in the mid–1870s, but they never met. Conan Doyle once wrote that he "probably brushed elbows with [him] in the crowded portal" [of Old College], but as Doyle entered university in October 1876, and Stevenson passed his final law exams in July 1875, this seems unlikely. Stevenson, like Walter Scott, was one of Conan Doyle's great literary heroes, and he was strongly influenced by him. In 1883 Doyle's story "J. Habakuk Jephson's Statement," inspired by the Marie Celeste mystery, was published anonymously in the *Cornhill Magazine*, and many readers attributed it to the pen of Stevenson. *A Study in Scarlet* (1887) was also heavily influenced by Stevenson's *The Dynamiter* (1885). In later life, when Stevenson was in the South Seas, they corresponded with each other, and Conan Doyle considered visiting him in Samoa. Stevenson was always appreciative of Doyle's work. "I have a great talent for compliment," he wrote, "accompanied by a hateful, even a diabolic, frankness." Stevenson actually read the Sherlock Holmes story "The Adventure of the Engineer's Thumb" to his native servants. The Samoans, however, had no understanding of what a fictional story was, but Stevenson still managed to mesmerize them.

In 1907 Conan Doyle paid homage to Stevenson's skills as a wordsmith in *Through the Magic Door*, his own personal tribute to the writers who held a special place on his book shelves:

He wrote, in my judgment, two masterpieces in his life, and each of them is essentially a short story, though the one happened to be published as a volume. The one is "Dr. Jekyll and Mr. Hyde," which, whether you take it as a vivid narrative or as a wonderfully deep and true allegory, is a supremely fine bit of work. The other story of my choice would be "The Pavilion on the Links"— the very model of dramatic narrative. That story stamped itself so clearly on my brain when I read it in Cornhill that when I came across it again many years afterwards in volume form, I was able instantly to recognize two small modifications of the text — each very much for the worse — from the original form. They were small things, but they seemed somehow like a chip on a perfect statue. Surely it is only a very fine work of art which could leave so definite an impression as that. Of course, there are a dozen other of his stories which would put the average writer's best work to shame, all with the strange Stevenson glamour upon them.... The main characteristic of Stevenson is his curious instinct for saying in the briefest space just those few words which stamp the impression upon the reader's mind. He will make you see a thing more clearly than you would probably have done had your eyes actually rested upon it.... Is Stevenson a classic? Well, it is a large word that. You mean by a classic a piece of work which passes into the permanent literature of the country. As a rule, you only know your classics when they are in their graves. Who guessed it of Poe, and who of Bor-

row? The Roman Catholics only canonize their saints a century after their death. So with our classics. The choice lies with our grandchildren. But I can hardly think that healthy boys will ever let Stevenson's books of adventure die, nor do I think that such a short tale as "The Pavilion on the Links" nor so magnificent a parable as "Dr. Jekyll and Mr. Hyde" will ever cease to be esteemed. How well I remember the eagerness, the delight with which I read those early tales in "Cornhill" away back in the late seventies and early eighties. They were unsigned, after the old unfair fashion, but no man with any sense of prose could fail to know that they were all by the same author. Only years afterwards did I learn who that author was.... No, I never met him. But among my most prized possessions are several letters which I received from Samoa. From that distant tower he kept a surprisingly close watch upon what was doing among the bookmen, and it was his hand which was among the first held out to the striver, for he had quick appreciation and keen sympathies which met another man's work half-way, and wove into it a beauty from his own mind.... I cannot forget the shock that it was to me when driving down the Strand in a hansom cab in 1894 I saw upon a yellow evening poster "Death of Stevenson." Something seemed to have passed out of my world. I was asked by his executors to finish the novel "St Ives," which he had left three-quarters completed, but I did not feel equal to the task.

Conan Doyle kept up his admiration for Stevenson to the end. The epitaph on his tombstone is a line taken from Stevenson's poem "My Wife," and reads, "Steel True, Blade Straight."

FURTHER INFORMATION: The Stevenson family moved to 17 Heriot Row in 1857, a Georgian street in Edinburgh's New Town which today still exudes affluence and pedigree. It is not open to the public; but it does operate as a bed and breakfast and is available to hire for dinners, weddings or any other special occasions. Tel: +44(0)131 556 1896. Email: *mail@stevenson-house.co.uk*. www.stevenson-house.co.uk.

SEE ALSO: Joseph Bell (p. 12), Sir Walter Scott (p. 38), George Borrow (p. 25), Edgar Allan Poe (p. 98), William Burton (p. 6), Churchyard of All Saints (p. 139).

West End

16 Charlotte Square
Former home of Sir Patrick Heron Watson, MD (1832–1907), probable inspiration for the fictitious Dr. John H. Watson

17 **Heriot Row.**

"Nobody in Scotland is willing to die till they have seen Watson."

We will never know the real inspiration for Sherlock Holmes's devoted sidekick, Dr. Watson, but a strong contender has to be Conan Doyle's former teacher, forensic expert Dr. Patrick Heron Watson. A son of the manse, Watson was one of the four surviving sons of the Rev. Charles Watson who had been a minister at Burntisland in Fife. His third son, Patrick, was born in Edinburgh in 1832, graduating in medicine at Edinburgh University in 1853. Shortly after the completion of his term as house-surgeon at Edinburgh's Royal Infirmary he joined the army Medical Corps in 1855 for service in the Crimean War. Before embarking for action he bought himself a uniform, a lamp, a robe of lynx skin, a raccoon coat coming down to his ankles, fur boots and a revolver. On reaching Constantinople he was posted to the military hospital at Scutari. Writing home to his mother he recalled the grim conditions of a barrack hospital: "The deaths in the Barrack Hospital amount to 50 a day. They are carted off, sewn up in blankets, in arabahs [a Turkish bullock cart] and laid in layers in trenches; officers are distinguished only by having a white-wood coffin. My first view of this was an arabah upset in the mud with the bodies all in a heap. In fact the Barrack Hospital is a lazar-house, a dead house. Everything there is bad and I look forward with no very pleasant feelings to being quartered there."

During Heron Watson's first month at the hospital, 300 out of 1,200 patients, one in every four, died, the majority of fever, dysentery or other infection, much originating within the hospital itself, his theater of operations for the next five months. "The nuns are far better than the nurses," he wrote, "and if I were ill I would rather have a nun to attend me. Some of the nurses have had fever and upon my word they are almost no loss. A bevy of good cooks would be a good deal more useful and not half so troublesome." He was also displeased concerning "the absurd puff about Miss Nightingale in The Times of 8 February, where it speaks about her angelic form. From what I have seen of her, which certainly has been in the distance, she is a very dowdy old maid, about whom the less

16 Charlotte Square.

romance the better." Nine months later Heron Watson was shipped home following attacks of typhus and dysentery.

In 1856 he returned to Edinburgh and became private assistant to James Miller, Professor of Surgery, whose daughter he later married. In 1860 was appointed assistant surgeon in Edinburgh Royal Infirmary, becoming a full surgeon in 1863. In 1858 he became lecturer on surgery in the extra-mural school of medicine of the Royal Colleges of Medicine and Surgery and it was while in this post, which he held for many years, that Conan Doyle would have had contact with him.

Although no friend of Florence Nightingale and the nurses of the Crimea, Heron Watson was an early pioneer for the medical education of women and was one of the first to open his class of surgery in the extra-mural school to women students. He also refused to be pigeon-holed as a surgeon, and remained both a physician and a surgeon, attaining success in both fields.

Rutherford Morison, a fellow surgeon and contemporary of Heron Watsons, described him after his passing in 1907: "There was a stronger individuality about him than anyone else I have known. His old house-surgeons will remember his military walk; correct attire; neat, plainly written notes; ready command of language peculiarly his own; his courteous manner; his independence of character. We will revere those memories for we loved the man."

FURTHER READING: W. N. B. Watson, "An Edinburgh Surgeon of the Crimean War — Patrick Heron Watson" (A paper read to the Scottish Society of the History of Medicine on 28 February 1964); P. Pincoffs, *Experiences of a Civilian in Eastern Military Hospitals* (Edinburgh, UK: Williams & Norgate, 1857); *Report Upon the State of the Hospitals of the British Army in the Crimea and Scutari* (London, UK: Eyre & Spottiswoode, 1855).

SEE ALSO: Royal Infirmary (p. 12), Maiwand Lion (p. 105), Sophia Jex-Blake (p. 33), The Criterion (p. 78).

23 Rutland Street

Former Home of Dr. John Brown (1810–82), physician, essayist and friend of Mary Doyle

They ken your name, they ken your tyke [dog],
They ken the honey from your byke [bees'nest];
But mebbe after a' your fyke [trouble],
(The truth to tell)
It's just your honest Rab they like,
An' no yoursel'.
— "To Doctor John Brown," *Underwoods* (1887), Robert Louis Stevenson

In June 1863, shortly after the death of their two-year-old daughter, Mary, Conan Doyle's parents joined the Philosophical Institution, a popular Edinburgh literary and debating society. Charles no doubt attended a few soirées, but for Mary it was a meeting of minds where she delighted in the debates and immersed herself in their extensive library. The most rewarding attraction of the Philosophical Institution, however, had to be making the acquaintance of its illustrious members, not least, the great physician and essayist Dr. John Brown (1810–82), known affectionately as the "Scottish Charles Lamb," with whom Mary Doyle became close friends.

Dr. John Brown didn't leave the world much to remember his literary talents by, but what lit-

23 Rutland Street.

tle he did leave ranks him amongst the world's foremost essayists. Most of his writings were contained in the three-volume *Horae Subsecivae* (Leisure Hours, 1858–82), which includes his masterpiece set in the streets of Edinburgh, "Rab and His Friends" (1859), one of the best insights into the human nature of dogs ever written.

The son of a minister, he was born in Biggar and moved to Edinburgh in 1822 at age 12. He qualified as a doctor and lived for 60 years in the city, counting among his many friends Ruskin, Thackeray and Mark Twain, who described him as having "a sweet and winning face, as beautiful a face as I have ever known. Reposeful, gentle, benignant; the face of a saint a peace with all the world and placidly beaming upon it the sunshine of love that filled his heart."

John Brown would have met the young Arthur Conan Doyle on many occasions, and Conan Doyle most certainly would have read Brown's short story "Rab and his Friends." There is a particularly moving scene in the story which could have persuaded a young boy considering a career in medicine to contemplate another path through life. Set in the days before anesthetic (chloroform was first used in Edinburgh by obstetrician James Young Simpson in 1847) and Pasteur's germ theory, the scene describes an operation at the city's Minto House Hospital, which then stood in Chambers Street. A local carter's wife named Ailie has "a kind o' trouble in her breest" and is operated on by surgeons in an amphitheater filled with excited medical students. Also present in the theater is her husband, James, and their dog, Rab:

> The operating theatre is crowded; much talk and fun, and all the cordiality and stir of youth. The surgeon with his staff of assistants is there. In comes Ailie: one look at her quiets and abates the eager students. That beautiful old woman is too much for them; they sit down, and are dumb, and gaze at her. These rough boys feel the power of her presence. She walks in quickly, but without haste; dressed in her mutch, her neckerchief, her white dimity short-gown, her black bombazine petticoat, showing her white worsted stockings and her carpet shoes. Behind her was James with Rab. James sat down in the distance, and took that huge and noble head between his knees. Rab looked perplexed and dangerous; forever cocking his ear and dropping it as fast.
>
> Ailie stepped up on a seat, and laid herself on the table, as her friend the surgeon told her; arranged herself, gave a rapid look at James, shut her eyes, rested herself on me, and took my hand. The operation was at once begun; it was necessarily slow; and chloroform — one of God's best gifts to his suffering children — was then unknown. The surgeon did his work. The pale face showed its pain, but was still and silent. Rab's soul was working within him; he saw that something strange was going on, — blood flowing from his mistress, and she suffering; his ragged ear was up, and importunate; he growled and gave now and then a sharp impatient yelp; he would have liked to have done something to that man. But James had him firm, and gave him a GLOWER from time to time, and an intimation of a possible kick; all the better for James, it kept his eye and his mind off Ailie.
>
> It is over: she is dressed, steps gently and decently down from the table, looks for James; then, turning to the surgeon and the students, she courtesies, and in a low, clear voice begs their pardon if she has behaved ill. The students — all of us — wept like children; the surgeon happed her up carefully, and, resting on James and me, Ailie went to her room, Rab following. We put her to bed.

Further Reading: E. T. Maclaren, *Dr John Brown and His Sister Isabella* (Edinburgh, UK: David Douglas, 1890); Dr. J. Brown (son) and D. W. Forrest, editors, "Letters of Dr. John Brown" (1907).

5 Castle Terrace
First married home of Joseph and Edith Bell

In 1865 Joseph Bell married Edith Erskine Murray, and on 27 May they moved into their first married home at Castle Terrace, beneath the city's most popular tourist attraction, Edinburgh Castle. In January of the same year Bell wrote: "My professional prospects still look bad. Few patients, hardly any remunerative ones and classes smaller than last years." A few weeks later the managers of the Royal Infirmary appointed him as clinical assistant surgeon to the legendary James Syme, a post which would be most beneficial all round.

Bell, however, was not at his physical best during 1865, and was still convalescing from an incident which occurred in the summer of the previous year when Edinburgh was in the grip of a serious diphtheria epidemic, an acute respiratory

5 Castle Terrace.

infection which could be life-threatening to children. The bacteria and the toxin destroy the mucous membrane, so that a thick coating is formed and the patient develops a serious inflammation of the throat. The membranous coating in the throat can become detached and obstruct the airways, making breathing difficult and sometimes causing asphyxiation. Joseph Bell had developed a technique of sucking out the poisonous coating from a child's throat with a special pipette — a practical but dangerous procedure, which infected him with diphtheria. He recovered, but it left him with a high-pitched voice and a limp (post-diphtheritic paralysis), which Conan Doyle observed as "walking with a curious jerky gait."

The year after his marriage, in 1866, he published his surgical handbook for students, the *Manual of the Operations of Surgery*, a tome which stayed in print until the turn of the century, and would have been well thumbed by the young Conan Doyle. In 1871 he was promoted to full surgeon at the Royal Infirmary.

The Bells had three children, but just as things were changing for the better, his wife was stricken with puerperal peritonitis and died on 9 November 1874. Bells black hair is said to have turned white almost overnight.

FURTHER INFORMATION: Joseph Bell's other residencies in Edinburgh inluded his birthplace at 22 St Andrews Square (1837–38); Canaan Lodge, Canaan Lane (1838); 120 George Street (c.1839–49); 8 Shandwick Place (1849–65); 20 Melville Street (1871–84); 2 Melville Crescent (1884–1911), and Mauricewood, Milton Bridge, Penicuik (1894–1911).

SEE ALSO: Royal Infirmary (p. 12), Surgical Hospital (p. 15), Surgeon's Hall Museum (p. 21), Mauricewood (p. 36), St. Andrew's Square (p. 26), Livingston Mission Hall (p. 9), Robert Louis Stevenson (p. 27), Dean Cemetery (p. 35).

5 Lothian Road
St. Cuthbert's Churchyard

Grave of Thomas De Quincey (1785–1859), opium-addicted essayist mentioned in "The Man with the Twisted Lip"

"Isa Whitney, brother of the late Elias Whitney, D.D., principal of the Theological College of St. George's, was much addicted to opium. The habit grew upon him, as I understand, from some foolish freak when he was at college; for having read De Quincey's description of his dreams and sensations, he had drenched his tobacco with laudanum in an attempt to produce the same effects. He found, as so many more have done, that the practice is easier to attain than to get rid of, and for many years he continued to be a slave to the drug, an object of mingled horror and pity to his friends and relatives. I can see him now, with yellow, pasty face, drooping lids, and pin-point pupils, all huddled in a chair, the wreck and ruin of a noble man." — Arthur Conan Doyle, "The Man with the Twisted Lip" from *Adventures of Sherlock Holmes* (1893)

Thomas De Quincey's life has become synonymous with two words — opium and debt — and outside his bestselling *The Confessions of an English Opium-Eater*, which made his name, little of his work is ever discussed, perhaps because most of it was journalism, written to put bread on the table for his eight children. He moved to Edinburgh in 1826 to escape his spiralling debts in London. There he became encumbered by more and more debt, for which he was eventually imprisoned in 1831. One of his sons died at age two in 1832, and his wife died in 1837. As if this wasn't enough suffering for De Quincey, another of his sons died shortly afterwards fighting, ironically, in the Chinese Opium Wars. De Quincey died in 1859, in a flat (now demolished) in Lothian Street, a street Conan Doyle would have walked down everyday on his way to Old College from his house in George Square. De Quincey also frequented Conan Doyle's favorite bookshop — James Thin, opposite Old College. He was described by Mr. Thin "as a meagre, nervous, shrivelled little man, who went skulking about after nightfall as if he could not stand the garish light of day." Death must have come as a great relief to De Quincey after such a tortuous and stressful life.

FURTHER INFORMATION: To find De Quincey's grave enter the churchyard from Lothian Road, walk straight down the path and turn right up the short steps just before the church. Follow the path around. De Quincey's grave is situated against the center of the wall facing King's Stables Road. The land around the church has been a burial ground for over 1,000 years, but internments ceased at the end

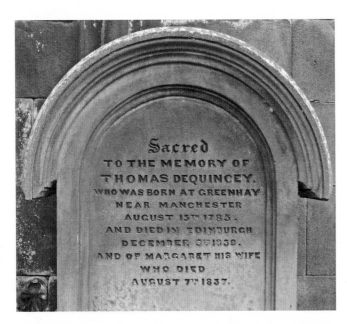

Grave of Thomas De Quincey, St. Cuthbert's Churchyard.

as if a blasphemy had been committed. His face betrayed his feelings only too clearly.... A woman doctor had been an abstract thing before, repugnant but distant. Now she was there in actual practice, with a brass plate up just like his own, competing for the same patients. Not that he feared competition, but he objected to this lowering of his ideal of womanhood.... It revolted him the more to recall the details of her education. A man, of course, could come through such an ordeal with all his purity, but it was nothing short of shameless in a woman." — Arthur Conan Doyle, "The Doctors of Hoyland," from *Round the Red Lamp* (1894)

As far as women were concerned, the British medical profession in the mid–19th century could be likened to a closed monastic order. Women were definitely taboo. Conan Doyle's short story "The Doctors of Hoyland" was his brief affirmation to the female

of the 19th century. In 1738, incidents of grave-robbing, to supply local medical schools with corpses, were becoming commonplace and the perimeter walls were raised to 8 feet. By 1803 it had become such a scourge that a crenellated watchtower was built to house guards throughout the night; this can still be seen today in the southwest corner of the churchyard.

FURTHER READING: G. Lindop, *Opium Eater: A Life of Thomas De Quincey* (London, UK: Weidenfeld & Nicolson, 1993); E. Sackville West, *A Flame in Sunlight: The Life and Work of Thomas De Quincey* (London, UK: Bodley Head, 1974); R. Morrison: *The English Opium Eater* (London, UK: Weidenfield & Nicolson, 2009).

SEE ALSO: James Thin (p. 19).

Haymarket

4 Manor Place

Former medical practice of Sophia Jex-Blake (1840–1912), pioneer of 19th century medical reform

"He had never seen a woman doctor before, and his whole conservative soul rose up in revolt at the idea. He could not recall any Biblical injunction that the man should remain ever the doctor and the woman the nurse, and yet he felt

Manor Place.

struggle for equality in the masculine domain of Victorian medicine. In the story Dr. James Ripley's rural practice comes under threat from a young female doctor, whose quick-witted intelligence and medical skills are a head and shoulders above his own. Conan Doyle's inspiration for the heroine of the story was clearly his recollections of Sophia Jex-Blake, whose crusade for women's rights led to her becoming Scotland's first woman doctor.

Sophia Jex-Blake was born in Hastings in 1840 into a middle-class, conservative family. After failing to gain entry to Harvard Medical School, she arrived in Edinburgh in 1869 in the hope of appealing to the university to admit women to study medicine. The Senatus Academicus decided by a majority to admit women for instruction in separate classes, and so in theory, doors were opening that had previously been firmly shut. Seven women, including Jex-Blake, enrolled for classes, amidst much opposition from professors and students. The university then discovered that its regulations did not permit them to graduate, and they were palmed off with a certificate of proficiency. After persistent crusading by Sophia Jex-Blake and her associates, Parliament eventually passed an act in 1876, the year Conan Doyle entered medical school, giving universities the authority to grant degrees to women. It took Sophia Jex-Blake eight years to qualify as a doctor, eventually establishing a practice in Manor Place. Had she not been the passionate, dedicated and courageous person she was, equality in the field of medicine would have taken considerably longer.

FURTHER READING: M. Todd, *The Life of Sophia Jex-Blake* (London, UK: Macmillan, 1918); S. Roberts, *Sophia Jex-Blake: A Woman Pioneer in Nineteenth Century Medical Reform* (New York: Routledge, 1993).

SEE ALSO: Sir Patrick Heron Watson (p.28).

Holyrood
Holyrood Park
Salisbury Crags
Mentioned in The Lost World

"When I finished my last letter I stated that we were within seven miles from an enormous line of ruddy cliffs, which encircled, beyond all doubt,

the plateau of which Professor Challenger spoke. Their height, as we approached them, seemed to me in some places to be greater than he had stated—running up in parts to at least a thousand feet—and they were curiously striated, in a manner which is, I believe, characteristic of basaltic upheavals. Something of the sort is to be seen in Salisbury Crags at Edinburgh."—Arthur Conan Doyle, *The Lost World* (1912)

The Lost World is a classic tale of adventure and discovery in which a scientific expedition hacks its way through the Amazon rainforest to reach an isolated plateau trapped in a prehistoric world inhabited by apemen and dinosaurs. Conan Doyle's reference in comparing the cliffs of the plateau to Salisbury Crags is understandable to any who have seen them. Formed from steep dolerite and columnar basalt, the crags are located within Holyrood Park, a 650-acre geological spectacle encompassing ancient volcanoes, fossilized beaches, and lochs. Walking beneath the crags it's not hard to imagine a pterodactyl swooping down at you, or apemen hurtling their victims over the edge onto bamboo spikes below. Conan Doyle would have seen the crags every day of his student life as they dominated the eastern horizon on his daily walk from his home in George Square to the medical faculty at Old College in South Bridge. The crags could easily qualify as *The Lost World* plateau in miniature (they are a mere 150 feet, compared to 1,000 feet in the novel), a catalyst if you like for a fertile imagination, but the genuine article lay elsewhere.

More plausible is the 1,300 foot cliffs of Mount Roraima on the borders of Venezuela, Brazil and Guyana, and another was the descriptions of the table-top hills in the Mato Grosso by the ill-fated explorer Percy Fawcett:

Above us towered the Ricardo Franco Hills, flat-topped and mysterious, their flanks scarred by deep quebradas [ravines]. Time and the foot of man had not touched those summits. They stood like a lost world, forested to their tops, and the imagination could picture the last vestiges there of an age long vanished. Isolated from the battle with changing conditions, monsters from the dawn of man's existence might still roam those heights unchallenged, imprisoned and protected by unscalable cliffs. So thought Conan Doyle when later in London I spoke of these hills and showed photographs of them. He mentioned an

Salisbury Crags (Chris Foster).

idea for a novel on Central South America and asked for information, which I told him I should be glad to supply. The fruit of it was his "Lost World" in 1912, appearing as a serial in the "Strand Magazine," and subsequently in the form of a book that achieved widespread popularity.

Professor Challenger, the expedition's autocratic leader, was inspired by Conan Doyle's former physiology professor, William Rutherford (1839–99). A short, stocky individual with an "Assyrian beard" and a booming voice who held an irresistible attraction to his students through his eccentric and often bizarre behavior. The name Challenger was derived from HMS Challenger, a British corvette which carried out a pioneering marine research expedition around the globe in 1873–76, and was led by Conan Doyle's natural history professor, Charles Wyville Thomson. In the novel, the soldier of fortune, Lord John Roxton, was based on Roger Casement, the Irish revolutionary who was executed for treason in 1916; and the journalist narrator, Edward Dunn Malone, was based on the Irish journalist, Edmund Dene Morel. The original artwork for the novel, and Conan Doyle's knowledge of prehistoric flora and fauna was mostly derived from E. R. Lankester's *Extinct Animals*.

FURTHER INFORMATION: The main entrance to Holyrood Park is adjacent to The Palace of Holyroodhouse, the ruling monarch's residence

in Edinburgh, at the bottom of the Royal Mile. In 1925 a silent feature film was made of *The Lost World*, and in April of the same year it became the world's first in-flight movie when it was screened onboard an Imperial Airways flight from London to Paris. The same year Col. Fawcett and his son disappeared in the Mato Grosso searching for "The Lost City of Z," a name given by Fawcett to a mysterious city said to have been visited by a Portuguese explorer in 1753.

FURTHER READING: Col. P. H. Fawcett, *Exploration Fawcett* (Phoenix, 2001, first published 1953, arranged from Fawcett's manuscripts, letters, log-books and records by his son, Brian Fawcett); E. R. Lankester, *Extinct Animals* (1905; repr., Whitefish, MT: Kessinger, 2008).

SEE ALSO: Professor William Rutherford (p. 39), Roger Casement (p. 96), George Square (p. 23).

Dean Village

Dean Path
Dean Cemetery
Grave of Dr. Joseph Bell (1837–1911); Conan Doyle's teacher and inspiration for Sherlock Holmes

Following the death of Joseph Bell on 4 October 1911, a staggering number of people attended his funeral, one of the largest ever seen in Edinburgh. Thousands more lined the streets. This turnout, however, was nothing to do with Conan Doyle having described Bell as his inspiration for Sherlock Holmes being "the literary embodiment of my memory of a professor of medicine at Edinburgh University." The tribute was for Joseph Bell the professor, the physician and the man.

The following extract from the *British Medical Journal*'s obituary for Joseph Bell faithfully sums up the feeling of the time:

Dr. Joseph Bell died at his country house, Mauricewood, Milton Bridge, Midlothian, on October 4th. His health broke down in February last, and although he rallied and was able to be out to enjoy a drive, he did not resume practice. A week or two ago serious heart symptoms recurred, and ended his life. Dr. Bell was a marked figure in Edinburgh. Nearly to the end of his life he retained his buoyant and even boyish disposition. He was bright, cheerful, and happy. He had many admiring friends. He was a kindly man, and unknown to all but a few, he did very many fine and helpful actions to those in trouble. Till his illness in February last he carried on a large family practice. He was a brilliant and impressive teacher. He missed nothing as a clinician. Among his pupils in the Edinburgh Royal Infirmary was Sir Arthur Conan Doyle, who, it is generally believed, took him as the prototype of the famous detective of the "Sherlock Holmes" stories. Sir Arthur Conan Doyle says of his old teacher: "Personally I can say very little of Dr. Joseph Bell, for I have never met him in his own house, and really only know him as my professor. As such I shall always see him very clearly, his stiff, bristling, iron-grey hair, his clear, half-humorous, half-critical grey eyes, his eager face, and swarthy skin. He had a very spare figure, as I remember him, and walked with a jerky energetic gait, his head carried high, and his arms swinging. He had a dry humour, and a remarkable command of the vernacular, into which he easily fell when addressing his patients. His skill as a surgeon and his charm as a lecturer are, of course, proverbial."

As a doctor he was greatly loved by his patients, in whatever rank of life they were. He lightened their burdens and cheered their lives by his fine sympathy and brightness and by his encouraging words. His nature was essentially bright, happy, and youthful. He will be long missed by a wide circle of friends and patients. His funeral took place from St. George's United Free Church on the afternoon of October 7th. There was a large

Grave of Joseph Bell, Dean Cemetery.

attendance of the office-bearers of his church, of the Royal Colleges of Physicians and Surgeons, of the University, of the Royal Infirmary, of the Longmore Hospital, of the Queen Victoria's Jubilee Institute of Nurses, of army veterans, of the Children's Hospital, and of the public.—*British Medical Journal*, October 14, 1911.

FURTHER INFORMATION: Joseph Bell's grave is marked by a white marble cross situated roughly midway along the northern wall of the older and main section of Dean Cemetery, bordering Ravelston Terrace.

SEE ALSO: Surgical Hospital (p. 15), Surgeon's Hall Museum (p. 21), Old College (p. 10), Royal Infirmary (p. 12), St. Andrew's Square (p. 26), Castle Terrace (p. 31), Mauricewood (p. 36), Livingston Mission Hall (p. 9), Robert Louis Stevenson (p. 27).

MIDLOTHIAN

Penicuik
Mauricewood

Country retreat of Joseph Bell and where he died in 1911

[Sherlock Holmes] has definitely retired from London and betaken himself to study and bee-farming on the Sussex Downs, notoriety has be-

come hateful to him, and he has peremptorily requested that his wishes in this matter should be strictly observed.—Arthur Conan Doyle, "The Adventure of the Second Stain" from *The Return of Sherlock Holmes* (1905)

In 1894 Joseph Bell purchased Mauricewood, a modest Victorian mansion with a small estate on the northern fringes of Penicuik at the foot

Joseph Bell.

often surrounded by his grandchildren, who nicknamed him "Gigs" because of his fondness for the horse-drawn carriage, Joe Bell withdrew slowly, but never completely, from the world of medicine.

He died at 73 on 4 October, 1911, at Mauricewood, from a combination of heart disease, uremia and albuminuria. His final days were recorded in the *Edinburgh Medical Journal* for October 1911 by his friend and colleague, Dr. John Playfair:

> During all the weeks and months of illness, never a murmur nor fretful word was heard from him, and his cheerfulness, even after a bad night was remarkable. I shall never forget, at the morning visit, and in response to my knock at his bedroom door, the loud and cheery come in, or come in, dear boy, so glad to see you. Then he gave me, with many humorous touches, a description of his night.... All orders and suggestions were gratefully and readily accepted and carried out with unfailing punctuality — this, too, although he was no ardent believer in the power of medicine. He realized that the best he could ever hope for would be a life of quiet invalidism. He accepted the outlook with perfect resignation and composure.... When he began to feel the end might be drawing near, he calmly and quietly asked us what we thought his prospects of life now were, requesting us to state our opinions plainly and frankly and to keep nothing back. A strong, simple Christian faith sustained him, not only then but through some of life's severest afflictions, and enabled him with a rare and lofty courage unshrinkingly to contemplate and prepare for the inevitable.

of the Pentland Hills. By the time he was almost sixty in 1896 he was seriously contemplating retirement. He still had one of the largest practices in the city. He was chief surgeon of the Royal Hospital for Sick Children, did charitable work for the Royal Hospital for Incurables, and had recently been elected to the post of University of Edinburgh assessor. A workload from which nobody would have criticized him from wanting to wind down, and where better to do it than at Mauricewood, then an idyllic country retreat on the edge of Edinburgh.

"He loved to romp here with his grandchildren; to welcome his friends," commented his granddaughter in 1943. "Such were its delights, his garden might have been the island valley of Avilon." And so, immersed in his flower garden,

FURTHER INFORMATION: Mauricewood is located in Milton Bridge, Penicuik, about nine miles from central Edinburgh. Built in 1836, it was extended in 1897 by Joseph Bell. It is not open to the public.

SEE ALSO: Surgical Hospital (p. 15), Surgeon's Hall Museum (p. 21), Old College (p. 10), Royal Infirmary (p. 12), St. Andrew's Square (p. 26), Castle Terrace (p. 31), Livingston Mission Hall (p. 9), Robert Louis Stevenson (p. 27), Dean Cemetery (p. 35).

BORDERS

Dryburgh
Dryburgh Abbey

Tomb of Sir Walter Scott (1771–1832), literary hero of Conan Doyle

"It is a great thing to start life with a small number of really good books which are your very own. You may not appreciate them at first. You may pine for your novel of crude and unadulterated adventure. You may, and will, give it the preference when you can. But the dull days come, and the rainy days come, and always you are driven to fill up the chinks of your reading with the worthy books which wait so patiently for your notice. And then suddenly, on a day which marks an epoch in your life, you understand the difference. You see, like a flash, how the one stands for nothing, and the other for literature. From that day onwards you may return to your crudities, but at least you do so with some standard of comparison in your mind. You can never be the same as you were before. Then gradually the good thing becomes more dear to you; it builds itself up with your growing mind; it becomes a part of your better self, and so, at last, you can look, as I do now, at the old covers and love them for all that they have meant in the past. Yes, it was the olive-green line of Scott's novels which started me on to rhapsody. They were the first books I ever owned — long, long before I could appreciate or even understand them. But at last I realized what a treasure they were. In my boyhood I read them by surreptitious candle-ends in the dead of the night, when the sense of crime added a new zest to the story. Perhaps you have observed that my 'Ivanhoe' is of a different edition from the others. The first copy was left in the grass by the side of a stream, fell into the water, and was eventually picked up three days later, swollen and decomposed, upon a mud-bank. I think I may say, however, that I had worn it out before I lost it. Indeed, it was perhaps as well that it was some years before it was replaced, for my instinct was always to read it again instead of breaking fresh ground.... But of all the sons of men, I don't think there are many greater than he who lies under the great slab at Dryburgh." — Arthur Conan Doyle, *Through the Magic Door* (1907)

Conan Doyle wanted more than anything to be remembered as an author of historical fiction, but despite writing extremely competent

Tomb of Sir Walter Scott, Dryburgh Abbey.

historical novels, they never eclipsed the popularity of Sherlock Holmes. He was of course following in the footsteps of his literary mentor, Sir Walter Scott, who, in 1814, with his first novel, *Waverley*, invented the romantic and historical novel virtually overnight, and would soon enjoy a readership across the entire literate world. He was a novel-writing machine, and no one could outdo him for style, plot and gross domestic product.

Scott's novels were the first books the young Conan Doyle owned, and although unable yet to fully comprehend them, he knew they were masterpieces of English literature. In later life he was a little more critical, adding, "There is, I admit, an intolerable amount of redundant verbiage in Scott's novels. Those endless and unnecessary introductions make the shell very thick before you come to the oyster." The shell is perhaps even thicker today, and the oyster lost on many, for the days of the mass readership for the great historical novel are long passed; but that in no way diminishes Scott's achievements. Few people read him today, but even less read Conan Doyle's romances.

Nestling on the banks of the River Tweed, this imposing 12th-century monastic ruin seems a fitting resting place for "the mighty minstrel." Scott's tomb is situated in one of the ruined aisles that once belonged to his forebears — the Haliburtons of Merton, an ancient baronial family and from whom his paternal grandmother was descended. Lady Scott was buried there in May 1826; Sir Walter himself on 26 September 1832; his son, Colonel Sir Walter Scott, in February 1847; and John Gibson Lockhart, his "son-in-law, biographer, and friend," in November 1854.

FURTHER INFORMATION: Dryburgh Abbey (+44 (0)1835 822381) is situated five miles southeast of Melrose, near the village of St. Boswells. From the A68 take the B6404, St. Boswells to Kelso road, and turn off at the B6356, signposted to Dryburgh Abbey. Parking is available close to the abbey, which is open all year. Only medieval ruins remain and Scott's tomb is in the north transept.

Ancrum
The Churchyard
Grave of Professor William Rutherford (1839–99), inspiration for Professor Challenger

"He sat in a rotating chair behind a broad table, which was covered with books, maps, and diagrams. As I entered, his seat spun round to face me. His appearance made me gasp. I was prepared for something strange, but not for so overpowering a personality as this. It was his size which took one's breath away — his size and his imposing presence. His head was enormous, the largest I have ever seen upon a human being. I am sure that his top-hat, had I ever ventured to don it, would have slipped over me entirely and rested on my shoulders. He had the face and beard which I associate with an Assyrian bull; the former florid, the latter so black as almost to have a suspicion of blue, spade-shaped and rippling down over his chest. The hair was peculiar, plastered down in front in a long, curving wisp over his massive forehead. The eyes were blue-gray under great black tufts, very clear, very critical, and very masterful. A huge spread of shoulders and a chest like a barrel were the other parts of him which appeared above the table, save for

two enormous hands covered with long black hair. This and a bellowing, roaring, rumbling voice made up my first impression of the notorious Professor Challenger."— Arthur Conan Doyle, *The Lost World* (1912)

Conan Doyle's memorably outlandish physiology professor, William Rutherford, died of influenza on 21 February 1899, thirteen years before he was immortalized by him as Professor Challenger in *The Lost World*. Whether Professor Rutherford would have taken delight or umbrage at his fictional counterpart is open to debate, but what is beyond doubt is that Conan Doyle did not overly embellish him as his temperament and oddball pronouncements were confirmed by many of his students and contemporaries. His obituary appeared in the *British Medical Journal* a few weeks after his death, written anonymously by "an old fellow student and close friend." The following extract sums up this extraordinarily determined, industrious, and often misunderstood man:

It is probable that no more difficult task could be undertaken than an appreciation of William Rutherford. Proud, shy, sensitive, resentful of injustice, he was no Laodicean, but one whose moral qualities made him loved and hated, misunderstood and admired, misjudged and enthusiastically applauded.... His manner and mode of speech have always been alluded to. They were often spoken of as dictated by superciliousness, hauteur, vanity, carelessness of the feelings of others. No doubt he thought it right to maintain his dignity, but the manner in which he did so was due to the overdoing of brusqueness to hide his real shyness, the affectation of calmness to hide his diffidence. He was at heart an exceedingly sensitive man, and was greatly afflicted by self-consciousness. The kindness of one pleased, as the unkindness of another hurt excessively; he dwelt upon and exaggerated both. His important investigations on the bile and on other subjects led him to perform experiments by vivisection. He thought it his duty to do it, and he rightly did it. But he was viciously attacked by certain people, Christian and other, and he felt it terribly — almost morbidly. There had been, for instance, such a thing as refusal to meet him at dinner, and he shrank from all but professional society for a time.

Under this strain, and weakened by unremitting toil, for a time his nervous system yielded, his mental balance and usual soundness of judgement were affected. Moreover, what recreation he indulged in was rather a variation of labour in the shape of metaphysical speculation and a study of

The marble stone marking Professor Rutherford's grave is engraved with the Rutherford motto, "Nec sorte nec fato"—"Neither by chance nor by fate," beneath a heraldic Martlet.

Oriental religions. In this state he misinterpreted and unjustifiably resented on more than one occasion the gestures and actions of some with whom he was associated in his work. He was fiercely assailed in return, and efforts were made to drive him from his chair...

Professor Rutherford by his will bequeathed to the University of Edinburgh his medical library, his microscopical specimens and diagrams used in connection with the class of physiology, and also a portrait of himself. The funeral took place at Ancrum Church on the morning of February 25th. The funeral procession was headed by some four hundred students walking four abreast.

FURTHER INFORMATION: The village of Ancrum is situated just off the A68 between St Boswells and Jedburgh. Ancrum churchyard, one of the most idyllic in the Border country, is located about half a mile north west of the village on the B6400 and is clearly signposted. Professor Rutherford's grave is in the far corner of the small burial area behind the ruins of the church, where his marble stone is engraved with the Rutherford motto, "Nec sorte nec fato"—"Neither by chance nor by fate," beneath a heraldic Martlet.

SEE ALSO: Salisbury Crags (p. 34), Roger Casement (p. 96).

Hawick
Where Conan Doyle stood for parliament in 1905

"The electors have returned me to the bosom of my family." — Conan Doyle's comment after his defeat in the 1905 election

Conan Doyle got more than he bargained for when he stood in the parliamentary election of 1905 as the Liberal Unionist candidate for "The Border Burghs," consisting of the Scottish towns of Hawick, Galashiels and Selkirk. These towns were all reliant on the woollen trade for their existence, each one a city-state, and each one with its own way of doing things. An outsider, even if he had lived in these valleys for fifty years, would still remain an outsider. Conan Doyle, although born a Scot, was still not a Borderer. He was an incomer. A stranger in a strange land with no hope of cracking what he de-

At the northeast end of Hawick High Street, a statue of a horse and rider commemorates the defeat of an English raiding party and the capture of the English flag, an event frequently reenacted at the annual Common Riding.

scribed as "the innate conservatism of the Scottish character."

He put up a good fight, but lost the election which ended his career in politics. As usual he gave it his best shot, and apart from the usual round of speeches and heckling, he did what had to be done to ingratiate himself with the locals, which included joining "what is known as the 'common riding' at Hawick."

The Common Riding is an annual summer event and local holiday celebrated throughout the towns of the Scottish Borders. Hawick's Common Riding takes place every June, and celebrates both the capture of an English Flag in 1514 and the ancient custom of riding the marches or boundaries of the common land. Conan Doyle was no great horseman and the proceedings proved gruelling, and at times fren-

zied, for him. His comment was that "sooner or later someone will be killed … and horses must be lamed every year." The Hawick Common Riding always ends with the crowd singing the town song, described by Conan Doyle as "an interminable ballad." "Teribus ye teri odin" was the war cry of the men of Hawick at the Battle of Flodden Field in 1513, and the people from Hawick call themselves "Teries," after the song. Conan Doyle, however, had no wish to become a Terie, and "no desire to face another Hawick Common Riding."

FURTHER INFORMATION: Conan Doyle set his 1892 Napoleonic tale, *The Great Shadow* on the eastern side of the Scottish Borders, safely distanced from Hawick.

SEE ALSO: Livingston Mission Hall (p. 9).

AYRSHIRE

Isle of Arran
Goat Fell

Where Conan Doyle climbed "the Mountain of the Wind"

And steer for Arran's isle;
The sun, ere yet he sunk behind
Ben-ghoil, "the Mountain of the Wind,"
Gave his grim peaks a greeting kind,
And bade Loch-Ranza smile.
— Sir Walter Scott, "Lord of the Isles" (1815)

Arran is a Gaelic word meaning "lofty isle," and it's the largest island in the Firth of Clyde. So varied is its landscape that it is frequently referred to as Scotland in miniature. The northern half of the island is extremely mountainous. In 1884 Conan Doyle and a friend, both budding amateur photographers, climbed "the Mountain of the Wind," Goat Fell (2,866 feet), Arran's highest summit to capture its spectacular views. Conan Doyle wrote:

The view of Arran as one approaches it is magnificent. A ring of yellow sand runs round the greater portion of the island, behind which rise up sloping green braes and dark fir forests. Behind these again are the rugged group of mountains, which form the north and centre of the island,

the whole culminating in the majestic Goatfell, which towers up to nearly three thousand feet.... It might have been some enchanted island which floated upon the calm azure sea. Behind us one the long line of the Scottish coast, with the one great gap which indicated the mouth of the Clyde, and away to the north the long jagged ridge of the Argyleshire hills. To the south stretched the Irish sea, broken only by the tall, white dome-like summit of Ailsa Craig, the strange solitary rock which stands out like a gigantic Druidical monolith amid the waste of waters...

Anyone who ventures into Arran must be prepared to rough it in the matter of edibles. Meat is a rare and scarce commodity. Bacon and eggs can generally be relied on, and fish are usually to be had. There are plenty of potatoes, and with a little butter the traveller can generally arrange a succulent and nutritious meal without the aid of a butcher. Prices are extremely reasonable, and our board and lodging — we had a large room, which combined sitting-room and bedroom — only cost us a few shillings a day...

We had determined to ascend Goatfell — a feat which seemed a great thing to my companion, who had done little mountaineering in the course of his life. We started at about seven in the morning, after a substantial porridge breakfast, with our two faithful followers bearing our camera-cases and plate-carriers. We ourselves were burdened with knapsacks containing provisions for the day. The morning was bright, but a chilliness in the air warned us that summer had fled. As we emerged from the forests of the Duke of Hamilton (in which the red deer swarmed upon every side, and climbed the sloping uplands beyond) the view was a marvellous one. From Bute and the Mull of Cantire, in the north almost as far as Wigtonshire, in the south the whole coast line of Scotland lay revealed. Down beneath us the blue ocean was flecked with the white sails of yachts and fishing boats, while here and there a dark cloud showed where some great steamer was ploughing its way to the great Scotch seaport. We expended a couple of plates — one of which was afterwards unfortunately ruined by fogging — upon the scene, and then turning to our task, continued to clamber up the mountain The declivity is not very steep until the last few hundred yards when it becomes almost precipitous, but we managed, thanks to our young islanders, to convey not only ourselves but our instruments also in safety to the summit. To the north the country seemed a very abomination of desolation — a world of wild peaks, of rugged chasms, and brown gnarled rocks, all inextricably jumbled together. I have been up several of the Alps, but have never seen a grander mountain view than is to be seen from the summit of Goatfell.

Having had our luncheon upon the summit, and smoked a pensive pipe while we admired the great panorama before us, we erected our cameras and took several pictures each, most of which turned out satisfactorily. By the time the afternoon was far gone and it was only by hard walking that we succeeded in accomplishing the descent and reaching Brodick before night fell. A dreamless sleep rewarded us after our unwonted exertions and rested our weary limbs.... It was with unfeigned regret that we took our leave next day of the beautiful island and its primitive inhabitants.

FURTHER INFORMATION: Those wishing to visit the Isle of Arran and tackle the ascent of

The summit of Goat Fell — where Conan Doyle "smoked a pensive pipe."

Goat Fell can do so comfortably in a day trip from the mainland. The ferry sails from Ardrossan to Brodick and takes around an hour. Goat Fell can be reached by a variety of routes from Brodick, and although signposted, consulting local maps and guidebooks are advisable as the route is a mix of roads, tracks and mountain paths. For ferries consult www.calmac.co.uk. For local information consult www.ayrshire-arran.com. In an earlier trip to Arran in 1877, Conan Doyle unexpectedly met Dr. Joseph Bell who was grouse shooting on the island. Conan Doyle also used Arran as a setting for the uncollected stories "Touch and Go: A Midshipman's Story" and "Our Midnight Visitor."

FURTHER READING: J. M. Gibson and R. L. Green, *Essays on Photography* (London, UK: Secker & Warburg, 1982); P. Dillon, *Walking in the Isle of Arran* (Minthrope, UK: Cicerone, 2008).

SEE ALSO: Joseph Bell (p. 12), Isle of May (p. 45).

DUMFRIES AND GALLOWAY

Dumfries
Craigs Road
High Cemetery

Grave of Charles Altamont Doyle, father of Arthur Conan Doyle

"My poor husband's condition was brought on by drink, he has had delirium tremens several times. Just thirty years ago — December 1862 — he had such a bad attack that for nearly a year he had to be on half pay and for months he could only crawl and was perfectly idiotic, and could not tell his own name. Since then he has been from one

fit of dipsomania to another. Using the most awful expedients, many times putting himself within reach of the law — to get drink — every article of value he or I possessed carried off secretly, debts to a large amount contracted to our trades people, bills given etc. — all for goods which never entered our doors, but were at once converted into money.... There is a public house in Edinburgh where I am told they have a most valuable collection of his sketches, given for drink.... He would strip himself of all his underclothes, take the very bed linen, climb down the water spout at risk of his life, break open the children's money boxes. He even drank furniture varnish. All our friends said the only way to save his life was to out him where he could get no drink. He only kept his position in the office because being very talented he could do what was wanted better than the others and also that amiable disposition endeared him to our kind friends, Mr. Matheson and Mr. Andrew Kerr. To know him was to love him."
— Letter from Mary Doyle to Dr. James Rutherford, Physician Superintendent at Crichton Royal Hospital, dated 3 December 1892.

Born of Irish-Catholic parentage, Arthur Conan Doyle was the fourth of ten children of Mary Foley and Charles Altamont Doyle. Charles came from an artistic family and was himself a talented artist. He was born in London in 1832 into an Irish-Catholic family and his father, John Doyle, was a popular political cartoonist. His mother, Marianne Conan, died shortly after Charles was born. He had two sisters and four brothers. One of them, Richard "Dicky" Doyle, became a celebrated illustrator for *Punch*. The family home was immersed in art, and Charles fondly remembered the family entertaining "the most distinguished and Literary and Artistic Men of London," including Thackeray, Dickens, Rossetti, Millais and Landseer. All three of his brothers prospered in the London art world, but Charles was sent to Edinburgh at the age of nineteen to take up a post as an assistant surveyor with Edinburgh's Office of Works. In 1855, at the age of twenty-two, Charles married seventeen-year-old Mary Foley, the granddaughter of his landlady.

In his *Life of Sir Arthur Conan Doyle* (1949), John Dickson Carr gives a fairly accurate description of Charles in his early married life: "He loved fishing, because when you fished the nagging world let you alone. To his family he

was becoming a dreamy, long-bearded stranger, with exquisite manners and an unbrushed top hat. Each day he trudged the long walk from home to his office at Holyrood Palace, and back again to pat the children's heads absent-mindedly, as he might have stroked his pet cats." He was also a staunch Irish patriot and a devout Catholic. He suffered from short-sightedness and although melancholic, had a liking for puns and playful humor. He did occasional book illustration and sketching, but his artistic career came to nothing, and the humdrum life of an assistant surveyor seemed to be his destiny. He started drinking, no doubt to forget the dire straits and boredom of his daily existence, but it soon became an addiction, making life for his wife and family intolerable. Like many drunkards he sank deeply into debt, became indolent, and was frequently absent from work, resulting in early retirement in 1876.

His behavior eventually became too much for his family to bear and he was admitted to Blairerno House, an institution for alcoholics in Kincardineshire, described in the Medical Directory for 1882 as follows:

"INTEMPERANCE — Home for Gentlemen in Country House in the North of Scotland. Of very old standing. Home comforts. Good Shooting. Trout fishing and Cricket. HIGHEST REFERENCES. Apply MR D. FORBES, BLAIRERNO HOUSE, DRUMLITHIE, FORDOUN, KINCARDINESHIRE." The proprietor, Mr. David Forbes, lived there with his family; and together with their small staff, cared for eighteen male residents. Charles Doyle was registered as an "architect and artist." Mary Doyle recalled her husband being a resident at Blairerno "for some years" and regularly attempting to escape to gratify his need for alcohol. In 1885 he was transferred to Montrose Lunatic Asylum, Scotland's oldest public asylum, established in 1781. When Charles Doyle arrived there, it had around 500 inmates. Contrary to the popular belief about Victorian asylums, Montrose, and especially its physician superintendent, Dr. James Howden, were extremely enlightened, believing that "we must not lose sight of the great principle of non-restraint which has revolutionised the treatment of the insane, so that the modern asylum has the character and aims of a Hospital and a Sanatorium rather than of a Prison or a Poorhouse."

Alcoholics, however, were not usually admitted to public asylums, simply because they were heavy drinkers. Charles Doyle's drinking excesses had caused brain damage resulting in impairment of memory. Problems with short-term memory were detected, suggesting he had what is known today as Korsakoff's psychosis, a type of dementia observed during the last stages of severe chronic alcoholism, which involves being in a confused state, loss of bodily control and short-term memory loss. He also developed epilepsy. Despite his failing physical and mental health, Charles continued to sketch and paint, producing some remarkable work, some of which he contributed to *The Sunnyside Chronicle*, the asylum magazine. Asylum amusements included theatrical entertainments, concerts, conjuring shows, magic lantern exhibitions, readings, dances, picnics, walks and even a visit from the D'Oyly Carte Opera Company. Many of these he captured with brush and pen in his sketchbooks. An inscription in one of his sketchbooks reads: "Keep steadily in view that this Book is ascribed wholly the the produce of a MADMAN. Whereabouts would you say was the deficiency of intellect? or depraved taste? If in the whole book you can find a single evidence of either, mark it and record it against me."

Under the constant delusion that he was being kept at Montrose under false pretenses, Charles' health was in fact in rapid decline. He was also preoccupied with the notion that he was about to die. "During last week was very queer," records his medical notes for 14 July 1885. "Complained at first of great langour, then of an overpowering presentiment that he was going to die, that he would die in 48 hours: he was not in the least depressed by the thought, but he took refuge in his prayer book, & had two long audiences with a priest, and prayed frequently.... Mr Forbes [of Blairerno] informs me that he was often thus, and he has seen him lie down & die, but he always comes to life again."

In 1891 he was transferred to the Royal Edinburgh Asylum where it was recorded that his memory was "much impaired for recent events," with a diagnosis of "epileptic insanity." The following year he was moved to the Crichton Royal Institution in Dumfries where he died in 1893 at the age of 61. A few days before he died, it was recorded in his notes that he was "pleasant & easily pleased. Solemnly presented me with an empty paper which he assured me contained gold dust & was a reward for professional attendance. He said he had collected it in the sunlight on the bed." A week later he died "in a fit during the night."

There is no doubt that Charles Doyle was an artist of great artistic vision, who, given other circumstances, could have excelled at his craft. Arthur Conan Doyle described his father as "a great and original artist ... the greatest, in my opinion, of the family.... His brush was con-

Arthur Conan Doyle in 1865, aged 6, with his father Charles.

cerned not only with the fairies and delicate themes of the kind, but with wild and fearsome subjects, so that his work had a very peculiar style of its own, mitigated by great natural humour. He was more terrible than Blake and less morbid than Wiertz. His originality is best shown by the fact that one hardly knows with whom to compare him."

FURTHER INFORMATION: A Celtic cross marks the grave of Charles Altamont Doyle and his three daughters: Annette Conan (1856–90), Catherine Angela (1858–58) and Mary Monica (1861–63). The inscription reads: "UNTIL THE DAY BREAK, AND THE SHADOWS FLEE AWAY," a quotation from the Bible, Song of Solomon, 2:17 and 4:6. Keys for access to the Cemetery Gates are available from High Cemetery Lodge, Craigs Road, Dumfries 9.00 A.M.— 2.00

P.M. Charles' asylum artwork from an 1889 sketchbook was published in 1978 as *The Doyle Diary*. Sunnyside Royal Hospital is situated two miles north of Montrose, beside the village of Hillside.

FURTHER READING: M. Baker, *The Doyle Diary, The Last Great Conan Doyle Mystery* (New York: Padington Press, 1978); A. Beveridge, "What became of Arthur Conan Doyle's father? The last years of Charles Altamont Doyle," paper presented at the 2007 Annual Conference of the International Council on Archives Section on University and Research Institution Archives, University of Dundee, Scotland, August 14, 2007.

SEE ALSO: Picardy Place (p. 3), St. Mary's Cathedral (p. 4).

FIFE

Isle of May
Where Conan Doyle went "After Cormorants with a Camera"

"The Isle of May seemed to offer 'fresh fields and pastures new' both for myself and to my camera."—Arthur Conan Doyle

Conan Doyle was a lifelong enthusiast of photography, and probably caught the bug from his boyhood friend Willie Burton who contributed technical articles for photographic journals, including the *British Journal of Photography*. Conan Doyle also wrote for the BJP, contributing to their regular feature called "Where to go with a Camera." One of these trips, while still a medical student in 1881, was to the Isle of May, the largest of the islands of the Firth of Forth, noted for its colonies of seabirds and grey seals. The resulting article was called "After Cormorants with a Camera," and was published by the BJP on 14 and 21 October. Accompanied by two gun-toting student friends, "Chawles" and "The Doctor," he crossed the Firth from Edinburgh to Anstruther in Fife loaded down with the Victorian photographer's paraphernalia, including a half-plate camera,

tripod, various lenses, developing chemicals and plates. After a few drinks at the Anstruther Arms, they boarded the coach for "the ancient and honourable Burgh of Crail," four miles along the coast, where they spent the night at the Golf Hotel. "The quaint little hostelry looked preeminently homely and comfortable," wrote Conan Doyle, "while a savoury smell of beefsteaks and onions from a kitchen door left artfully ajar whetted an appetite already painfully keen.... At about six in the morning an inarticulate howl from a slipshod chambermaid summoned us regretfully from our beds.... Arriving at the harbour we were greeted by a grizzly and splay-footed mariner, old enough, apparently, to be the father of Coleridge's hero."

Although the two sailors crewing the boat smelt of whisky and had "a roll in their gait," the party didn't seem too concerned and set sail for the Isle of May. Landing in the rocky cove which served as the island's harbor they scrambled ashore while the crew stayed with the boat and their luncheon basket. At the top of the cliff pathway stood the lighthouse, the only inhabited building on the island, and here Conan Doyle set about the business of photography,

The Isle of May viewed from the North Horn (Sean D. Langton).

while his friends started shooting just about everything that moved "making havoc among the sea birds." "'Not a bad morning's work,' said Chawles a few hours later, 'Forty-three cormorants, nine rock pigeons, two mallets, a curlew, and a bo'sun gull — pretty good for two guns!'" By midday Conan Doyle and his two bloodthirsty friends went off in search of their lunch box, only to observe, from the cover of some bushes, the "grizzly" old crewman swigging out of their whisky bottle. No doubt his two friends discussed shooting the culprit, but Conan Doyle quickly, and surreptitiously, photographed the crime scene and obtained the conclusive piece of evidence, deciding not to do anything about the "old sinner" until the photograph was developed.

Later, when they were all sitting down to lunch, Conan Doyle said sternly to the old crewman, "You've not been drinking anything out of the basket, have you? ... He put his gnarled old hand upon his breast: 'Maybe ye dinna' ken,' he said, 'that I'm an elder o' the free kirk o' Scotland.'" After lunch Chawles and The Doctor continued their killing spree, and when the light began to fail, Conan Doyle did a bit of sea fishing. They spent the night with the lighthouse keeper and his family and departed the next day through "a heavy Scotch mist" for the Golf Hotel at Crail.

After refreshments at the Golf they boarded the Anstruther coach, and Old Sinbad, as they now called their old crewman came to see them off. "'Sinbad, we are sorry even for a moment to have suspected an elder of the church of such a crime as theft,' said The Doctor, 'We think some apology is due to you, and you will find it inside this packet.' So saying, he solemnly handed him a little parcel containing a print of the old sailor as he appeared when industriously pouring water into the whisky bottle. The driver cracked his whip and we shot away along the country road; but the last we saw of Crail was old Sinbad, too much horrified to speak, glaring at the dumb accuser before him."

FURTHER INFORMATION: The Isle of May lies 5 miles off the Fife coast and is about a mile long and a quarter of a mile wide. In 1956 it was designated a National Nature Reserve (www. nnr-scotland.org.uk) because of its profusion of seabirds. Over 250 species have been recorded on the island. The Isle of May ferry is operated by Anstruther Pleasure Trips, 28 St. Adrians Pl., Anstruther, Fife, KY10 3DX. Tel: +44(0)1333 310103/310054. Email: info @isleofmayferry.com. www.isleofmayferry.com. The ferry sails once a day, weather permitting, on the tide April to September. Tickets from the kiosk at Anstruther Harbour. Round trips take 4 to 5 hours, with 2 to 3 hours on the island. The Golf Hotel, 4 High St., Crail, is located 10 miles south east of St. Andrews and 4 miles west of Anstruther on the A917. Tel: +44(0)1333 450206. www.thegolfhotel-crail.com.

FURTHER READING: Arthur Conan Doyle, edited by J. M. Gibson and R. L. Green, *Essays on Photography* (London, UK: Secker & Warburg, 1982).

SEE ALSO: Arran (p. 41).

ANGUS

Kirriemuir
Brechin Road

*Birthplace of J. M. Barrie (1860–1937), friend
and collaborator of Conan Doyle*

"We were in our rooms in Baker Street one evening. I was (I remember) by the centre table writing out 'The Adventure of the Man without a
Cork Leg' (which had so puzzled the Royal Society and all other scientific bodies of Europe),
and Holmes was amusing himself with a little
revolver practice. It was his custom of a summer
evening to fire round my head, just shaving my
face, until he had made a photograph of me on
the opposite wall, and it is a slight proof of his
skill that many of these portraits in pistol shots
are considered admirable likenesses." — J. M.
Barrie, "The Adventures of the Two Collabora-
tors," a parody on Holmes

Conan Doyle and J. M. Barrie were predes-
tined to become allies and friends. Both were
Scots of a similar age from humble back-
grounds. Both attended Edinburgh University
in the 1870s, although, as far as we know, they
never met there. And, for a couple of working-
class Scots, they had a strange passion for the
essentially English game of cricket.

Conan Doyle first met Barrie at a literary
dinner hosted by his friends and colleagues on
The Idler, a magazine edited by the novelist
Jerome K. Jerome. Barrie had his own cricket
team called the "Allahakbarries" of which Conan Doyle became a member, along with other
literary notables including H. G. Wells, A. E.
W. Mason, G. K. Chesterton and A. A. Milne.
"A grand bowler," one team member wrote of
Conan Doyle, "knows a batsman's weakness by
the colour of the mud on his shoes."

When Conan Doyle was lecturing in Scotland in 1893, Barrie invited him to Kirriemuir
to stay with his family. "Splendid types of folk
who have made Scotland great," wrote Conan
Doyle, "Kirriemuir could by no means understand Barrie's success, and looked upon their
great son as an inexplicable phenomenon. They
were acutely aware, however, that tourists were
arriving from all parts to see the place on account of Barrie's books. 'I suppose you have
read them,' I said to the wife of the local hotel
man. 'Aye, I've read them, and steep, steep, weary
work it was,' said she."

James Mathew Barrie was born on 9 May
1860 in Kirriemuir, the ninth child of Margaret
Ogilvy and David Barrie, a hand-loom weaver.
His parents had ten children in all: seven daughters and three sons. David, his mother's favorite
son, died tragically, aged fourteen, in a skating
accident when James was six. His mother was
"always delicate from that hour," he recalled,
and constantly thinking of her boy who was
gone. She never recovered from her loss, and
throughout his childhood Barrie tried desperately to replace him, yearning for his mother's
love. Chiefly remembered today as the creator
of "Peter Pan," Barrie became one of the most
praised and successful dramatists of his day.
Wealth and fame, however, failed to bring him
happiness, and he spent much of his life trying
to win the love denied him as a child. His gen-
erosity could be overwhelming, his affection
intense and possessive. Small in stature, shy, se-
cretive, and with unpredictable moods, Barrie
was an odd and complex genius.

Shortly after his visit to Barrie's family home
at Kirriemuir, Conan Doyle received a telegram
from Barrie summoning him to his Suffolk
home, stating, "Come at once if convenient —
if inconvenient, come all the same." Barrie was
worried because he was contracted to the theatrical manager, Richard D'Oyly Carte, to
write a libretto for a light opera called *Jane
Annie*, but due to ill health, he knew he would
not finish it on time. He asked Conan Doyle
to help him complete it as part author. Conan
Doyle readily agreed, although afterwards he
regretted it. "The only literary gift which Barrie
has not got is the sense of poetic rhythm," he
later wrote, "and the instinct for what is per-
missible in verse. Ideas and wit were in abundance. But the plot itself was not strong." The
production folded seven weeks later, but on the
opening night Conan Doyle and Barrie were

J. M Barrie's birthplace in Kirriemuir. The building on the left, edged by daffodils, is the communal laundry house, where a 7-year old Barrie staged his first play and upon which Wendy's house in Neverland was modeled.

DD8 4BX. Tel: +44(0)1575 5726 46. Open April to September. After Barrie's death in 1937, his birthplace had a narrow escape when it was proposed that the house be sold and dismantled stone by stone for a buyer in the USA. Fortunately for Scottish literary history, a local philanthropist bought it and donated it to the National Trust. The house is now a museum and includes manuscripts, diaries, photographs, Barrie's own writing desk, examples of the original costumes worn at the first production of "Peter Pan" and a contract which Barrie made with the six-year-old Princess Margaret after he had incorporated some words she had said to him into one of his plays. Barrie bequeathed the copyright of "Peter Pan" to London's Great Ormond Street Hospital for Sick Children and immortalized his "wee red toonie" (Kirriemuir) in *A Window in Thrums* (1899). A statue to Peter Pan can be seen in Kirriemuir High Street.

given a loud applause before the curtain rose. "At the end a youthful friend came into our box," Barrie later recounted, "and Doyle expressed my feelings in saying to him reprovingly, 'Why did you not cheer?' but I also sympathised with our visitor when he answered plaintively, 'I didn't like to, when no one else was doing it.'"

FURTHER INFORMATION: J. M. Barrie's birthplace, 9 Brechin Road, Kirriemuir, Angus,

FURTHER READING: A. Birkin, *J. M. Barrie and the Lost Boys* (New Haven, CT: Yale University Press, 2003); L. Chaney, *Hide-and-Seek with Angels: A Life of J. M. Barrie* (London, UK: Arrow Books, 2006).

SEE ALSO: Rutherfords (p. 20), St. Margaret's Church. (p. 88).

ABERDEENSHIRE

Peterhead
Queen Street
Clifton House Hotel
Former Home of John Gray, Conan Doyle's captain on the Greenland whaler Hope

"He who has once been within the borders of that mysterious region, which can be both the most lovely and the most repellent upon earth, must always retain something of its glamour. Standing on the confines of known geography I

have shot the southward flying ducks, and have taken from their gizzards pebbles which they have swallowed in some land whose shores no human foot has trod. The memory of that inexpressible air, of the great ice-girt lakes of deep blue water, of the cloudless sky shading away into a light green and then into a cold yellow at the horizon, of the noisy companionable birds, of the huge, greasy-backed water animals, of the slug-like seals, startlingly black against the dazzling whiteness of the ice — all of it will come back to a man in his dreams, and will seem little more than some fantastic dream itself, go removed is it from the main stream of his life. And then to play a fish a hundred tons in weight, and worth two thousand pounds."—Arthur Conan Doyle, *Through the Magic Door* (1907)

Whaling began in northeast Scotland around the mid–18th century and was one of the most dangerous ways imaginable to make a living wage. The prospect of entire crews disappearing was high, and at least fifty whalers from the northeast ended up beneath the ice of the Arctic whaling grounds. The dangers from drowning, frostbite, scurvy and being crushed or stranded by ice floes was ever-present, but enormous amounts of money could be made and nothing stood in the way of profit. A man could earn more on a whaling trip than he could in an entire year of toiling in the jute mills. Today the whaling industry is socially, morally and ethically unacceptable, but in history it was an industry that made and lost fortunes as well as hundreds of lives.

In 1880 Conan Doyle was unexpectedly plunged into the world of the Arctic whaler when a fellow medical student, who had signed up for a whaling cruise as a ship's surgeon, was unable to go. He asked Conan Doyle if he would like to take his place, and on the spur of the moment, Conan Doyle agreed. At this time Conan Doyle was only a third-year medical student who had only a rudimentary knowledge of surgery, but adventure and money were the attraction. A seven-month cruise at two pounds ten shillings a month and three shillings a ton oil money was an offer he couldn't refuse.

A week later he was in Peterhead stowing his belongings into a cabin locker aboard the whaler *Hope*, captained by John Gray, "a really splendid man, a grand seaman and a serious-minded Scot." It would be a whale and seal hunting expedition that would prove to be the equal of any yarn from the pen of Jack London or Herman Melville, and Conan Doyle would draw on his experiences for the rest of his days. "To play a salmon is a royal game," he wrote, "but when your fish weighs more than a suburban villa ... it dwarfs all other experience." Four days out from the Shetland Isles he awoke to find the whole sea covered with ice fields, an end-

of-the-world seascape he recounted meticulously in his 1890 story:

The Captain of the Polestar, "Being an extract from the singular journal of John M'Alister Ray, student of medicine": September 11th.—Lat. 81 degrees 40' N.; long. 2 degrees E. Still lying-to amid enormous ice fields. The one which stretches away to the north of us, and to which our ice-anchor is attached, cannot be smaller than an English county. To the right and left unbroken sheets extend to the horizon. This morning the mate reported that there were signs of pack ice to the southward. Should this form of sufficient thickness to bar our return, we shall be in a position of danger, as the food, I hear, is already running somewhat short. It is late in the season, and the nights are beginning to reappear.... Amsterdam Island, at the north-west corner of Spitzbergen, is visible upon our starboard quarter—a rugged line of volcanic rocks, intersected by white seams, which represent glaciers. It is curious to think that at the present moment there is probably no human being nearer to us than the Danish settlements in the south of Greenland—a good nine hundred miles as the crow flies. A captain takes a great responsibility upon himself when he risks his vessel under such circumstances. No whaler has ever remained in these latitudes till so advanced a period of the year.... A fine lead appeared in the pack this morning, as I had expected, and we were able to cast off our ice-anchor, and steam about twelve miles in a west-sou'-westerly direction. We were then brought to a halt by a great floe as massive as any which we have left behind us. It bars our progress completely, so we can do nothing but anchor again and wait until it breaks up, which it will probably do within twenty-four hours, if the wind holds. Several bladder-nosed seals were seen swimming in the water, and one was shot, an immense creature more than eleven feet long. They are fierce, pugnacious animals, and are said to be more than a match for a bear. Fortunately they are slow and clumsy in their movements, so that there is little danger in attacking them upon the ice.

The crew of the *Hope* returned to Peterhead with four whales, its hold loaded with a cargo sixty-six tons. Conan Doyle had more money than he "had ever possessed before," including his £50 share of the crew's profits, but it was also a triumph of maturity and worldliness. "I went on board the whaler a big, straggling youth," he once remarked, "I came off a powerful, well-grown man."

FURTHER INFORMATION: Captain Gray died at his home in Queen Street in 1892. His house is now a hotel. Memorabilia relating to Peterhead's whaling days and Conan Doyle adorn its walls. Clifton House Hotel, 96 Queens Street, Peterhead, Aberdeenshire, AB42 1TT, Scotland. Tel: +44 (0)1779 477838. www.cliftonhotelpeterhead.co.uk

Stories inspired by Conan Doyle's Arctic experience include: "The Firm of Girdlestone," "The Captain of the 'Pole-Star,'" and "The Gully of Bluemansdyke."

FURTHER READING: G. Sutherland, *The Whaling Years: Peterhead 1788–1893* (UK: University of Aberdeen, 1993).

INVERCLYDE

Firth of Clyde

Conan Doyle's trip "Doon the Watter"

> Duncan fleech'd and Duncan pray'd
> Ha, ha, the wooing o't!,
> Meg was deaf as Ailsa Craig
> Ha, ha, the wooing o't!
> — Robert Burns, "Duncan Gray"

In early 1881 Conan Doyle took off with some friends on a week-long photographic trip to Ireland, which he later recounted in an article titled, "To the Waterford Coast and Along It." They traveled by train from Edinburgh to Glasgow and boarded the steamer for Ireland at Greenock's old Princes Pier. Conan Doyle's description of the landscape of the then thriving Firth of Clyde, once a cradle of shipbuilding and seafaring, is a memorable travelogue of a now vanished Scotland:

> We all proceeded to Greenock together by rail, to await the steamer there. We filled in the interval very pleasantly by wandering over the old town and inspecting one of the shipbuilding yards, which we had hardly left before our steamer came churning down the river, and we found ourselves with our chattels on board of the good ship "Rathlin." There was a shouting, a throwing off of warps, and a cheer from our friends on the shore, and we were fairly started for the land of Ire.
>
> I know no such place where a photographer may have such an *embarras des richesses* as on the Clyde in a steamer when the sea is calm. There were hardly any passengers besides ourselves and a few commercial travellers with a couple of young ladies, so that we could plant our cameras where we liked upon the poop. As we steamed along a great moving panorama seemed to be unrolled before us. The huge half-finished ships which lined the bank, with their gaunt ribs sticking up to heaven like skeletons of some antediluvian saurian, gradually gave place to green meadows and country scenery, which alternated with the pretty little watering places which dot the coast from Greenock to Ardrossan. Steamers from Ireland and America ploughed past us, and a

Waverley, the world's last seagoing paddle steamer, sailing "doon the watter."

host of little yachts played all round. We wasted
several plates in endeavouring to secure some of
these as they passed. Even when the camera is on
the shore it is surprising how easy it is to miss a
large object which is crossing the field. Many
times have I borne home what I imagined to be a
splendid of yacht or steamer, only to find, as I
watched the detail coming up, nothing but a single monotonous line of horizon. When, however,
the stand of your camera is also moving at eight
or ten miles an hour the difficulty is proportion-
ately increased, and the chances are, as we found,
very much against a successful result. Our landscapes, however, and views of the banks were all
that could be desired.

As the sun sank down towards the horizon we
had got well out to the mouth of the Clyde. The
water was calm as a mill pond and reflected the
scarlet tinge of the clouds. Away to the north
were the rugged mountains of Argyllshire and of
the great islands, wrapped in that purple evening
mist which Waller Paton loves. Ahead of us was
Arran with its peak of Goat Fell enveloped in
fleecy clouds. To the south the strange precipitous upheaval called Ailsa Crag reared itself out
of the ocean — a grim looking place, which has
been the last spot upon earth that the eyes of many
a drowning man have rested on. The whole scene
was as beautiful a one as an artist could love to
dwell upon.... We passed Ailsa Crag before it was

quite dark, but it was too late by that time for us
to do it justice in a plate. However, we had succeeded in several distant views, so we had no
cause to be discontented. As we passed the captain ordered the steam-whistle to be blown,
which had the effect of sending up an innumerable cloud of seabirds from their nests on the
rock. For some minutes the air was simply alive
with kittiewakes, gulls, solan geese, gannets,
blackbacks, and other birds, whose screams and
cries drowned every other sound. then we
steamed on, and the great Crag was left far astern
until it was simply a dark loom in the darkness.

FURTHER INFORMATION: The halcyon days
of the Clyde steamer and the tradition of sailing "doon the watter" (down the waters of the
River Clyde) have passed into history, but every
July and August a taste of the old glory days return when *Waverley*, the world's last seagoing
paddle steamer, provides excursions around the
Clyde during the summer season. For details
contact Waverley Excursions at +44 (0)141 221
8152. www.waverleyexcursions.co.uk

FURTHER READING: J. M. Gibson and R. L.
Green, *Essays on Photography* (London, UK:
Secker & Warburg, 1982).

SEE ALSO: Arran (p. 41), Isle of May (p. 45).

GLASGOW

West End

Charing Cross
49 West Princes Street

*Scene of the murder for which Oscar Slater was
wrongly convicted and sentenced to penal servitude for life*

"The whole case will, in my opinion, remain immortal in the classics of crime as the supreme
example of official incompetence and obsti-
nacy." — Arthur Conan Doyle

Conan Doyle campaigned against criminal
injustice throughout his life, but the case of
Oscar Slater, who was found guilty of a murder
he never committed, was one of Doyle's most
public and exasperating crusades. Oscar Joseph
Slater (originally Leschziner) was born in 1872
in Upper Silesia, Germany, to Jewish parents.
In the early 1890s he was working in London

as a bookmaker and a dealer in precious stones
using various surnames — Sando, George, Anderson, Schmidt and Slater. In 1908 he was in
Glasgow living the life of a gambler, a thief and
a pimp — a member of a low-life criminal un-
derbelly who could easily have passed for a
lackey of Professor Moriarty. All these unsavory
traits, however, did not make him a murderer,
but they did combine to seal his fate.

The story began a few days before Christmas
on 21 December 1908, on a rainy night in West
Princes Street, then a fairly prosperous area of
Glasgow's West End. In a second floor flat at
number 49, a wealthy 82-year-old spinster,
Marion Gilchrist, was found bludgeoned to
death in her dining room by her maidservant,
Helen Lambie. The doctor's report described
that the cause of death was due to "extensive
wounds and fractures of bones of face and skull

Scene of the crime — 49 West Princes Street.

... fractures of breast bone and ribs, together with shock and bleeding therefrom, that the said injuries were produced by forcible contact with a blunt weapon, and that the violence was applied with considerable force."

She was murdered shortly after 7 P.M. Helen Lambie had gone out to buy an evening newspaper. On her return to the front door of the flat, she found the downstairs neighbor, Arthur Adams, knocking at the door. Adams had heard a disturbing thud and had come upstairs to investigate. Lambie unlocked the door and they both entered the broad hallway. A man appeared coming out of the bedroom on their right and disappeared swiftly down the stairs and into the street below. Adams presumed Lambie knew this man as she did not seem at all surprised by his presence. "But where is your mistress?" asked Adams. As Lambie entered the dining room she let out a scream. Miss Gilchrist was lying by the fireplace in a bloody pool with a rug covering her head.

The police concluded that Miss Gilchrist must have known her murderer, as there was no sign of a forced entry. The motive was unclear. Perhaps robbery, but although she had a large jewelry collection hidden around the house, over three thousand pounds worth, only one item, a crescent-shaped diamond brooch, was discovered missing. They questioned Adams and Lambie about the man who rushed past them from the bedroom, but neither could give an accurate description. Lambie hardly saw him and Adams was not wearing his spectacles. But the description the police ended up with was of "a man between twenty-five and thirty years of age, 5 feet 8 or 9 inches in height, slim build, dark hair, clean shaven; dressed in light grey overcoat and dark cloth cap."

On Christmas Eve a further witness, Mary Barrowman, claimed the suspect rushed past her in the street, and gave a description which so conflicted with the original one that the police decided there must have been two culprits. On Christmas Day a bicycle dealer named Allan McLean claimed a fellow member of his local gambling club, a German Jew by the name of Oscar, had been trying to sell a pawn ticket for a diamond brooch.

The police tracked down Oscar Slater's address to 69 St. George's Road, only a few hundred yards from the murder scene, but he was not at home, nor was his mistress. On Christmas Day they had left Glasgow for Liverpool and boarded the Lusitania for New York traveling under the names of Mr. and Mrs. Otto Sando. Despite the fact that the clue that had led them to Slater was false — the brooch had been pawned by Slater over a month before the murder and bore no resemblance to the missing one — the police had Slater arrested in New York. A lightweight hammer was found in his possession which police presumed was the murder weapon. Extradition, however, was not necessary, as Slater returned to Glasgow willingly in the hope of clearing his name. Unfortunately Slater did not take into consideration the inadequacy of the Scottish legal system and the incompetence of the Glasgow police, for the High Court of Justiciary in Edinburgh found him guilty of murder by a majority verdict and sentenced him to hang. This was later commuted to penal servitude for life and he was incarcerated at Peterhead Prison in northeast Scotland, where he remained for eighteen and a half years.

Almost immediately there was a public outcry, as it was clear that an injustice had been done. The Scottish lawyer and amateur criminologist, William Roughead, published a booklet entitled "Trial of Oscar Slater," which allowed the public to read a transcript of the trial and consider its extremely fickle evidence. Conan Doyle had also been following the case and had decided to act, claiming that "this unhappy man had in all probability no more to do with the murder for which he had been condemned than I had." In 1912 he published, with Roughead's help, "The Case of Oscar Slater," an in-depth study in which he systematically laid out the inconsistencies of the whole affair. For example — the hammer found on Slater was too light and fragile to do any damage other than "fixing a tin-tack"; Slater was traveling under an assumed name in order to deceive his wife; the statements of the witnesses were contradictory and the theft of the brooch was a red-herring covering up the theft of a document, such as a will. Questions were raised in the House of Commons, but the Secretary of State for Scotland (then the principal minister of Her Majesty's Government in Scotland) declared that "no new considerations have, in my opinion emerged such as would justify me in reopening the case." In 1914 John Trench, one of the detectives involved in the original investigation, was dismissed from the force for disclosing information, allegedly concealed by the police, implicating a relative of Marion Gilchrist.

The case languished for another fifteen years; and although efforts were made to reopen it, they came to nothing. Conan Doyle, however, had not forgotten Slater, and wrote "From time to time one hears some word of poor Slater from behind his prison walls like the wail of some wayfarer who has fallen into a pit and implores aid from the passers-by." In 1927 Conan Doyle's own "Psychic Press" published a book entitled *The Truth About Oscar Slater*, by Glasgow journalist, William Park. The book claimed that Marion Gilchrist knew her murderer and that they had quarrelled over a document she possessed. He then pushed her to the floor where she struck her head against the coal box, and proceeded to bludgeon her to death with a heavy chair. The visitor then grabbed the document and fled past Helen Lambie, whom she recognized as a nephew of Miss Gilchrist, a person the libel laws prevented William Park from naming. Helen Lambie later supposedly claimed that the police had coached her to identify Slater, and one newspaper claimed she had been bribed by the police. These revelations raised fresh doubts about the reliability of the verdict and no doubt contributed to the Secretary of State for Scotland releasing Slater on November 8, 1927. But the real reason was probably to avoid an official enquiry into the case.

He was released on license, but not granted a pardon. Conan Doyle led a campaign to reopen the case, clear Slater's name and win compensation. A fund was raised to pay Slater's legal fees and included a £1,000 guarantee from Conan Doyle. The subsequent hearing, which lasted ten days, quashed Slater's conviction on a technicality and awarded him £6,000 compensation. Conan Doyle expected Slater to reimburse those who had contributed to his legal costs, but Slater thought he should not be expected to bear the costs of the case and refused to pay. Conan Doyle was incensed, but Slater eventually contributed £250 towards costs, and sent £200 to William Park, author of *The Truth About Oscar Slater*. Slater eventually settled in Ayr on the southwest coast of Scotland where he lived a life of respectability, remarrying at the age of sixty-six. He died, aged seventy-five, in 1948. There are many theories to what actually happened that night at 49 West Princes Street, none of which to this day have been proved, save for the fact that Oscar Slater was not guilty.

FURTHER INFORMATION: An extensive collection of papers relating to the trial of Oscar Slater, principally papers from the Lord Advocate's Department, the Scottish Office Home and Health Department and the High Court of Justiciary, may be examined in the public search room at The National Archives, West Register House, 17a Charlotte Square, Edinburgh EH2 4DJ. Tel: +44(0)131 535 1400. www.nas.gov.uk. Oscar Slater's letter from Peterhead Prison asking for legal help and news cuttings relating to John Trench can be consulted at Glasgow City

Oscar Slater after being released in 1928.

Archives, The Mitchell Library, 210 North Street, Glasgow G3 7DN. Tel: +44(0)141 287 2910. www.csglasgow.org/archives. The nearby Carnarvon Bar (formerly Oscar Slater's pub) at 129 St. Georges Road, has a few painted portraits of Oscar Slater hanging on its walls.

FURTHER READING: A. C. Doyle, *The Case of Oscar Slater* (London, UK: Hodder & Stoughton, 1912); W. L. Park, *The Truth About Oscar Slater* (London, UK: Psychic Press, 1926); P.

Hunt, *Oscar Slater: The Great Suspect* (New York: Collier, 1963); J. House, *Square Mile of Murder* (Edinburgh, UK: Chambers, 1961). W. Roughead, editor, *Trial of Oscar Slater* (Edinburgh, UK: Hodge, 1950); T. Toughill, *Oscar Slater: The Mystery Solved* (Edinburgh, UK: Canongate, 1993).

Gorbals
Corner of Ballater Street and Gorbals Street
Site of the birthplace of Allan Pinkerton, founder of Pinkerton's Detective Agency

"But you've heard of Pinkerton's?"
"I've read of some folk of that name."
"Well, you can take it from me you've no show when they are on your trail. It's not a take-it-or-miss-it Government concern. It's a dead earnest business proposition that's out for results, and keeps out till, by hook or by crook, it gets them. If a Pinkerton man is deep in this business we are all destroyed." — Arthur Conan Doyle, *The Valley of Fear* (1915)

Written in the early months of 1914, *The Valley of Fear* is a detective novel in two parts. The first part, "The Tragedy of Birlstone," was described by the pioneer of the "locked room" mystery, John Dickson Carr, as "a very nearly perfect piece of detective-story writing." The second part, however, abandons Sherlock Holmes, and immerses itself in the coal mining communities of Pennsylvania, basing its plot loosely around a real-life Pinkerton detective who infiltrated, and eventually put an end to, the Molly Maguires, a covert and militant organization which claimed to defend the rights of Irish miners in Pennsylvania in the 1870s. Contrary to popular belief, the Pennsylvania "Mollies" were not crusaders against injustice, but a well-organized group of Irish extremist thugs, who intimidated, terrorized and murdered to achieve their own ends. In the story the "Mollies" are known as the Scowrers, and the man from Pinkertons is Birdy Edwards; but Conan Doyle made a point of distancing himself from the real facts of the events, changing names and obscuring origins. "The Irish are very touchy on such matters," he told the editor of the *Strand Magazine*. "I make it vague and international with nothing to offend anyone." Conan Doyle was right to tread warily as the trial that sent nineteen Mollies to the scaffold at Pottsville, Pennsylvania, in 1876, was still within living memory. The Pinkerton agent who brought them to justice was an extremely courageous and diligent immigrant Irishman named James McParland, who managed to gain access to the Mollies' inner circle and bring about their downfall at great risk to his own life. Proving that, when Conan Doyle's character in *The Valley of Fear* nervously states, "If a Pinkerton man is deep in this business we are all destroyed," it was no idle remark.

Allan Pinkerton was born in 1819 to William Pinkerton, a hand loom weaver, and Isabella McQueen, a cotton mill worker, in a top floor tenement flat on the corner of Muirhead Street and Rutherglen Loan (now demolished) in the Gorbals area of Glasgow. It was then a slum area on the south bank of the River Clyde, a rabbit warren of grimy streets, filthy alleyways, belching factory chimneys and open sewers, housing a predominantly Irish Catholic population. The Pinkerton's, however, were neither Irish nor Catholic, they were Scottish atheists and are listed in parish records as far back as the early 17th century. After his father's death in 1830, ten-year-old Allan left school and learned the trade of a cooper. In 1838 he went "on the tramp" for four years searching out seasonal work as a cooper throughout Scotland and the north of England. During this time he became an ardent supporter of parliamentary reform and joined various militant groups, which eventually resulted in him becoming, in his own words, "a wanted criminal fleeing to the new world." In 1842 he sailed for Montreal with his new bride. Hit by a hurricane, their ship ran aground on reefs off the Canadian coast, where they were reputedly robbed of most of their possessions by the local Indians. Making their way inland, they eventually put down roots in the small Scottish settlement of Dundee, northwest of Chicago, where Allan set up his own cooperage business. After alerting the law to the activities of a gang of counterfeiters on a nearby island, he was offered the job of deputy sheriff of Kane County, which eventually led to him being offered the post of the first detective on the Chicago police force. In the early 1850s he set up his own detective agency, using groundbreaking infiltration and

Top: Allan Pinkerton, President Abraham Lincoln, and General John A. McClernand, at Antietam, Maryland, October 3, 1862. This was taken shortly after the Battle of Antietam, the first major battle of the American Civil War, fought near Sharpsburg, Maryland, and Antietam Creek. *Bottom*: The corner of Ballater Street and Gorbals Street, birthplace of Allan Pinkerton.

surveillance techniques still in use today. His logo was a human eye and his motto was "We Never Sleep." The Chicago underworld nicknamed him "The Eye," the origin of the phrase Private Eye. Pinkerton's Detective Agency tackled everything from bank robbery to fraud, pursuing wrongdoers from Jesse James to Butch Cassidy. They headed a federal intelligence network during the American Civil War and foiled a plot to assassinate Abraham Lincoln. The Pinkerton agent, like the Canadian Mountie, always got his man. Allan Pinkerton, however, did not die in a blaze of gunfire as might have been expected. In June of 1884 he went for a short walk, tripped on the sidewalk, fell over and bit into his tongue. Three weeks later he died from the effects of gangrene and septicemia. He was 64 years old.

FURTHER INFORMATION: The site of Allan Pinkerton's birth was demolished at the end of the 19th century. The offices of the Procurator Fiscal now stand on the site at the corner of Ballater and Gorbals St. Further down Gorbals St., on the corner of Belford Lane, stands a derelict tenement, the oldest surviving building in the Gorbals, a grim reminder of its slum heritage. Allan's mother, Isabella, worked in Thomson's Mill, which stood on the site now occupied by the Glasgow Central Mosque, opposite the Procurator Fiscal offices. Allan Pinkerton is buried in Graceland Cemetery, 4001 N Clark St., Chicago.

FURTHER READING: J. MacKay, *Allan Pinkerton: The First Private Eye* (Secaucus, NJ: Castle, 2007); Allan Pinkerton, *The Molly Maguires and the Detectives* (New York: Haskell House, 1982); J. Lukas, *Big Trouble* (New York: Simon & Schuster, 1997); J. D. Horan, *The Pinkertons: The Detective Agency That Made History* (Modesto, CA: Bonanza, 1967).

NORTH YORKSHIRE

Masongill
Masongill Cottage

Home of Mary Doyle from 1882 to 1917

> 'Twere good there were rest above,
> For life is labour and pain,
> And love is a grief, for those who love
> Seldom are loved again.
> — Bryan Charles Waller (1853–1932),
> "Annette's Music"

In the late summer of 1876, seventeen-year-old Arthur Conan Doyle arrived back at the family home at 2 Argyle Park Terrace in Edinburgh, having finished his boarding school education at Stonyhurst. Much to his annoyance his mother had taken in a lodger. Dr. Bryan Charles Waller was just six years older than Conan Doyle and a qualified doctor. He was a published poet, and William Thackeray had dedicated *Vanity Fair* to his father, but to Conan Doyle he was a cuckoo in the mam's nest. Bryan Waller has always been a mysterious figure in the Doyle household, but exactly what his true relationship was with Conan Doyle's mother has never been determined. Was he a philanthropic friend or a secret lover? Whatever their relationship was, they remained very attached to each other for the rest of their lives; but to date no-one has been able to uncover what was at the root of their peculiar tête-à-tête.

A few months previously, in June of 1876, Conan Doyle's dipsomaniac father had been admitted to a home for alcoholics, leaving Mary Doyle without a husband and a wage-earner. She was also pregnant at this time with her ninth, and last child — a girl, born in March 1877. She was christened Bryan Mary Julia Josephine Doyle, a distinctly odd name to give a female child, although not unheard of. The implica-

tion is that Mary Doyle and Bryan Waller were very close. How close is a matter for debate. It was also rumored that Waller was in love with Mary's daughter, Annette, a love which appears to have been spurned. Annette, who died in an influenza epidemic in Portugal in 1889, was immortalized in "Annette's Music," Waller's poem of lost love.

At this point in his life Conan Doyle was unsure what career path to go down, and his mother, with Waller's backing, encouraged him to take up medicine. Waller, who at this time was lecturing in pathology at the university, coached him through the entrance exams, and he entered Edinburgh University Medical Faculty in the fall of 1876.

In the spring of 1877 Waller inherited his family's estate at Masongill in North Yorkshire, financially securing his future; and by late summer the Doyle family had moved from their overcrowded apartment in Argyle Park Terrace across The Meadows park to a much more salubrious and spacious house at 23 George Square, a few doors away from the former home of Conan Doyle's literary hero, Sir Walter Scott. The house was leased by Waller who was now practicing as a consultant pathologist. In 1881 the family moved to nearby Lonsdale Terrace, again leased by Waller. The following summer of 1882, Bryan Waller, together with the mam and her brood, retired to his estate in Yorkshire where he would spend the rest of his days as a country gentleman.

Waller resided at Masongill House, and the mam at Masongill Cottage, where she lived for over thirty years. With her husband now safely institutionalized, and the dreary struggle of her Edinburgh life behind her, she set about rebuild-

Masongill Cottage (Phillip Bergem).

Edmund Waller (1606–87). When asked by King Charles II why his poem "To the King, upon his Majesty's Happy Return" was a lesser piece of verse than his eulogy to Oliver Cromwell, Edmund Waller shrewdly replied, "Sir, we poets never succeed so well in writing truth as in fiction." This was a legacy Conan Doyle could tap into on his doorstep, and its threads found its way into his future works from *Micah Clarke* to Sherlock Holmes. He visited Masongill often, and was married to his first wife, Louise, at the nearby church of St. Oswald in August 1885, with

ing her life under the wing of her benefactor. She even discarded her religion, converting from Catholicism to Anglicanism, worshiping in the local church of St. Oswald in Thornton in Lonsdale. Waller eventually married Ada Roberts, a local governess, who became increasingly resentful of his relationship with Mary Doyle. The marriage, which was childless, was deemed loveless, and her meanness and snobbery are all that history remembers her by. Waller's legacy was much the same.

Conan Doyle never publicly expressed his opinion of Waller, and never mentioned him in his memoirs, save for the statement: "My mother had adopted the device of sharing a large house, which may have eased her in some ways, but was disastrous in others." He could not fail, however, to have had misgivings about a man who had stepped in as confidante and financial prop for his mother, dislodging what he must have seen as his own rightful duty. Whatever his qualms were about this puzzling relationship, he kept them to himself, but it was not all as adverse as it seemed. Waller's heritage was one Conan Doyle would have coveted. His ancestors fought at Agincourt and commanded Cromwell's troops during the English Civil War. Waller himself was an accomplished poet and a direct descendant of the poet

Bryan Waller serving as a witness. Needless to say, Mary Doyle was well liked by the local community, which is more than can be said for Waller, an inveterate snob, who insisted that locals doff their caps to him in reverence. His legs were bandy, and legend has it that his legs had to be tied together to make him fit into his coffin, which prompted an undertaker's assistant to exclaim, "There you are, you old bugger, and nobody will be raising their cap to you where you've gone." But the last words on Bryan Waller has to be from Conan Doyle himself, who faithfully recreated him as Pinfold the Vicar, in his 1889 novel, *Micah Clarke*:

> The Vicar, whose name was Pinfold, possessed in this manner great power in the town, and he was a man with a high inflamed countenance and a pompous manner, he inspired no little awe among the quiet inhabitants. I can see him now with his beaked nose, his rounded waistcoat and his bandy legs, which looked as if they had given way beneath the load of learning which they were compelled to carry. Walking slowly with right hand stiffly extended, tapping the pavement at every step with his metal-headed stick, he would pause as each person passed him, and wait to see that he was given the salute which he thought due to his dignity. This courtesy he never dreamed of returning, save in the case of some of his richer parishioners, but if by chance it were omitted he would hurry after the culprit, and,

shaking his stick in his face, insist upon his doffing his cap to him.

FURTHER INFORMATION: Masongill lies on the border between Lancashire and North Yorkshire about a mile north of the A65. Mary Doyle lived at Masongill until June, 1917, when she moved to Bowshot Cottage, West Grinstead, in Sussex, to be near her daughter Connie. Two of Conan Doyle's sisters were also married in the church of St. Oswald at Thornton-in-Lonsdale. The church dates back to the 13th century, but the tower is all that remains of the original Norman structure. A fire destroyed the church in 1933, and what stands today is a replica of the 1870 building. Copies of Conan Doyle and Louise's marriage certificate can be viewed at the church. To arrange access phone +44 (0)152 4261579.

FURTHER READING: A detailed portrait of Bryan Waller can be found in Owen Dudley Edwards' *The Quest for Sherlock Holmes* (Edinburgh, UK: Mainstream, 1983).

SEE ALSO: George Square (p. 23), Stonyhurst (p. 63), Charles Altamont Doyle (p. 42).

Harrogate
Swan Road
The Old Swan Hotel

Where Agatha Christie was found after her disappearance in 1926, a mystery for which Conan Doyle employed the power of psychic investigation

"Very few of us are what we seem." — Agatha Christie

In December 1926 the crime novelist, Agatha Christie, mysteriously disappeared for ten days. The reason behind her disappearance still remains a mystery, and although many explanations have been suggested over the years, it is still a story without a conclusive ending. Agatha Christie's mother had died in the spring of 1926, plunging Agatha into severe despondency. She also discovered that her husband, former World War I aviator, Archibald Christie, was having an affair with another woman named Nancy Neele. Her husband wanted a divorce, but Christie resisted. On the morning of Friday, 3 December, their maid overheard them arguing at breakfast,

after which her husband departed for a rendezvous with Nancy Neele at a house in Godalming. That evening Christie drove off in her Morris-Cowley car, which was found abandoned the next day at Newlands Corner, just a few miles from Godalming. In the car was a suitcase of clothes and a driver's license in the name of Agatha Christie. Close by was a small pond known as the Silent Pool, which Christie had used as a location for a dead body in a previous novel.

The police naturally assumed she had drowned herself and dredged the pool, but no body was found. A massive manhunt of the surrounding area was got underway, involving thousands of volunteers, bloodhounds, and airplanes. *The Times* newspaper published the following police report:

> Missing from her home, the Styles, Sunningdale, Berks., Mrs. Agatha May Clarissa Christie, wife of Colonel Christie, aged 35, height 5ft., 7in., hair reddish and shingled, eyes grey, complexion fair, well built, dressed in grey stockinet skirt, green jumper, grey and dark grey cardigan, small green velour hat, wearing a platinum ring with one pearl. No wedding ring. Had black handbag with her, containing probably £5 to £10. Left home in a Morris-Cowley car at 9:45 P.M. on Friday, leaving a note saying she was going for a drive. Next morning the car was found abandoned at Newlands Corner, Surrey.

All of these efforts achieved nothing, and the police were baffled. Crime novelist Edgar Wallace, proffered his own theory: "The disappearance seems to be a typical case of 'mental reprisal' on somebody who has hurt her. To put it vulgarly, her first intention seems to have been to 'spite' an unknown person who would be distressed by her disappearance. That she did not contemplate suicide seems evident from the fact that she deliberately created an atmosphere of suicide by abandonment of her car."

After she had been missing for a week, the police decided to consult Conan Doyle. His usual deductive reasoning, however, was not employed to solve this mystery. Conan Doyle judged it a case for psychic investigation, and using one of Christie's gloves, handed it over to a psychic named Horace Leaf. Leaf's supposed skill was psychometry, the ability to discover facts about an event or person by touching inanimate objects associated with them. "The method is very simple," wrote Leaf. "An article worn or handled by an individual, held in the hand of the psychometrist or pressed against the forehead may call up in his mind thoughts, feelings, and even visions related to that individual." Conan Doyle claimed he "gave him no clue at all as to what I wanted or to whom the article belonged. He never saw it until I laid it on the table at the moment of consultation, and there was nothing to connect either it or me with the Christie case. The date was Sunday last. He at once got the name Agatha." Leaf went on to say: "The person who owns it is half dazed and half purposeful. she is not dead, as many think. she is alive. You will hear of her, I think, next Wednesday." Conan Doyle may have given Leaf "no clue," but the nationwide press coverage of the case and the likelihood that the police would seek advice from Conan Doyle would have been apparent to even the most amateurish psychometrist, let alone the eminent Leaf.

While all this public furor was happening, a woman calling herself Teresa Neele had checked in to Harrogate's Hydropathic Hotel (now the

The Old Swan Hotel, formerly The Hydropathic Hotel.

Old Swan Hotel) on Saturday, 4 December. Mrs. Neele, said to be recovering from a bereavement, was perceived by a member of the hotel's resident band, Bob Tappin, to bear a strong resemblance to Agatha Christie. Tappin informed the police, who summoned her husband for verification. "There is no question about the identity," stated Archibald Christie. "It is my wife. She has suffered from the most complete loss of memory and I do not think she knows who she is." Later, in a statement to the press, he said: "My wife is extremely ill. Three years have dropped out of her life. She cannot recall anything that has happened during that period. The fact that she lives in Sunningdale has no significance for her, and she does not seem to realize that her home is at the Styles. As to what has happened since she left there her mind is a complete blank. She has not the slightest recollection of going to Newlands Corner or of proceeding eventually to Harrogate."

It was an explanation which effectively ended all inquiry, but the public and the press found it unconvincing with many unanswered questions. One theory, amongst many, was that Christie was trying to frame her husband for murder. Another that it was a deliberate torment towards her husband in an effort to win him back. Conan Doyle offered no theory, but trusted that the police would see the value of using psychometry in the future. Agatha Christie did eventually divorce her husband, freeing him to marry Nancy Neele. In 1930 she married archaeologist Max Mallowan. Her comments on Conan Doyle's involvement in the manhunt for her were never recorded, but in her 1952 novel, *Mrs. McGinty's Dead*, Poirot is addressed by a character who states: "I have my methods Watson. If you'll excuse me calling you Watson. No offence intended. Interesting, by the way, how the technique of the idiot friend has hung on. Personally, I myself think the Sherlock Holmes stories grossly overrated."

FURTHER INFORMATION: The Old Swan Hotel, Swan Road, Harrogate, HG1 2SR. Tel: +44(0)844 879 9071. www.macdonaldhotels.co.uk/oldswan/

SEE ALSO: Major-General Alfred Drayson (p. 131), Houdini (p. 133), Psychic Bookshop (p. 89), Albert Hall (p. 90).

WEST YORKSHIRE

Cottingley
Cottingley Beck

Where the Cottingley Fairy photographs were taken

"But remember always, as I told you at first, that this is all a fairy tale, and only fun and pretence; and, therefore, you are not to believe a word of it, even if it is true." — Charles Kingsley, *The Water Babies* (1863)

Dear Jo,

Dad came home from France the other week, and we all think the war will be over in a few days. We are going to get our flags to hang upstairs in our bedroom. I am sending two photos, both of me, one of me in a bathing costume in our back yard, Uncle Arthur took that, while the other is me with some fairies up the Beck, Elsie took that one.

Frances Griffiths was writing to her friend Johanna Parvin in Cape Town, 9 November 1918. On the back of the fairy photo, she wrote: "Elsie and I are very friendly with the Beck Fairies. It is funny I never used to see them in Africa. It must be too hot for them there."

The photo Frances Griffiths posted of herself to her South African friend in 1918 was taken by her cousin Elsie Wright at the rear of her house beside a stream known as Cottingley Beck. It has become one of the world's most famous images. Not because of the picturesque Beck, or Elsie's photographic skills, but because of the fairies dancing in front of Frances' face. The photograph, the first of five taken by the girls, startled the world and confirmed to many, including Arthur Conan Doyle, the existence of fairies. They were of course faked, but what started as a harmless prank escalated into a deception of global magnitude which Frances and Elsie only confessed to over sixty years later in 1983.

Elsie was sixteen years old in 1917 and was the only child of Polly and Arthur Wright, a local handyman with an interest in photography. She was a talented artist who attended Bradford Art College, and for a time worked in a photographic lab. In April 1917, Polly's sister, Annie, and her ten-year-old daughter, Frances, returned from South Africa and moved in with the Wrights at 31 Main Street. Despite the age difference, Elsie and Frances became firm friends, and their favorite retreat was the wooded Beck [stream] beyond the back garden, where, armed with sandwiches, drinks and dolls, they would withdraw into their own private world. In July 1917 they also took along a few hat pins, some zinc oxide bandage tape, Arthur Wright's Butcher Midg ¼-Plate Camera, and a few cardboard cut-outs of fairies copied by Elsie from *The Princess Mary Gift Book*.

The resulting photograph was developed by Arthur in his own dark room. He was convinced it was a fake, but the girls were adamant they had photographed real fairies. A few weeks later Frances took a photo of Elsie with a cut-out gnome; and after this further mischievous episode, Arthur refused to lend them the camera again. And this was where the prank should have ended. A couple of amusing photographs pasted into the family album, reminisced by friends and family after Christmas dinner and a few sherries. Elsie's mother, however, was a Theosophist.

In the summer of 1919 Polly Wright attended a meeting of the local Theosophical Society in nearby Bradford. The subject of fairies was discussed; and after the meeting Polly approached the lecturer and related the story of her daughter's fairy photographs. The photos were soon brought to the attention of leading Theosophist, Edward Gardner, who subsequently passed them on to Conan Doyle, who at that time was collecting material for an article on fairies for the *Strand Magazine*. Conan Doyle was a strong believer in spiritual beings, and desperately wanted to believe in the photographs, but had to get them checked for authenticity. Gardner, also a believer, was asked to verify the negatives, while Doyle would consult the Kodak Company. Gardner's research confirmed that the photographs were not fakes, but Kodak's response was more guarded and advised proceeding with caution.

Doyle was about to embark on a lecture tour of Australia and New Zealand to promote his spiritualist beliefs, commitments which prevented him from personally investigating the Cottingley controversy. Instead, he asked Gardner to help him, offering £50 for his assistance. He also sent a letter to the Wright family, enclosing one of his books for Elsie, and offering £5 for the use of the photographs in the *Strand Magazine* article on fairies. Gardner was accordingly invited to Cottingley by the Wrights and left a camera with the girls hoping for further fairy photographs.

It was now July 1920, three years since the first two photographs were taken; but a few weeks later Elsie and Frances captured their cutout fairies on three more photographs. Gardner wrote ecstatically to Conan Doyle: "The wonderful thing has happened!" Doyle's reply from Melbourne was equally exultant. "Any doubts which had remained in my mind as to honesty were completely overcome," he wrote, "for it was clear that these pictures ... were altogether beyond the possibility of fake." In November 1920 Conan Doyle's article on fairies, along with the first two Cottingley photographs, appeared in the Christmas issue of the *Strand Magazine*. In 1922 Doyle published his book *The Coming of the Fairies* which included all five of the Cottingley photographs.

The public were bewildered. Few of his spiritualist colleagues stood by him, fearing ridicule; and the press had a field day. But Conan Doyle was resolute in his beliefs, publishing a second edition of *The Coming of Fairies* in 1928, in which he stated "The discovery by Columbus of a new terrestrial continent is a lesser achievement than the demonstration of a completely new order of life inhabiting the same planet as ourselves."

By now, fear of diminishing their own reputations — as well as those of Garner and Conan Doyle — committed Elsie and Frances to perpetuating their fabrications indefinitely. The girls were probably enjoying the attention and hoped that maybe there was money to made. Their identities and address had been kept secret, but the press soon tracked them down to Cottingley. And for over sixty years the media pursued them relentlessly wherever they were living, hoping for a confession. But whether in newspaper, or on radio and television, they never admitted fabricating the photographs. Their "confession" finally appeared in *The Times* in 1983. Frances was 75 and Elsie was 81. Conan Doyle died in 1930, happy in the "knowledge" that the photographs were genuine, but Gardner heard the truth, aged 96, at his Theosophical Retirement Home in New Zealand. No comment was recorded.

FURTHER INFORMATION: The village of Cottingley is situated between Shipley and Bingley on the A650. Cottingley Beck still survives today, as does the waterfall which flows along the bottom of 31 Main Street's garden, but it is now overshadowed by modern housing. At the time of writing part of the stream has been fenced off and declared dangerous. Photographs and papers, including Conan Doyle's letters relating to the Cottingley Fairies, are held by Leeds University Library (+44(0)113 34 35518), www.library.leeds.ac.uk

FURTHER READING: *Princess Mary's Gift Book* (London, UK: Hodder & Stoughton, 1915); Arthur Conan Doyle, *The Coming of Fairies* (London, UK: Hodder and Stoughton, 1922); Joe Cooper, *The Case of the Cottingley Fairies* (London, UK: Robert Hale, 1990).

SEE ALSO: Leeds University (p. 62).

Leeds
Leeds University
The Brotherton Library

Home to a collection of miscellaneous material on the Cottingley fairy photographs

"The series of incidents set forth in this little volume represent either the most elaborate and ingenious hoax ever played upon the public, or else they constitute an event in human history which may in the future appear to have been epoch-making in its character. It is hard for the mind to grasp what the ultimate results may be if we have actually proved the existence upon the surface of this planet of a population which may be as numerous as the human race, which pursues its own strange life in its own strange way, and which is only separated from ourselves by some difference of vibrations. We see objects within the limits which make up our colour spectrum, with infinite vibrations, unused by us, on either side of them. If we could conceive a race of beings which were constructed in material which threw out shorter or longer vibrations, they would be invisible unless we could tune ourselves up or tone them down. It is exactly that power of tuning up and adapting itself to other vibrations which constitutes a clairvoyant, and there is nothing scientifically impossible, so far as I can see, in some people seeing that which is invisible to others. If the objects are indeed there, and if the inventive power of the human brain is turned upon the problem, it is likely that some sort of psychic spectacles, inconceivable to us at the moment, will be invented, and that we shall all be able to adapt ourselves to the new conditions. If high-tension electricity can be converted by a mechanical contrivance into a lower tension, keyed to other uses, then it is hard to see why something analogous might not occur with the vibrations of ether and the waves of light." — Arthur Conan Doyle, *The Coming of Fairies* (1922)

The five Cottingley Fairy photographs, taken between 1917 and 1920 by Frances Griffiths and Elsie Wright are amongst the most famous photographic images in the world. And although since proved to be fakes, they are still a source of media interest today. They captivated Conan Doyle to the extent that he wrote a book called *The Coming of Fairies* about the "facts" of the phenomenon. His belief in the fairy world seriously damaged his credibility. When he died in 1930 the photographs had still not been officially discredited. Frances and Elsie finally confessed they were fakes in 1983, sixty-four years after the first photographs were taken.

Miscellaneous articles connected to the events, including cameras, photographs, negatives and correspondence, etc., have been scattered widely over the years and have ended up in various public and private collections. Frances and Elsie made considerable sums selling their collections through auction houses. The Brotherton Collection at Leeds University has a substantial collection of artifacts, including the five glass plates of the fairies, donated by Leslie Gardner, son of Edward Gardner who first brought the photographs to Conan Doyle's attention. Other artifacts in the collection include books, videos, journals, newspaper cuttings, letters, photographs and glass negatives.

FURTHER INFORMATION: Leeds University Library is one of the major academic research libraries of the United Kingdom. There are three main libraries on the university campus: The Health Sciences Library, The Edward Boyle Library and the Brotherton Library (located in the Parkinson Building), which covers Arts and Social Sciences and is also home to Special Collections. Members of the public can visit for the day. http://www.leeds.ac.uk/library/spcoll/. Tel: +44(0)113 34 35663.

Email: library@leeds.ac.uk. Please bring some form of ID.

The original cameras used by Frances Griffiths and Elsie Wright are on display at the National Media Museum in Bradford, www.nationalmediamuseum.org.uk

SEE ALSO: Cottingley Fairies (p. 61).

LANCASHIRE

Hurst Green
Stonyhurst College
Alma mater of Arthur Conan Doyle

"My object will be, if possible, to form Christian men, for Christian boys I can scarcely hope to make." — Thomas Arnold (1795–1842), English historian, Headmaster of Rugby School from 1828

When he was nine years old, in September

1868, Arthur Conan Doyle was packed off to study at Stonyhurst, a Jesuit boarding school in the north of England. The fees were paid by his father's staunch Roman Catholic family, a move which they hoped would steer him towards the path of righteousness and distance him from the pressures of an alcoholic father. He would remain at Stonyhurst for seven years, returning to his family only for the annual six-week summer holiday. And although other boys

Stonyhurst College (Phillip Bergem).

returned home for Christmas, he had to remain because he was deemed to live too far away. His adult recollections of Stonyhurst very much reinforce the concept of the Victorian English public school system, which, although it produced educated, upright, Christian gentlemen, it did so at great mental cost to many. Ironically his experience among the Jesuits fueled his doubts about Catholicism, which he eventually rejected in 1880. And although he seemed to have weathered Stonyhurst reasonably well, he still encountered loneliness, corporal punishment, dreary food, a formulaic syllabus, and systems that "weaken self-respect and self-help." He did, however, discover he had "some literary streak," and rejoiced in telling his fellow pupils stories, for which he charged an apple or a pastry. He also excelled at sport and developed his lifelong love for cricket.

His first two years were spent at Hodder, the preparatory school for Stonyhurst, situated about a mile from the main school and where all boys under twelve were schooled and quartered. Here he first encountered "the black-robed Jesuit guardians," who were to be his masters for the next seven years. For the most part he enjoyed his time at Hodder and was fortunate in having a benevolent principal, one Father Cassidy, whom he described as "more human than Jesuits usually are." "I hope you are quite well,"

he wrote to his mother from Hodder in November 1869, "I am as well as I ever was. I send you a picture Mr. Cassidy gave me for knowing my Greek Grammar. in that old box [a festive holiday box] I would like 1 plum-pudding 1 chicken & german sausage 1 piece of tongue. 1 doz oranges 1 half doz apples 1 plum cake 1 shortbread cake a packet of butterscotch and as a novelty a few sticks of gundy [a chewy confectionary] and 1 quill pen some paper and some sweets & some liquorice. send it to the red lion."

From Hodder he moved up to the main college, where he later wrote, "the general curriculum, like the building, was mediaeval but sound." Studies consisted predictably of Euclid, mathematics and the classics taught with such drudgery as to leave "a lasting abhorrence." Pupils were never allowed to be alone. Masters participated in games, walks, and at night patrolled the dormitories. Public school immorality, prevalent at other schools, was never allowed to surface at Stonyhurst. Dry bread and hot milk was dished up for breakfast, pudding was only on the dinner menu twice a week, and snacks were "bread and beer," a curious concoction consisting of dry bread and a brown liquid which bore no resemblance to beer. Despite a monotonous and wearisome diet, the pupils, according to Conan Doyle, "were all very healthy on this regime." Corporal punishment was draconian and dispensed using and instrument called a tolley, "a piece of india-rubber of the size and shape of a thick boot sole." Punishment was nine lashes on each hand, and Conan Doyle seemed to be beaten more than others in an effort to quell his rebellious nature. His masters despaired for his future prospects, and when he informed one of them he was considering becoming a civil engineer, he remarked, "Well, Doyle, you may be an engineer, but I don't think you will ever be a civil one."

Stonyhurst, however, did not defeat him, but strengthened him. In his final year he edited the college magazine. And defying all his master's

Arthur Conan Doyle at Stonyhurst (fourth from left, back row).

bequeathed to them by Thomas Weld, a former St. Omer pupil. Stonyhurst College is located near the village of Hurst Green on the B6243, 13 miles from Preston. The college and its gardens are open to the public during the summer and guided tours are available. For admission times, ticket prices, etc., consult www.stonyhurst.ac.uk or phone +44(0)1254 826345. Conan Doyle left Stonyhurst at the age of 16 and was sent for a few months to Stella Matutina, a school run by the Jesuits at Feldkirch in Austria.

predictions, he surprised all by taking honors, emerging from this Jesuit bastion at sixteen "with more credit than seemed probable from my rather questionable record."

FURTHER INFORMATION: The Jesuit college was founded in 1593 at St. Omer, northern France, to provide a Catholic education for English families prevented from educating their children in their faith at home. The college moved to Bruges in 1762 and in 1773 to Liege. In the wake of the French Revolution, the Jesuits settled on the Stonyhurst estate which was

FURTHER READING: A. Hewitson, *Stonyhurst College, Present and Past: Its History, Discipline, Treasures and Curiosities* (Lancashire, UK: Preston Chronicle, 1878); H. Chadwick, *St. Omers to Stonyhurst: A History of Two Centuries* (London, UK: Burns & Oates, 1962); J. Keating and G. Gruggen, *Stonyhurst: Its Past History and Life in the Present* (Charleston, SC: BiblioBazaar, 2009).

SEE ALSO: Newington Academy (p 9).

CHESHIRE

Bebington
Poulton Lancelyn
Poulton Hall

Ancestral home of Richard Lancelyn Green (1953–2004), world authority on Sir Arthur Conan Doyle

"Priscilla West left Oxford for London in haste, increasingly fearful for her brother's welfare. She arrived at his luxury flat at noon and rang the bell. No one answered. The police were called and broke down the front door. Mrs. West waited anxiously downstairs as the officers searched the flat. Their footsteps stopped in the bedroom.

Richard Lancelyn Green was found lying dead in his double bed. He was surrounded by stuffed toys and a bottle of gin. Around his neck was a shoelace in which a wooden kitchen spoon, which had been used to twist the cord tight, was still entangled. The 50-year-old millionaire bachelor had been garroted." — David Smith, *The Observer*, 23 May 2004.

Up until his strange and untimely death in 2004, Richard Lancelyn Green had amassed the world's largest private collection of material on Conan Doyle and Sherlock Holmes. Collecting had become an all-consuming, fanatical obsession that reached back to his childhood. After his death the collection was bequeathed to the city of Portsmouth, but so vast was its content that it took two weeks to pack and load it into numerous vehicles. He died in extremely suspicious circumstances. The coroner deemed suicide the most likely explanation, but also commented that it had been a "very unusual death." Murder was suspected, but never proved. To date, no one has solved the mystery.

Green was born on 10 July 1953, at Poulton Hall, his family's seat since before the Norman Conquest. His father, Roger Lancelyn Green, a biographer and children's author, had been an academic at Oxford with C. S. Lewis and J. R. R. Tolkien. His mother, June Green, was a drama teacher. An Oxford graduate, Richard Lancelyn Green began his fascination with all things Doylean when he was around five years old. He built a replica of 221B Baker Street in his attic. And anything relating to Sherlock Holmes and Conan Doyle he meticulously archived, including books, original manuscripts, letters — even a hypodermic syringe containing the "seven per cent solution" of cocaine. He wrote and edited numerous Sherlockian books, but he will be best remembered for co-editing *A Bibliography of Arthur Conan Doyle* with John Gibson, which was awarded a Special Edgars Award from the Mystery Writers of America in 1984. From 1996 to 1999 he was Chairman of the Sherlock Holmes Society of London. At the time of his death, he was still researching a project that had been close to his heart for many years: a planned three-volume biography of Conan Doyle — 1859 to 1890 (youth and tiro writings); 1891 to 1914 (the years of maximum creativity); 1915 to 1930 (the finale). Much to his chagrin he was constantly prevented from moving forward because of the inaccessibility of Conan Doyle's papers due to legal wrangling. Further salt in the wound happened in 2004 when a "lost archive" of 3,000 letters, notes and book drafts of Conan Doyle's were auctioned in London, a collection Lancelyn Green believed should have been donated to the British Library.

His sister, Priscilla, told *The Observer* newspaper after his death that "he was clearly very stressed about these papers.... He became delusional.... The coroner's open verdict is the right one. Richard was very disturbed but I wouldn't have said suicidal. I have one or two recent files from his computer and they are models of lucid argument. Just occasionally there is a sense of helplessness about it all." Whatever the truth of the matter, Scotland Yard will not reopen the case unless fresh evidence comes forward, which now seems unlikely.

FURTHER INFORMATION: Poulton Hall is open to the public by request only. If you are interested in visiting, please apply in writing to S. R. Lancelyn Green Esq., Poulton Hall, Poulton Lancelyn, Bebington, Wirral, Cheshire CH63 9LN. www.poultonhall.co.uk

Richard Lancelyn Green's Conan Doyle Collection is located at the City Museum on Museum Road Portsmouth. www.portsmouthcitymuseums.co.uk.

FURTHER READING: R. L. Green and J. M. Gibson, *A Bibliography of Arthur Conan Doyle* (Oxford, UK: Clarendon Press, 1983); R. L. Green, editor, *The Further Adventures of Sherlock Holmes* (London, UK: Penguin Books, 1985); R. L. Green, editor, *Sherlock Holmes Letters* (London, UK: Secker & Warburg, 1986).

SEE ALSO: Portsmouth Museum (p. 134).

DERBYSHIRE

Winnats Pass
Blue John Cavern

Setting for "The Terror of Blue John Gap"

"My view is — and it was formed, as is shown by my diary, before my personal adventure — that in this part of England there is a vast subterranean lake or sea, which is fed by the great number of streams which pass down through the limestone. Where there is a large collection of water there must also be some evaporation, mists or rain, and a possibility of vegetation. This in turn suggests that there may be animal life, arising, as the vegetable life would also do, from those seeds and types which had been introduced at an early period of the world's history, when communication with the outer air was more easy. This place had then developed a fauna and flora of its own, including such monsters as the one

Winnats Pass (Dave Pape).

which I had seen."—Arthur Conan Doyle "The Terror of Blue John Gap" (1912)

The Blue John Cavern is one of four caves open to the public around Castleton, and is so called because the semiprecious mineral Blue John was mined there. Derbyshire Blue John is a purple-blue fluorite, which the Victorians mined for its attractive blue and yellow coloring. The name derives from the French bleu-jeune (blue-yellow). For nearly 300 years tourists have been exploring the miles of underground tunnels and caverns in this area in search of adventure, returning home with a chunk of Blue John as a souvenir. Conan Doyle was no exception, and when in 1878 he took on a summer post as a doctor's assistant in Sheffield, he made sure to visit the nearby limestone caves of the Peak District, notably the Blue John Cavern, which

inspired his subterranean horror story, "The Terror of Blue John Gap."

The plot centers around a young doctor who is recovering from tuberculosis and recuperates on a farm in the Peak District. Fresh air and long walks are the order of the day. During one of his strolls he encounters Blue John Gap, an old Roman mine with a network of endless caves. He also discovers that something or someone has been stealing sheep locally, and trails of blood lead to the mouth of Blue John Gap. Armed with a gun, ropes and candles, he descends into the depths of the hillside. What he found deep in the earth was so horrible that he eventually dies from his traumatic encounter. Fortunately he left behind his journal, and like the giant rat of Sumatra, it's a story for which the world is not yet prepared.

FURTHER INFORMATION: The Blue John Cavern is just off the A6187 at the top of Winnats Pass in the Peak District, a few miles west of Castleton and is well signposted. It is open all year, but not suitable for people with heart conditions, bronchial illness or babes in arms. For guided tours phone +44(0)1433 620638 or consult www.bluejohn-cavern.com.

SEE ALSO: Residences of Arthur Conan Doyle (p. 146).

STAFFORDSHIRE

Great Wyrley
Station Road
St. Mark's Vicarage

Former home of George Edalji, who was wrongly convicted of the Great Wyrley Outrages

"George, where do you live?"
"The Vicarage, Great Wyrley."
"And where is that?"
"Staffordshire, Father."
"And where is that?"
"The centre of England."
"And what is England, George?"

"England is the beating heart of the Empire, Father."

"Good. And what is the blood that flows through the arteries and veins of the Empire to reach even its farthest shore?"

"The Church of England."

"Good, George."

— Julian Barnes, *Arthur & George* (2005)

Shapurji Edalji had been a Parsee, a follower of the Zoroastrianism religion in India. In his youth he converted to Christianity and became a minister of the church. In 1876 he was appointed vicar of St. Marks at Great Wyrley, and, together with his Scottish wife, he settled down to a parish life of writing sermons and visiting the sick and poor. They had three children: George, Maude and Horace. Although life was a contented one at the Vicarage, the family was the frequent victim of hoaxes, hate mail, and racist abuse. Dead birds were dropped into the milk churn, excrement was smeared on the doorstep, goods delivered that were never ordered, and malicious letters continually arrived in the mail: "Every day, every hour, my hatred is growing against George Edalji. And your damned wife. And your horrid little girl. Do you think, you Pharisee, that because you are a parson God will absolve you from your iniquities?" Many of these letters were signed by God, Beelzebub or the Devil. Local police investigations into the campaign of harassment against the Edaljis were half-hearted, incompetent, and failed to find the culprits. The abuse,

which persisted erratically for almost twenty years, would suddenly disappear, only to reappear when they were least expecting it again. In the end it became part of the routine of life, and the family learned to live with it.

George, Shapurji Edalji's oldest child, was a shy, polite, introverted boy, with poor eyesight. He was raised not to be wasteful or dishonest, but to be charitable, loving and good. He didn't mix well with school friends or the village children. Had no interest in sport, theater, pubs, or gambling. His ambition was to become a solicitor, which he achieved in 1899, qualifying with Second Class Honors. He set up office in the nearby city of Birmingham and looked forward to an ordered life of conveyancing and drawing up wills. Everything was as he hoped it would be.

In 1903 there had been a spate of horrific animal mutilations in the Great Wyrley area. Horses, cows and sheep were ripped under the belly in the dead of night and left to bleed to death. These motiveless crimes of senseless cruelty were thought to be the work of a local, but the police were at their wit's end as to the perpetrator. On June 29th a letter arrived at the local police station:

I have got a dare-devil face and can run well, and when they formed that gang at Wyrley they got me to join. I knew all about horses and beasts and how to catch them best. They said they would do me if I funked it, so I did, and caught them both lying down at ten minutes to three, and they roused up; and then I caught each under the belly, but they didn't spurt much blood, and one ran away, but the other fell. Now I'll tell you who are in the gang, but you can't prove it without me. There is one named Shipton from Wyrley, and a porter they call Lee, and he's had to stay away, and there's Edalji the lawyer. Now I haven't told you who is at the back of them all, and I shan't unless you promise to do nothing

The Vicarage viewed from the side of St. Marks (Hazel and John Sant).

at me. It is not true we always do it when the moon is young, and the one Edalji killed on April 11 was full moon. I've never been locked up yet, and I don't think any of the others have, except the Captain, so I guess they'll get off light.

The letter was signed by a William Greatorex, and although semiliterate, the letter sounded to the police as if it's author was familiar with the facts of the case. William Greatorex was discovered to be a local schoolboy whose handwriting did not match the letter. Lee, Shipton, and the "Captain" were unknown to the police, but they were acquainted with George Edalji. Other letters followed. One threatened to "do twenty wenches like the horses ... little girls." The police were nervous. Special constables were brought in, and the force was under immense public pressure to apprehend the guilty party.

On the night of the 17th of August, 1903, one of the Wyrley Colliery's ponies was slashed across the abdomen. It was the eighth incident, making a total of sixteen animals mutilated. The police searched the Edalji's vicarage and found what they claimed was incriminating evidence against George: razors, a blue serge coat with bloodstains and animal hair, and a pair of muddy boots. George was arrested at his Birmingham office. The resulting trial, for which the prosecution produced dubious witnesses and circumstantial evidence, found him guilty and he was sentenced to seven years penal servitude. He was released three years later in 1906, a weary, confused man, who still pinned his hopes on clearing his name.

Conan Doyle claims in his autobiography that he first became acquainted with the Edalji case when reading by chance an "obscure paper" called *The Umpire* in late 1906, but there was never any chance involved, as George Edalji had actually sent him correspondence regarding his case personally. Once Conan Doyle suspected that an injustice had been committed, he acted swiftly and arranged to meet George at London's Grand Hotel in Charing Cross. Observing him reading a newspaper, he quickly diagnosed acute myopia, a nearsightedness which immediately eliminated him from the act of wandering around a field at night slitting the

stomach of a horse. George Edalji was as blind as a bat and could not see further than a few inches in front of his face — a fact that never surfaced during his trial. Conan Doyle was convinced that racism was the key to his troubles and offered his services, pledging to win him a free pardon and compensation. Conan Doyle made investigations locally in Great Wyrley. He consulted world's leading eye experts and handwriting experts. He investigated racial prejudice amongst the local police, commenting that the Chief Constable "was quite honest in his dislike of George Edalji, and unconscious of his own prejudice.... As I trace the course of events, this dislike of their chief's filtered down until it came to imbue the whole force, and when they had George Edalji they did not give him the most elementary justice." Concluding his investigations, Conan Doyle petitioned the Home Secretary, the ultimate authority, for George's pardon and compensation. The outcome was a Royal Pardon, but no compensation was offered on the grounds that, although they accepted he was not guilty of cattle maiming, they still held the view that he was guilty of writing the malicious letters to the police. In other words, what this Home Office ruling was effectively saying was, that although they did not agree with the verdict of the jury, they still maintained that he brought the whole thing down on own his own head and had to accept the consequences. No one, therefore, was to blame.

Although George did not fully clear his name, he did receive a pardon which enabled him to practice once again as a solicitor, and his case led to the creation of the Court of Criminal Appeal. In 1934 George Edalji wrote his last public statement on the case in the *Daily Express*:

The great mystery, however, remained unsolved. All kinds of theories were advanced. One is that the outrages were the work of a lunatic seized from time to time with blood lust. Another was that they were done with the idea of bringing the parish and the police into disrepute, or possibly the work of some dismissed policeman. One curious theory was suggested to me. A man belonging to Staffordshire told me the outrages were committed, not by a human being, but one or more boars. He suggested that these animals were sent out at night after being given some kind of dope which made them ferocious. He said he had seen one of these boars. The boar theory seemed to me then — as it does now — too fantastic to be taken seriously.

FURTHER INFORMATION: The Vicarage, now surrounded by a high hedge, is behind the church, and is not open to the public.

Letters and papers, 1902–1904, concerning the trial of George Edalji are located in the Archives and Heritage Service of the Birmingham Central Library. Parliamentary Reports, papers relating to the case of George Edalji, are located in the Social Sciences section of the Birmingham Central Library. Tel: +44(0)121 303 4511.

FURTHER READING: J. Barnes, *Arthur & George* (London, UK: Jonathan Cape, 2005); A. C. Doyle, "The Case of Mr. George Edalji" (1907); G. Weaver, *Conan Doyle and the Parson's Son* (New York: Vanguard Press, 2006); the Rev. S. Edalji, *A Miscarriage of Justice: The Case of George Edalji* (1905).

SEE ALSO: St. Margaret's Church (p. 88).

NORFOLK

Cromer
Hall Road
Cromer Hall

Probable inspiration for Baskerville Hall in The Hound of the Baskervilles

"The avenue opened into a broad expanse of turf, and the house lay before us. In the fading light I could see that the centre was a heavy block of building from which a porch projected. The whole front was draped in ivy, with a patch clipped bare here and there where a window or a coat-of-arms broke through the dark veil. From this central block rose the twin towers, ancient, crenelated, and pierced with many loopholes. To right and left of the turrets were more modern wings of black granite. A dull light shone through heavy mullioned windows, and from the high chimneys which rose from the steep, high-angled roof there sprang a single black column of smoke."
— Conan Doyle's description of Baskerville Hall, in *The Hound of the Baskervilles* (1902)

As a candidate for the original Baskerville Hall, the gothic splendor of Cromer Hall possesses many of the vital components and bears a striking resemblance to Conan Doyle's original. It even had its own Yew Alley, which featured prominently in the story; and although, once upon a time, "the whole front was draped in ivy," the woody evergreen has long disappeared.

Conan Doyle first made its acquaintance in 1901 when, suffering from enteric fever, he returned from the Boer War. To regain his health he took off on a golfing holiday to Norfolk with his friend Bertram Fletcher Robinson. During their stay they dined with the Cabell family at Cromer Hall. During dinner Benjamin Cabell related the story of his ancestor Richard Cabell, a 17th century Dartmoor squire, on whose death a pack of hounds are alleged to have gathered and howled around his house.

Although there are many hound legends in West Country folklore, Conan Doyle would also have been told of East Anglia's own legendary Black Shuck, a ghostly black hound who is said to have roamed the countryside for centuries. His most memorable appearance was recorded on 4 August 1577 at Blythburgh in Suffolk, when he burst into the local church, savaged two of the congregation, and breathed scorch marks on the church door — marks which can still be seen on the door to this day. The event was recorded by the Rev. Abraham Fleming in 1577 in *A Straunge and Terrible Wunder*: "This black dog, or the divel in such a linenesse (God hee knoweth al who worketh all) runing all along down the body of the church with great swiftnesse, and incredible haste, among the people, in a visible fourm and shape, passed between two persons, as they were kneeling upon their knees, and occupied in prayer as it seemed, wrung the necks of them bothe at one instant clene backward, in somuch that even at a moment where they kneeled, they strangely dyed."

Sounds like an appropriate finale to the traditional fire and brimstone service, but whatever the truth of it all, we can safely assume that

Conan Doyle's Norfolk holiday sowed the seeds of inspiration.

FURTHER INFORMATION: Cromer Hall is not open to the public, but is located just a short walk from Cromer Railway Station. On exiting the station turn left into Holt Road. Cromer Hall is on Hall Road, the next on your right. Conan Doyle and Fletcher Robinson stayed at the famous Royal Links Hotel, which was destroyed by fire in the 1940s on the Overstrand Road overlooking the sea.

FURTHER READING: *Cromer Hall: Seat of the Cabell Family* (Norwich, UK: Paragraph, 2007); M. Newell and J. Dodds, *Black Shuck: The Ghost Dog of Eastern England* (Suffolk, UK: Jardine Press, 1999).

SEE ALSO: High Moorland Visitor Centre (p. 111), Bertram Fletcher Robinson (p. 114), Lopes Arms (p. 116), Undershaw (p. 107).

Happisburgh
Hill House Pub

Where Conan Doyle was inspired to write "The Adventure of the Dancing Men"

"I think that I can help you to pass an hour in an interesting and profitable manner," said Holmes, drawing his chair up to the table and spreading out in front of him the various papers upon which were recorded the antics of the dancing men.... 'I have here in front of me these singular productions, at which one might smile had they not proved themselves to be the forerunners of so terrible a tragedy. I am fairly familiar with all forms of secret writings, and am myself the author of a trifling monograph upon the subject, in which I analyze one hundred and sixty-three separate ciphers; but I confess that this is entirely new to me. The object of those who invented the system has apparently been to conceal that these characters convey a message, and to give the idea that they are mere random sketches of children.'"—Arthur Conan Doyle, "The Adventure of the Dancing Men" (1904)

In the summer of 1903 Conan Doyle was taking a break in Norfolk. His sister Connie and her husband, Willie Hornung, had rented a summer house at East Ruston, and his mother was also holidaying there. Conan Doyle was staying about three miles away on the coast at the Hill House Hotel (now the Hill House pub) in Happisburgh (pronounced Haisbro). From there he wrote a letter to Herbert Greenhough Smith, the editor of the *Strand Magazine*, stressing, "I have a strong bloody story." The story was another of Conan Doyle's favored Sherlock Holmes scenarios — the mystery locked in the past — and involved text written in a secret cypher in the shape of matchstick figures. The inspiration is said to have come from Gilbert Cubitt, the seven-year-old son of his hotel landlady. Gilbert had written his name as a matchstick men cryptogram and this is said to have inspired Conan Doyle to write "The Adventure of the Dancing Men," in the Green Room of the hotel which overlooked the bowling green.

The story is set in Norfolk where Conan Doyle describes the landscape "as singular a countryside as any in England.... On every hand enormous square-towered churches bristled up from the

The Hill House pub (Maureen Still).

flat green landscape and told of the glory and prosperity of old East Anglia." The plot revolves round doomed protagonist, Hilton Cubitt (named after little Gilbert, the landlady's son), a country squire who has lived for five centuries at Riding Thorpe (a fusion of local villages Ridlington and Edingthorpe), and who, in desperation, approaches Holmes to crack the mysterious code of the dancing men. Two plaques can be seen on the outside of the pub commem-

orating Conan Doyle's visit there in 1903, and if you are prepared to wait around until closing time on a Saturday night, you may even see dancing men (and women) for real.

FURTHER INFORMATION: Hill House, Happisburgh, Norfolk, NR12 OPW. Tel: +44(0) 1692 650004. Happisburgh is situated on the Norfolk coast about 1 mile east of the B1159. The nearest railway station is 8 miles away in North Walsham.

LONDON

Westminster

East End Road
East Finchley Cemetery
Grave of Sidney Paget (1860–1908)
Painter and illustrator best known for his portrayals of Sherlock Holmes

"The editor of the *Strand* was seeking an illustrator and remembered an artist named Paget who had been a representative for the Illustrated London News with the Gordon Relief Expedition. He forgot his Christian name, however, and sent the letter of commission to my father instead of Walter [his brother]." — Winifred Paget, daughter of Sidney Paget

Finding the right artist to illustrate a story is in itself an art. If successful, the story and the artwork become like two halves that only exist for each other and are forever set in stone. Lewis Carroll had Tenniel; Dickens had Phiz; and Conan Doyle had Sidney Paget. From the time when the first Sherlock Holmes's story, "A Scandal in Bohemia," appeared in the *Strand Magazine* in 1891, it was Sidney Paget's graphic interpretation of a wiry, hawk-like, pipe-smoking detective, which readers would forever equate with the great sleuth. Conan Doyle initially favored "a thin, razor-like face, with a great hawk's-bill of a nose, and two small eyes, set close together on either side of it," but Sidney Paget's creation, said to be based on his good-looking artist brother Walter, was the portrayal destined to become iconic. "From the point of view of my lady readers," remarked Conan Doyle, "it was as well."

Sidney Edward Paget was born on 4 October 1860, the fifth of nine children of Martha Clarke, a music professor, and Robert Paget, a vestry clerk. When he was twenty-one he entered London's Royal Academy Schools, the oldest art school in the UK, founded in 1769, where training was free and modelled on the French Académie de peinture et de sculpture. Former students included William Blake, J. M. W. Turner, John Constable and Edwin Landseer. One of Paget's fellow students was Alfred Morris Butler, who is said to have been the model for his drawings of Doctor Watson. As a professional illustrator Paget's drawings appeared not only in the *Strand*, but *Pictorial World*, *The Sphere*, the *Pall Mall Magazine*, *The Graphic*, the *Illustrated London News*, and many best-selling books. One of his commissions came personally from Conan Doyle who wanted Paget to paint his portrait in oils in 1897. The painting depicts the writer at his peak, and was described admirably by Julian Barnes in his 2005 novel, *Arthur & George*: "Sitting straight-backed in an upholstered tub chair, frock coat half open, fob chains on show, in his left hand a notebook, in his right a silver propelling pencil. His hair is now receding above the temples, but this loss is made irrelevant by the compensating glory of the moustache: it colonizes his face above and beyond the upper lip and extends in waxed toothpicks out beyond the line of the earlobes. It gives Arthur the commanding air of a military prosecutor; one whose authority is endorsed by the quartered coat of arms in the top corner of the portrait."

In 1893 Sidney Paget married Edith Hounsfield, with whom he had six children. Their daughter Winifred recalled:

> After their marriage in 1893, my parents set up their home in a village in Hertfordshire. Here my father built a studio in one corner of the orchard that surrounded the house. During the summer I fear he sometimes spent more time in that orchard than he did in the studio. When the time came for the next batch of drawings to go to the publisher he would have to sit up half the night working hard to get them finished. It was worth it I suppose for those sunny days spent haymaking in the orchard. I remember, too, the barrel organ that used to stop and play outside our gate and around which we children would dance and throw our pennies. Suddenly my father would appear and, with great abandon, turn cartwheels on the lawn. Then, with a wave and a grin he would just as suddenly disappear and return to work.... As a young man, my father lived in the country. It was then that he wore the surely now most famous of all hats, the deerstalker. Like most artists, he followed many pursuits, but I do not think deer-stalking was one of them! I imagine he chose this type of hat for himself as being suitable and comfortable for tramping round the countryside. This possibly inspired him to depict Holmes wearing a deerstalker on similar occasions. It seems to me to be a fitting headgear for the great detective out on the man-hunt. It may once more become the height of fashion as it has lately been seen adorning the head of young Prince Charles on his return from a visit to the country. Little did my father know that his deerstalker would still be talked about more than half a century after it first appeared in the pages of the *Strand Magazine*!

Legend has it that Sidney Paget died from the effects of ingesting lead-based paint caused by sucking on his paint brushes. If true, it was a strange, sad and untimely death for one of Britain's outstanding illustrators.

FURTHER INFORMATION: Sidney Paget's grave is located near the junction of East Avenue and Rosemary Avenue in East Finchley Cemetery, East End Road, East Finchley, London, N2 ORZ. Tel: +44(0)208 567 0913. Buses 143 and 143A both stop in East End Road outside of the Cemetery. The nearest underground stations are East Finchley and Finchley Central on the Northern Line.

SEE ALSO: *Strand Magazine* (p. 91).

2 Upper Wimpole Street
Former consulting rooms of Conan Doyle's ophthalmic practice

> "My mind," he said, "rebels at stagnation. Give me problems, give me work, give me the most abstruse cryptogram, or the most intricate analysis, and I am in my own proper atmosphere. I can dispense then with artificial stimulants. But I abhor the dull routine of existence. I crave for mental exaltation. That is why I have chosen my own particular profession, or rather created it, for I am the only one in the world."—Arthur Conan Doyle, *The Sign of Four* (1890)

From 1882 to 1891 Conan Doyle created a successful medical practice in Southsea and a parallel literary career that was beginning to return financial rewards; but like Sherlock Holmes in *The Sign of Four*, life had become a "dull routine of existence." "Suddenly, however," he wrote, "there came a development which shook me out of my rut, and caused an absolute change in my life and plans." The way out of his humdrum existence, believed Conan Doyle, was to specialize, and he had recently become interested in specializing upon the eye. Ophthalmology he deemed was his future, and where better to make a go at creating a lucrative consultancy than in London.

In March of 1891 Conan Doyle and his family moved into a flat at 23 Montague Place, Bloomsbury. He signed a lease for a consulting room and shared waiting room at 2 Upper Wimpole Street, a stone's throw from Harley Street, traditional home of the successful London specialist. Conan Doyle, however, was up against the best medical brains in the country; and, as he admitted to himself as a student, "was always one of the ruck, neither lingering nor gaining—a sixty-per-cent man." London had numerous eye specialists, and consulting an under qualified and unknown newcomer was a risk not worth taking. Predictably no patients crossed his threshold and the door slowly closed on medicine, but another opened which set in motion the golden age of crime fiction.

Up until this time, it was his novels that had gained him critical acclaim and financial reward, and not his short stories, which were a fragmented, muddled collection of no great literary merit. But short stories that were written

2 Upper Wimpole Street (Phillip Bergem).

standing merit behind them, with the possible exception of Wandering Willie's Tale in "Red Gauntlet." On the other hand, men who have been very great in the short story, Stevenson, Poe, and Bret Harte, have written no great book. The champion sprinter is seldom a five-miler as well.

In April 1891 Conan Doyle proved himself to be the world's greatest "champion sprinter" when he sent his first Sherlock Holmes short stories, "A Scandal in Bohemia" and "The Red-Headed League," to his agent, launching Conan Doyle the writer on the road to immortality and Conan Doyle MD to the annals of history.

Portland Place
The Langham Hotel
Where Conan Doyle dined with Oscar Wilde in 1889

> "There is no such thing as a moral or an immoral book. Books are well written, or badly written." — Oscar Wilde, *The Picture of Dorian Gray* (1891)

On the evening of August 30, 1889, the Philadelphia publisher Joseph M. Stoddart, managing editor of *Lippincott's Monthly Magazine*, invited Oscar Wilde, Arthur Conan Doyle and the Irish MP, Thomas Patrick Gill, to dinner

with a continuing theme, thought Conan Doyle, featuring the same popular character, and each one complete in itself, might excite and galvanize the reader into a loyal following. "Looking round for my central character," he wrote, "I felt that Sherlock Holmes, whom I had already handled in two little books, would easily lend himself to a succession of short stories." The short story, however, requires a special skill, which Conan Doyle was well aware of. Writing in *Through the Magic Door* (1907) he encapsulates the difficulty of its illusive mastery:

> Which are the great short stories of the English language? Not a bad basis for a debate! This I am sure of: that there are far fewer supremely good short stories than there are supremely good long books. It takes more exquisite skill to carve the cameo than the statue. But the strangest thing is that the two excellencies seem to be separate and even antagonistic. Skill in the one by no means ensures skill in the other. The great masters of our literature, Fielding, Scott, Dickens, Thackeray, Reade, have left no single short story of out-

The Langham Hotel.

at the prestigious Langham Hotel. Stoddart had come to London to organize an English edition of *Lippincott's*, and also hoped to commission some talented British writers into the bargain. The dinner was a great success and resulted in Wilde contributing *The Picture of Dorian Gray*, and Conan Doyle *The Sign of Four*, the second Sherlock Holmes story. Conan Doyle wrote:

> It was indeed a golden evening for me. Wilde to my surprise had read "Micah Clarke" and was enthusiastic about it, so that I did not feel a complete outsider. His conversation left an indelible impression upon my mind. He towered above us all, and yet had the art of seeming to be interested in all that we could say. He had delicacy of feeling and tact, for the monologue man, however clever, can never be a gentleman at heart. He took as well as gave, but what he gave was unique. He had a curious precision of statement, a delicate flavour of humour, and a trick of small gestures to illustrate his meaning, which were peculiar to himself. The effect cannot be reproached, but I remember how in discussing the wars of the future he said: "A chemist on each side will approach the frontier with a bottle"— his upraised hand and precise face conjuring up a vivid and grotesque picture. His anecdotes, too, were happy and curious. We were discussing the cynical maxim that the good fortune of our friends made us discontented. "The devil," said Wilde, "was once crossing the Libyan Desert, and he came upon a spot where a number of small fiends were tormenting a holy hermit. The sainted man easily shook off their evil suggestions. The devil watched their failure and then he stepped forward to give them a lesson. 'What you do is too crude,' said he. 'Permit me for one moment.' With that he whispered to the holy man, 'Your brother has just been made Bishop of Alexandria.' A scowl of malignant jealousy at once clouded the serene face of the hermit. 'That,' said the devil to the imps, 'is the sort of thing which I should recommend.'"

The result of the evening was that both Wilde and I promised to write books for Lippincott's Magazine—Wilde's contribution was "The Picture of Dorian Gray," a book which is surely upon a high moral plane, while I wrote "The Sign of the Four." in which Holmes made his second appearance. I should add that never in Wilde's conversation did I observe one trace of coarseness of thought, nor could one at that time associate him with such an idea. Only once again did I see him, many years afterwards, and then he gave me the impression of being mad. He asked me, I remember, if I had seen some play of his which was running. I answered that I had not.

He said: "Ah, you must go. It is wonderful. It is genius!" All this with the gravest face. Nothing could have been more different from his early gentlemanly instincts. I thought at the time, and still think, that the monstrous development which ruined him was pathological, and that a hospital rather than a police court was the place for its consideration.

FURTHER INFORMATION: The Langham Hotel has featured in three Sherlock Holmes stories: *The Sign of Four*, "A Scandal in Bohemia" and "The Disappearance of Lady Frances Carfax." The Langham Hotel, 1c Portland Place, Regent Street, London, W1B 1JA. Tel: +44(0)20 7636 1000. www.london.langhamhotels.co.uk

221B Baker Street
The Sherlock Holmes Museum

> "We met next day as he had arranged, and inspected the rooms at No. 221B, Baker Street, of which he had spoken at our meeting. They consisted of a couple of comfortable bed-rooms and a single large airy sitting-room, cheerfully furnished, and illuminated by two broad windows."—Arthur Conan Doyle, *A Study in Scarlet* (1888)

People have been writing to Sherlock Holmes at 221B Baker Street since as far back as 1890 when a copy of his monograph on tobacco ash was requested by a tobacconist in Philadelphia. Hundreds of letters have been received over the years, all of them addressed to 221B, his official London residence. Most of them are written tongue-in-cheek, in the hope of an official reply from his "secretary." Others are written by practical jokers, certifiable lunatics, and people who just need to get out more. For around seventy years, from 1932 to 2002, much of the correspondence was handled by various secretaries of the Abbey National Building Society, whose office location at Abbey House incorporated 215 to 229 Baker Street. Wrote former secretary Sue Brown, during her time in office,

> Mr. Holmes has received post from every quarter of the globe. There are fan letters, birthday wishes, Christmas cards (one each year is from Dr Watson), invitations to give lectures or attend weddings. Sometimes he learns that he is the potential winner of a fortune or that he has been specially selected to receive a trial subscription to a well-known periodical, but by far the largest number of letters contain details of intriguing

mysteries. He is asked to trace, as it may be, a peanut thief in Kansas or to bring to justice the chopstick murderer of Nagasaki or to end the nuclear arms race. A few bring news of Professor Moriarty some claiming that he has been spotted boarding a train in Neasden or that he is responsible for the theft of a painting from the Dulwich Gallery. Others again wish to know intimate details of the detective's private life. Was he left — or right-handed? Did he dislike gooseberry jam? Did he once wound Mrs. Hudson in the foot while cleaning a revolver? And did Mycroft Holmes wear glasses? These and other questions are hard to answer, and I have to remind his correspondents that Holmes is now spending much of his time in Sussex and is rarely, if ever, on hand to deal with the queries himself.

The exact location of 221B Baker Street has never been established, and the fact that it never existed when the first Holmes story was published in 1888 has never been an obstacle to those determined enough to find it. In the early 1920s a Dr. G. C. Briggs came to the conclusion that the address must be at 111 Baker Street (destroyed during World War II) because it was di-

221B Baker — official residence of The Sherlock Holmes Museum.

rectly opposite Camden House, mentioned in "The Adventure of the Empty House," the first Holmes story set after his supposed death at the Reichenbach Falls. By the 1930s upper Baker Street had been created and the number 221 became a genuine address and part of the Abbey National Building Society, then known as the Abbey Road Building Society. And so Abbey House, its head office, became the official residence of Sherlock Holmes.

This entitlement, however, was contested by The Sherlock Holmes Museum (also on Baker Street) and led to a lengthy dispute between the two organizations. The Sherlock Holmes Museum argued that it was a more relevant organization than a Building Society to deal with Sherlock's mail. And although both claimants' right to be known as the official residence are contrived and have no basis in fact, the dispute was finally settled in 2002 when Abbey National quit their Baker Street premises, making The Sherlock Holmes Museum the official 221B Baker Street, now endorsed up by an official heritage plaque.

The museum, which opened in 1990 and is privately run, is dedicated to all things Sherlockian. It includes the famous study "where visitor's can sit in Mr. Holmes's armchair by the fireside to pose for photos." And although 221B was a fictitious address, the museum Web site treads a fine line between fact and fiction, stating, "Visitors often ask whether Sherlock Holmes and Dr Watson really lived in the house, but unfortunately no official records of the lodgers who lived here in Victorian times exist. Local authority records do state that the house was registered as a lodging house between 1860–1934, and that the maids who worked in it were related to a Mr. Holmes."

Conan Doyle's youngest daughter, Dame Jean Conan Doyle (1912–97), expressed her displeasure of the museum in an interview with Jean Upton of ASH, the oldest women's Sherlockian Society:

> The Sherlock Holmes Museum on Baker Street caused Jean no end of irritation, particularly when it began to tell visitors (quite falsely) that it was the former lodgings of Arthur Conan Doyle. In the company of two friends, she visited the Museum anonymously one day in order to gain

Watson and Holmes's study at The Sherlock Holmes Museum (John Griffiths).

first-hand experience. Her friends felt the admission fee and cost of souvenirs were expensive, and Jean herself remarked, "Personally I deplore the Museum because of its false claims, especially those regarding my father, and I cannot envisage Holmes and Watson in such extremely cramped quarters."

FURTHER INFORMATION: The Sherlock Holmes Museum, 221B Baker Street, London NW1 6XE. www.sherlock-holmes.co.uk. Open every day except Christmas from 9:30 A.M. to 6 P.M. Nearest underground stations are Baker Street or Marylebone. ASH (Adventuresses of Sherlock Holmes) is based in New York City and was founded by a group of women students at Albertus Magnus College in the late 1960s. www.ash-nyc.com.

FURTHER READING: R. L. Green, editor, *Letter to Sherlock Holmes* (London, UK: Penguin, 1985).

SEE ALSO: Sherlock Holmes pub (p. 84).

Marylebone Road
Statue of Sherlock Holmes

"I would much rather have men ask why I have no statue than why I have one." — Marcus Porcius Cato (234 B.C.–149 B.C.)

A London memorial to Sherlock Holmes was always on the nation's consciousness ever since his supposed death in "The Final Problem" in 1893. Father Brown creator, G. K. Chesterton, was an early campaigner for a statue in the early 1930s. But the first life-size statue of Sherlock Holmes was actually erected at Meiringen in Switzerland, near the famous Reichenbach Falls in 1988, sculpted by British sculptor, John Doubleday. A few weeks later the Japanese unveiled their own contribution at Koshinzuka Park in Karuizawa, sculpted by Satoh Yoshinori. And in 1991 a third statue was erected close to Conan Doyle's birth site at Picardy Place in Edinburgh, sculpted by Gerald Ogilvie-Laing. By the mid–1990s there was still no statue to Sherlock Holmes in London, but a plan was afoot, and the driving force behind it was the Sherlock Holmes Society of London. The

Tribute to the sleuth — the Sherlock Holmes statue outside Baker Street underground station.

sculptor John Doubleday was approached and a company was set up to supervise the project and act as fundraisers. Most of the funding came from the Abbey National PLC whose headquarters were at 215–229 Baker Street, which encompasses the site of the fictitious 221B. The statue was eventually unveiled by Lord Tugendhat on 23 September 1999. Standing over 9 feet tall, minus its plinth, it has now become a London landmark outside Baker Street Tube Station.

SEE ALSO: Picardy Place (p 3).

109–117 Marylebone Road
Marylebone Library
The Sherlock Holmes Collection

A public archive devoted to all things Sherlockian

In 1951 the austerity and devastation of the Second World War was a very recent memory for the British people; and in an effort to raise the nation's spirit and confidence, the Festival of Britain was created, celebrating the very best in British art, design and industry. St. Marylebone Borough Council's contribution was an extensive exhibition on Sherlock Holmes on the first floor of the Abbey National Building in Baker Street. When the exhibition closed, it toured the United States for two years, before finally settling into its present home at Marylebone Library where it formed the core of The Sherlock Holmes Collection. Over the years a vast collection of Holmes memorabilia has been assembled, all of which is available to the general public.

The collection includes *The Canon*—works about Sherlock Holmes by Sir Arthur Conan Doyle. Translations of the Sherlock Holmes stories are also held, with at least one example in all the major languages. Since 1982 it has been Marylebone's policy to strengthen its coverage of Conan Doyle himself, and they have retrieved from within Westminster Libraries materials such as *The British Campaign in France and Flanders*. With the help of dealers and Sherlockian societies, they now have copies of all of Conan Doyle's works. There are also biographies, critical works, film scripts, Bradshaw's Railway Guide, a copy of William Gillette's only detective novel, and complete runs of the *Strand Magazine* from 1891 to 1930, *The Baker Street*

Journal, published by the Baker Street Irregulars of New York, *The Sherlock Holmes Journal*, published by the Sherlock Holmes Society of London, and *ACD—The Journal of the Arthur Conan Doyle Society*.

FURTHER INFORMATION: Marylebone Library (entrance in Gloucester Place), 109–117 Marylebone Road, London NW1 5PS. Nearest underground: Marylebone, Baker Street. The Collection is held at Marylebone Information Service, and is accessible by appointment only. The library is open seven days a week. Tel: +44 (0)20 76411206. Enquiries: ccooke@westminster.gov.uk. www.westminster.gov.uk

SEE ALSO: Portsmouth Museum (p. 134).

224 Piccadilly
The Criterion

Where Doctor Watson first heard the name of Sherlock Holmes

> "Young Stamford looked rather strangely at me over his wineglass. 'You don't know Sherlock Holmes yet,' he said; 'perhaps you would not care for him as a constant companion.'"—Arthur Conan Doyle, *A Study in Scarlet* (1888)

After qualifying as a doctor in 1878, Watson became an army surgeon and fought in the Second Afghan War (1878–80), where he was wounded by an Afghan bullet at the Battle of Maiwand in 1880. Convalescing at an army hospital in India he was struck down by enteric fever and was later invalided back to England. "I had neither kith nor kin in England, and was therefore as free as air — or as free as an income of eleven shillings and sixpence a day will permit a man to be," he exclaims in the opening chapter of *A Study in Scarlet*. He was staying at a private hotel in London's Strand, and with finances dwindling rapidly he had to find a "less pretentious and less expensive domicile" without delay. This penny-pinching attitude, however, did not appear to extend to the consumption of alcohol, for on New Years Day, 1881, he called in for a drink at one of London's top-class establishments, memorably recalled in the opening chapter of *A Study in Scarlet*:

> I was standing at the Criterion Bar, when some one tapped me on the shoulder, and turning round I recognised young Stamford, who had been a dresser under me at Barts. The sight of a

The Criterion — Watson's gateway to immortality.

friendly face in the great wilderness of London is a pleasant thing indeed to a lonely man. In old days Stamford had never been a particular crony of mine, but now I hailed him with enthusiasm, and he, in his turn, appeared to be delighted to see me. In the exuberance of my joy, I asked him to lunch with me at the Holborn, and we started off together in a hansom.

"Whatever have you been doing with yourself, Watson?" he asked in undisguised wonder, as we rattled through the crowded London streets. "You are as thin as a lath and as brown as a nut."

I gave him a short sketch of my adventures, and had hardly concluded it by the time that we reached our destination.

"Poor devil!" he said, commiseratingly, after he had listened to my misfortunes. "What are you up to now?"

"Looking for lodgings." I answered. "Trying to solve the problem as to whether it is possible to get comfortable rooms at a reasonable price."

"That's a strange thing," remarked my companion; "you are the second man today that has used that expression to me."

"And who was the first?" I asked.

"A fellow who is working at the chemical laboratory up at the hospital. He was bemoaning himself this morning because he could not get someone to go halves with him in some nice rooms which he had found, and which were too much for his purse."

"By Jove!" I cried, "if he really wants someone to share the rooms and the expense, I am the very man for him. I should prefer having a partner to being alone."

Young Stamford looked rather strangely at me over his wineglass. "You don't know Sherlock Holmes yet," he said; "perhaps you would not care for him as a constant companion."

"Why, what is there against him?"

"Oh, I didn't say there was anything against him. He is a little queer in his ideas — an enthusiast in some branches of science. As far as I know he is a decent fellow enough."

"A medical student, I suppose?" said I.

"No — I have no idea what he intends to go in for. I believe he is well up in anatomy, and he is a first-class chemist; but, as far as I know, he has never taken out any systematic medical classes. His studies are very desultory and eccentric, but he has amassed a lot of out-of-the-way knowledge which would astonish his professors."

"Did you never ask him what he was going in for?" I asked.

"No; he is not a man that it is easy to draw out, though he can be communicative enough when the fancy seizes him."

"I should like to meet him," I said. "If I am to lodge with anyone, I should prefer a man of studious and quiet habits. I am not strong enough yet to stand much noise or excitement. I had enough of both in Afghanistan to last me for the remainder of my natural existence. How could I meet this friend of yours?"

"He is sure to be at the laboratory," returned my companion. "He either avoids the place for weeks, or else he works there from morning to night. If you like, we shall drive round together after luncheon."

"Certainly," I answered, and the conversation drifted away into other channels.

As we made our way to the hospital after leaving the Holborn, Stamford gave me a few more particulars about the gentleman whom I proposed to take as a fellow-lodger.'

FURTHER INFORMATION: The Criterion, 224 Piccadilly, Piccadilly, London W1J9HP. Tel: +44(0)20 7930 0488. www.criterionrestaurant. com. A plaque at The Criterion commemorates the meeting between Watson and Stamford and reads as follows: "HERE, NEW YEAR'S DAY, 1881 AT THE CRITERION LONG BAR STAMFORD, DRESSER AT BART'S MET DR. JOHN H. WATSON AND LED HIM TO IMMORTALITY AND SHERLOCK HOLMES."

SEE ALSO: Ward, Lock & Company (p. 92), Maiwand Lion (p. 105).

107 Pall Mall
The Athenaeum
Conan Doyle's gentleman's club

> "There are many men in London, you know, who, some from shyness, some from misanthropy, have no wish for the company of their fellows. Yet they are not averse to comfortable chairs and the latest periodicals. It is for the convenience of these that the Diogenes Club was started, and it now contains the most unsociable and unclubbable men in town. No member is permitted to take the least notice of any other one. Save in the Strangers' Room, no talking is, under any circumstances, permitted, and three offences, if brought to the notice of the committee, render the talker liable to expulsion. My brother was one of the founders, and I have myself found it a very soothing atmosphere." — Arthur Conan Doyle, Holmes describing his brother Mycroft's club in Pall Mall, "The Adventure of the Greek Interpreter," *The Memoirs of Sherlock Holmes* (1894)

The gentleman's club is a peculiarly British male institution — a place where gentlemen can eat, drink, sleep, smoke, gamble, and join in intelligent conversation with their peers. In other words, it is a luxurious male bastion, devoid of feminine influence and fripperies, where women are taboo. By the middle of the 19th century these clubs were at their most prolific around Pall Mall and St. James's Street. Conan Doyle, a man not averse to male bonhomie, was a member of several throughout his life. But The Athenaeum was probably the most prestigious and was solely for artists, writers and scientists. Sir Walter Scott, Charles Dickens and William Thackeray had been past members, and legend has it that Dickens and Thackeray were reconciled here after years of rebuffing one another following a bitter quarrel.

In May 1907, the American periodical, *Munsey's Magazine*, published an article by Conan Doyle's journalist friend, Bertram Fletcher Robinson, entitled "People Much Talked About in London." In the article Robinson profiles many personalities, including Conan Doyle:

> In Pall Mall, too, it is likely that we shall meet some of the more famous of English literary men bound for that most exclusive of clubs — The Athenaeum. Here comes that kindly giant, Sir Arthur Conan Doyle, the creator of Sherlock Holmes, prince of detectives. He is of a fine British type, a clear-headed, sport-loving, big-hearted patriot.
>
> A mention of the Athenaeum Club reminds me of a story Sir Arthur told me of his first visit, after election, to that home of the respectabilities. He walked up to the hall-porter and, desiring to introduce himself to that important person's notice, asked if there were any letters for Conan Doyle. Now the Athenaeum is a favourite resort of the clerical dignitaries, and the hall-porter, who had small acquaintance with literature, replied "No, canon, there are no letters for you."
>
> Sir Arthur did not care to explain, and for some weeks he suffered much from the disapproving eye of the hall-porter. The suit of tweeds affected by the great novelist shocked that functionary deeply, and when one day Sir Arthur appeared in a long racing-coat, the spectacle had such an effect on him that

The Athenaeum — bastion of male bonhomie.

Doyle had to rush to the desk and explain that he was not a dignitary of the church, but a writer of tales to whom some latitude in dress might be allowed.

Named after the ancient Roman center for the study of literature and science, The Athenaeum was designed in 1827 by the architect Decimus Burton "as a meeting place for men who enjoy the life of the mind." Burton rounded off the building by enveloping a frieze around it depicting copies of the Elgin Marbles (recently rescued, or looted, depending on your point of view, from the Parthenon in Athens) displayed in the British Museum. The majority of members would have preferred the money designated for the frieze to have been used to build an ice house. The promoter of the frieze plan, however, was the Secretary of the Admiralty, J. W. Croker. Not a man to be trifled with, hence the witticism of the day:

> "I'm John Wilson Croker
> I do as I please;
> Instead of an Ice House
> I give you — a frieze!"

Breaking 150 years of tradition, The Athenaeum opened its doors to women members in 2002. Would Conan Doyle have approved?

FURTHER INFORMATION: The Athenaeum, 107 Pall Mall, London, SW1Y 5ER. Tel: +44 (0)20 7930 4843. www.athenaeumclub.co.uk

SEE ALSO: Fletcher Robinson (p. 114).

100 Strand
Simpson's-in-the-Strand

Dining establishment favored by Holmes and Watson

"Thank you, Watson, you must help me on with my coat. When we have finished at the police-station I think that something nutritious at Simpson's would not be out of place." — Arthur Conan Doyle, "The Adventure of the Dying Detective," *His Last Bow* (1917)

There is no doubt that Sherlock Holmes appreciated the finer things of life; and although his eating habits were erratic, he did appreciate a really good restaurant, especially one of the standard of Simpson's-in-the-Strand. Watson was also not averse to dining "at our Strand restaurant" with the great sleuth. "I met him by appointment that evening at Simpson's," he

Simpson's-in-the-Strand — antithesis of the fast food restaurant.

wrote in "The Illustrious Client," "where, sitting at a small table in the front window, and looking down at the rushing stream of life in the Strand, he told me something of what had passed."

Originally opening as a chess club and coffee house known as The Grand Cigar Divan, Simpson's takes pride in offering classic British dishes. For over 170 years it's silver-domed trolleys have been wheeled to the tables of its famous guests, including Arthur Conan Doyle, Charles Dickens, George Bernard Shaw, Benjamin Disraeli, Thomas Hardy, John Buchan, and Vincent Van Gogh.

FURTHER INFORMATION: Simpson's-in-the-Strand, 100 Strand, London WC2R 0EW. Tel: +44(0)20 7420 2494. www.simpsonsinthestrand.co.uk.

Nearest underground station Charing Cross or Embankment.

21 Wellington Street
Lyceum Theatre

Site of the first UK performance of William Gillette's play Sherlock Holmes

"It was a September evening, and not yet seven o'clock, but the day had been a dreary one, and a dense drizzly fog lay low upon the great city. Mud-coloured clouds drooped sadly over the muddy streets. Down the Strand the lamps were but misty splotches of diffused light, which threw a feeble circular glimmer upon the slimy pavement. The yellow glare from the shop-windows streamed out into the steamy, vaporous air, and threw a murky, shifting radiance across the crowded thoroughfare.... At the Lyceum Theatre the crowds were already thick at the side-entrances. In front a continuous stream of hansoms and four-wheelers were rattling up, discharging their cargoes of shirt-fronted men and beshawled and bediamonded women. We had hardly reached the third pillar, which was our

William Gillette as Sherlock Holmes.

rendezvous, before a small, dark, brisk man in the dress of a coachman accosted us."—Arthur Conan Doyle, *The Sign of Four* (1890)

Conan Doyle first encountered the Lyceum on a visit to London as a fifteen-year-old in 1874 when he attended a performance of *Hamlet*. In later years he used it as the rendezvous for Holmes, Watson, and Mary Morstan's curious patron, in *The Sign of Four*. But its most famous Doylean claim to fame has to be William Gillette's production of the play *Sherlock Holmes*, which opened at the Lyceum in September 1901 and ran for seven months. William Gillette (1853–1937) was an American actor, playwright and stage-manager, who is best remembered for his portrayal of Sherlock Holmes; and although he was not the first actor to play the great sleuth, he came to represent the definitive Holmes, appearing on stage as the character for thirty years in over 1,300 performances. He also appeared on film and radio as Holmes; and the American illustrator Frederic Dorr Steele, best known for illustrating Sherlock Holmes, used his likeness as a model.

Shortly after Conan Doyle's move to Undershaw, his new house in Surrey, during the fall of 1897, he wrote a play about Sherlock Holmes. Only a few years earlier, in 1893, he had killed him off by throwing him over the Reichenbach Falls. "The strain was something I could not endure any longer," he told a local journalist. "Of course had I continued I could have coined money, for the stories were the most remunerative I have written; but as regards literature, they would have been mere trash." Noble words, but now with a new house to pay for, and subsequent novels that hadn't set the world on fire, Conan Doyle needed to resuscitate his bank balance, and a play based around Holmes might be the solution.

Initially actor manager, Herbert Beerbohm Tree, was interested in staging the play, but it came to nothing. William Gillette then approached Conan Doyle, but wished to adapt and revise it to suit his own style. He even wanted to marry off Holmes and cabled Conan Doyle for clearance, to which he received the disinterested reply: "You may marry him, murder him, or do anything you like to him." The end result was a great success and the beginning of Sherlock Holmes as a piece of mass-market merchandise. Conan Doyle's response was to write "my only complaint being that you make the poor hero of the anaemic printed page a very limp object as compared with the glamour of your own personality which you infuse into his stage presentment."

FURTHER INFORMATION: Lyceum Theatre, 21 Wellington Street, London WC2E 7RQ. www.lyceum-theatre.co.uk

Nearest underground Covent Garden or Charing Cross. There has been a Lyceum Theatre on this site since 1765. The present building, which seats 2,000, dates from 1834 and was designed by Samuel Beazley.

Trafalgar Square
The National Gallery

The Paintings of Horace Vernet, ancestor of Sherlock Holmes

"It was after tea on a summer evening, and the conversation, which had roamed in a desultory, spasmodic fashion from golf clubs to the causes of the change in the obliquity of the ecliptic, came round at last to the question of atavism and hereditary aptitudes. The point under discussion was how far any singular gift in an individual was due to his ancestry, and how far to his own early training.

'In your own case,' said I, 'from all that you have told me it seems obvious that your faculty of observation and your peculiar facility for deduction are due to your own systematic training.'

'To some extent,' he answered, thoughtfully. 'My ancestors were country squires, who appear to have led much the same life as is natural to their class. But, none the less, my turn that way is in my veins, and may have come with my grandmother, who was the sister of Vernet, the French artist. Art in the blood is liable to take the strangest forms.'

'But how do you know that it is hereditary?'

'Because my brother Mycroft possesses it in a larger degree than I do.'" — Arthur Conan Doyle, "The Adventure of the Greek Interpreter," *The Memoirs of Sherlock Holmes* (1894)

Horace Vernet was a predictable choice as an ancestor of Sherlock Holmes as his paintings depicted history through battle scenes and military subjects, themes never far from the pen of Conan Doyle. Vernet was also a man of principles, another important criteria. When asked by Louis Napoleon to delete a general he found loathsome from a painting of a military review, Vernet replied, "I am a painter of history, sire and I will not violate the truth."

Horace Vernet was born in 1789, the son of the celebrated painter Carle Vernet. Contemptuous of the constrictions of classical art, Horace Vernet chose contemporary subjects in a natural style, a route which led to him depicting the everyday attitudes of the French soldier, in stark contrast to the idealized military paintings of the day. His battle scenes were also groundbreaking, with vast canvases representing the victories of Napoleon, including Jena, Friedland and Wagram. He

Napoleon at the Battle of Friedland (1807) by Horace Vernet. The Emperor is depicted giving instructions to General Nicolas Oudinot. Between them is depicted General Etienne de Nansouty and behind the Emperor, on his right is Marshal Michel Ney, Duke of Elchingen.

died in Paris in 1863, unaware of his bloodline to Sherlock Holmes.

FURTHER INFORMATION: The National Gallery, Trafalgar Square, London, WC2N 5DN. Tel: +44(0)20 7747 2423. Some of Horace Vernet's paintings can be viewed online at www.nationalgallery.org.uk

10–11 Northumberland Street
The Sherlock Holmes pub and restaurant
Home to part of the 1951 Festival of Britain Exhibition on Sherlock Holmes

"For me, it brought back a flood of memories.... A half-century ago, as I stood admiring the completeness of the panoply of familiar items, another acolyte, a dear little old lady standing nearby put to me this poser. 'Excuse me,' she queried somewhat tentatively, 'Is this his very room?' How, I thought to myself, can I truthfully answer this disarmingly naïve soul? A resolution came to me and I answered, 'I am told that that is so.' We exchanged smiles for my response appeared to please both of us."
Frank Darlington, from Port Townsend, Washington, U.S.A., recalling his visit to Holmes's Baker St. lodgings at the Abbey National building in 1951.

As part of the 1951 Festival of Britain celebrations, a Sherlock Holmes exhibition was held at the Abbey National building in Baker Street.

About a third of the floor area of the exhibition was devoted to a reproduction of the interior of 221B Baker Street. This part of the exhibition was later purchased by the brewery Whitbread & Co. and re-erected at their premises in Northumberland Street in 1957, since renamed The Sherlock Holmes. The bar is on street level and the restaurant is upstairs, where you can view the Baker Street room through a glass partition. Other Holmes and Doyle paraphernalia, including the mounted head of the hound of the Baskervilles, are scattered throughout the building. The restaurant menu is themed around the Holmes stories, so hopefully you will be able to taste culinary delights such as Devil's Foot Soup, Baskerville Salad and Mrs. Hudson's home baking. The smells from the kitchen are no doubt delightful, but there is another smell wafting on the air — that of the tourist trap!

FURTHER INFORMATION: The Sherlock Holmes, 10–11 Northumberland Street, Westminster, WC2N 5DB. Tel: +44(0)20 7930 2644. www.sherlockholmespub.com

The Sherlock Holmes is just a few minutes walk from Charing Cross and Embankment underground stations. By bus alight at Trafalgar Square or Charing Cross.

SEE ALSO: Sherlock Holmes Museum (p. 75).

Victoria Embankment
Scotland Yard
Former Headquarters of the Metropolitan Police

"It is an open secret that the credit of this smart capture belongs entirely to the well-known Scotland Yard officials, Messrs. Lestrade and Gregson. The man was apprehended, it appears, in the rooms of a certain Mr. Sherlock Holmes, who has himself, as an amateur, shown some talent in the detective line, and who, with such instructors, may hope in time to attain to some degree of their skill." — Arthur Conan Doyle, *A Study in Scarlet*

The routinely baffled detectives of Scotland Yard usually ended up getting the credit for solving mind-boggling crimes, but it was Sherlock Holmes who was invariably at the root of the problem-solving pro-

Raising a glass to the sleuth — The Sherlock Holmes Pub.

cess. Depicted as little more than careless and clumsy dolts, the intuitiveness of the Victorian police detective is not a feature of the Sherlock Holmes story. Although Conan Doyle's forensic knowledge was satisfactory, his knowledge of police procedure was in no way perfect. He once visited, perhaps for inspiration, the famous Black Museum at Scotland Yard. Holmes, however, needed perfect foils on which to project his genius, and that was unfailingly Watson and the Scotland Yard detective. Despite all that, if you dig deep enough, Conan Doyle did have a real regard for the force, as he states in "The Adventure of the Three Garridebs": "There may be an occasional want of imaginative intuition down there, but they lead the world for thoroughness and method."

The Yard — international symbol of law enforcement.

The name "Scotland Yard" is derived from its original location on Great Scotland Yard, Whitehall, but the exact origins of the name are vague. One interpretation has it as a site once used by the Kings of Scotland; another that the site was owned by a man named Scott; and yet another that stagecoaches left for Scotland from here. The first Scotland Yard was at 4 Whitehall Place, the original site of Great Scotland Yard. It became the headquarters in 1829 of the newly established Metropolitan Police formed by the Home Secretary, Sir Robert Peel (origin of the name "Bobby"). In 1890 larger headquarters, known as New Scotland Yard and designed by Norman Shaw, were opened on the Embankment. This red and white brick Victorian Gothic edifice became the classic face of Scotland Yard portrayed in popular fiction and cinema, including the works of John Creasey, P. D. James, Agatha Christie, and of course, Arthur Conan Doyle. It also held the famous telephone number Whitehall 1212.

Since 1967 Metropolitan Police headquarters have been located at 10 Broadway, SW1, along with the national crime database. This is where its national IT system is called Home Office Large Major Enquiry System, a mouthful which is conveniently known by the acronym HOLMES.

FURTHER INFORMATION: The Black Museum, officially known as The Crime Museum, was conceived in 1874 when an Inspector Neame began collecting items connected to criminal cases to assist in the practical instruction of police officers. The present two-room museum, based at 10 Broadway, contains an extensive collection of weapons and relics connected to many famous cases, including Dr. Crippen, Ruth Ellis, and Jack the Ripper. The museum is not open to the public; but if you are famous enough, doors may open, as they did for Conan Doyle, Harry Houdini, Gilbert & Sullivan, Laurel & Hardy, and members of the Royal family.

SEE ALSO: Kent Police Museum (p. 109).

Victoria Tower Gardens
Statue of Emmeline Pankhurst
Political activist and leader of the British suffrage movement

> "There is something that Governments care for far more than human life, and that is the security of property, and so it is through property that we shall strike the enemy. Be militant each in your own way. I incite this meeting to rebellion." — Emmeline Pankhurst

A few months before Conan Doyle's death in 1930, a statue was erected adjacent to the Houses of Parliament to Emmeline Pankhurst (1858–1928), figurehead of the suffrage movement.

Emmeline Pankhurst's statue basking in the shadow of her former nemesis — The Houses of Parliament.

Conan Doyle was no friend of women's suffrage, and his comments on the statue's erection were not recorded. In 1914, during a visit to America, sulphuric acid was poured through a mailbox next to his Windlesham home, but the militant response never deterred him from voicing his opposition to a movement which indulged in "window smashing, house burning and picture mutilating," warning that if "militant suffragettes continued in this vein ... they would surely be lynched by an angry public." The response of *The New York Times* to these comments was to print an article headlined: "CONAN DOYLE FEARS DRASTIC UPRISING AGAINST MILITANTS; Believes the Time Is Close at Hand When the English People Will Take the Law Into Their Own Hands and the Result Will Be Nothing Short of Lynching." Conan Doyle's immediate response to the American press's hyperbolic journalism was to call a press conference where "in a wretched humour," he stated the following:

> I open the late editions of your amazing papers and find myself headlined as desiring to lynch the militants! I must correct that or I shall not dare to return to England. I have many very good friends among the militants and among those who favor the militant movement. Now, what I did say to your reporters was that I was afraid the time was close at hand when some very drastic action would be taken. That I very much feared that the people would take the law into their own hands, and that the result would be nothing short of lynching. That would be a terrible outcome — I can conceive of nothing more horrible, except that I myself should subscribe to such an action! But the situation is very, very grave indeed — I do not think that you on this side of the water realize the seriousness of the pass to which we are coming.
>
> So far the Government has followed public opinion and so far public opinion has not demanded the suppression of the militants. But the patience of the public has just about reached the breaking point, and I am very much afraid that something is going to happen.

Although a supporter for the reform of the divorce laws, Conan Doyle remained an outspoken opponent of militant suffrage, believing its outcome to lead only to social chaos. The immensely brave struggle of the suffrage movement, however, was in the end, together with women's contribution during the First World War, responsible for the political shift which gave the vote to women over the age of 30 in 1918, and eventually to all women over the age of 21 in 1928.

FURTHER INFORMATION: The Houses of Parliament were a prime site for suffragette protest and many militant incidents took place there. On one occasion suffragettes chained themselves to the statue of Viscount Falkland in St. Stephen's Hall breaking the spur of his boot with their chains. The broken spur can still be seen today. For details of how to visit or join a conducted tour of the Houses of Parliament consult www.parliament.uk

SEE ALSO: Albert Hall (p. 90).

Dean's Yard
Westminster Abbey
Grave of Thomas Babington Macaulay (1800–1859)

Politician, historian and lifelong inspiration of Conan Doyle

"I can remember that when I visited London at the age of sixteen the first thing I did after housing my luggage was to make a pilgrimage to

Macaulay's grave, where he lies in Westminster Abbey, just under the shadow of Addison, and amid the dust of the poets whom he had loved so well. It was the one great object of interest which London held for me. And so it might well be, when I think of all I owe him." — Arthur Conan Doyle, *Through the Magic Door* (1907)

Conan Doyle admired many writers throughout his life, but it was Macaulay who became his lifeblood and mentor, and who buried a childhood love of history deep within him, turning it "into an enchanted land, a land of colour and beauty." Like Macaulay, Conan Doyle desperately tried to breath life into his own historical works, and more than anything he wanted to be remembered as one of England's great historical novelists. His destiny, much to his vexation, trod a different path; and history records him, somewhat misguidedly, as solely the creator of Sherlock Holmes, ignoring his substantial historical works. In 1907 he published a personal appraisal of his favorite books, titled *Through the Magic Door,* citing preferences from Sir Walter Scott to Robert Louis Stevenson. His description of Macaulay's influence, however, is one of reverence and lifelong adoration:

Reading is made too easy nowadays, with cheap paper editions and free libraries. A man does not appreciate at its full worth the thing that comes to him without effort. Who now ever gets the thrill which Carlyle felt when he hurried home with the six volumes of Gibbon's "History" under his arm, his mind just starving for want of food, to devour them at the rate of one a day? A book should be your very own before you can really get the taste of it, and unless you have worked for it, you will never have the true inward pride of possession.

If I had to choose the one book out of all that line from which I have had most pleasure and most profit, I should point to yonder stained copy of Macaulay's "Essays." It seems entwined into my whole life as I look backwards. It was my comrade in my student days, it has been with me on the sweltering Gold Coast, and it formed part of my humble kit when I went a-whaling in the Arctic. Honest Scotch harpooners have addled their brains over it, and you may still see the grease stains where the second engineer grappled with Frederick the Great. Tattered and dirty and worn, no gilt-edged morocco-bound volume could ever take its place for me.

What a noble gateway this book forms through which one may approach the study either of letters or of history! Milton, Machiavelli, Hallam,

Thomas Babington Macaulay — mentor to "an enchanted land."

Southey, Bunyan, Byron, Johnson, Pitt, Hampden, Clive, Hastings, Chatham — what nuclei for thought! With a good grip of each how pleasant and easy to fill in all that lies between! The short, vivid sentences, the broad sweep of allusion, the exact detail, they all throw a glamour round the subject and should make the least studious of readers desire to go further. If Macaulay's hand cannot lead a man upon those pleasant paths, then, indeed, he may give up all hope of ever finding them.

When I was a senior schoolboy this book — not this very volume, for it had an even more tattered predecessor — opened up a new world to me. History had been a lesson and abhorrent. Suddenly the task and the drudgery became an incursion into an enchanted land, a land of colour and beauty, with a kind, wise guide to point the path. In that great style of his I loved even the faults — indeed, now that I come to think of it, it was the faults which I loved best. No sentence could be too stiff with rich embroidery, and no antithesis too flowery. It pleased me to read that "a universal shout of laughter from the Tagus to the Vistula informed the Pope that the days of the crusades were past," and I was delighted to learn that "Lady Jerningham kept a vase in which people placed foolish verses, and Mr. Dash wrote verses which were fit to be placed in Lady Jerningham's vase." Those were the kind of sentences which used to fill me with a vague but enduring pleasure, like chords which linger in the musician's ear. A man likes a plainer literary diet as he grows older, but still as I glance over the Essays I am filled with admiration and wonder at the alternate power of handling a great subject, and of adorning it by delightful detail — just a bold sweep of the brush, and then the most delicate stippling. As he leads you down the path, he for ever indicates the alluring side-tracks which branch away from it. An admirable, if somewhat old-fashioned, literary and historical education night be effected by working through every book which is alluded to in the Essays. I should be curious, however, to know the exact age of the youth when he came to the end of his studies.

I wish Macaulay had written a historical novel. I am convinced that it would have been a great one. I do not know if he had the power of drawing an imaginary character, but he certainly had the gift of reconstructing a dead celebrity to a remarkable degree.

FURTHER INFORMATION: Westminster Abbey is next to Big Ben and the Houses of Parliament and is open to the public Monday to Saturday. Sunday is for worship only. The nearest underground is St. James' Park (District and Circle Lines) and Westminster (Jubilee, District and Circle Lines). No parking facilities are available. www.westminster-abbey.org

SEE ALSO: James Thin (p. 19).

St. Margaret's Street
St. Margaret's Church

Where Conan Doyle married Jean Leckie

"Sherlock Holmes Quietly Married" — *Buenos Aires Standard*, September 1907

Conan Doyle fell in love with Jean Leckie while still married to his first wife, Louise, who in 1893 had been diagnosed with tuberculosis and given only a few months to live. Louise, however, outlived her prognosis by thirteen years, dying at the age of 49 in 1906. Conan Doyle gave her the best care available, including trips to Switzerland and Egypt where it was thought the climate would be more beneficial to her health; but the endgame always lurked in the shadows. Sooner, rather than later, Louise would die.

Conan Doyle first met Jean Leckie, who was thirteen years younger than himself, in March 1897, but where this meeting took place is unclear. She was "the young daughter of a Blackheath family whom I had known for years," he wrote in his autobiography, "and who was a dear

friend of my mother and sister." It was love at first sight, but as far as we know they never consummated their relationship until they were married. Conan Doyle may have been playing with fire, but his integrity and morality were not to be sacrificed, although his mental suffering must have been immense.

For ten years he kept up an intimate, and allegedly, non-sexual relationship with Jean. Conan Doyle, of course, told all to his mother, as he did with everything in his life, and she appeared to sanction the relationship. In fact, everyone among his close circle, including Jean's parents, seemed to know about the liaison — everyone that is, except Louise.

Just over a year after Louise's death, Conan Doyle married Jean Leckie at a small private ceremony at St. Margaret's Church, adjacent to Westminster Abbey, on 18 September 1907. His brother Innes was best man and his sister Dodo's husband, the Rev. Cyril Angell, performed the ceremony before around thirty guests. The reception was held at the Hotel Metropole where 250 guests gathered to celebrate, including J. M. Barrie, Bram Stoker, Jerome K. Jerome,

St. Margaret's Church.

George Newnes, Greenhough Smith and George Edalji. Shortly afterwards the newlyweds left for a Mediterranean honeymoon.

FURTHER INFORMATION: St. Margaret's Church has stood on its present site since the 11th century and is dedicated to St. Margaret of Antioch, a figure whose historical existence is doubtful. The building has changed considerably over the years and was seemingly built in order to give the monks from the abbey next door peace from the public. The monks, who would worship at various times throughout the day, were disturbed by the people who came to hear Mass, and began building a small church next to the abbey where the public could still receive the ministrations of the church, but leave them in peace and tranquility. The Metropole Building in Northumberland Avenue (near to the Embankment) was once home to the Hotel Metropole, and now houses The Corinthia Hotel.

SEE ALSO: Windlsham (p. 123), George Edalji (p. 67), J. M. Barrie (p. 47).

Abbey House
2 Victoria Street
Site of the Psychic Bookshop

> "Ectoplasm Sowest London" — Telegraphic address of The Psychic Bookshop

In February 1925 Conan Doyle launched an enterprise that was dear to his heart — a psychic bookshop in city center London, "within a stone's throw of Westminster Abbey." This ground floor and basement shop was devoted to psychic literature, and later contained a museum displaying a collection of spirit photographs, seance equipment, etc. "It has long seemed to me," he wrote, "that one of the weak points in our psychic movement is the complete disconnection between our splendid literature and the man in the street."

In May 1927 he was interviewed by Leonard Crocombe for the *Strand Magazine* in an article titled "The World's Happiest Museum — Through a Room of Miracles with Sir A. Conan Doyle," and the following extract gives the reader a taste of the inexhaustible enthusiasm he had for his spiritualist beliefs:

> He wished [to make it] clear that the interview was not to be considered as propaganda for Spiri-

tualism and psychic phenomena. That was not his object in giving me this interview for the Magazine with which he has been associated as a leading contributor since the year of its foundation.... To reach this room of miracles you enter the Psychic Book Shop and Library, facing Westminster Abbey. Sir Arthur is proprietor of this shop, and beneath it is the long room in which he has arranged hundreds of objects, photographs, pictures — a thought-provoking record of certain phases of Spiritualist activities, and of the results of psychic research (between the two is an important difference), for the past fifty years or so. "My Museum may be the smallest in London," Sir Arthur said, "but it is as large as any museum ever need be, for the visitor will have to give several hours to its exhibits if he wishes really to examine them all thoroughly. It is, also, unique. We can give the history of every single thing in it, and I do not think the most hardened sceptic could go over the exhibits and retain any doubt as to the continuity of our life after physical death. That is surely the core of every religion, and my little Museum must be doing good work if it proves our survival of bodily death."

While I have been making my notes ... my guide has been fingering a large vase. "This room is full of incredible things," he said, "Things which, in the old days, would have been called miracles, or the results of miracles. A miracle, now and always, is simply the intrusion of some natural force which we do not yet understand. That is why it is incorrect to use the words 'supernatural' or 'supernormal' in connection with these manifestations of powers of whose methods we are as yet ignorant. Everything in Nature is 'natural' and 'normal,' whether we understand it or not. We can show you results here before we can accurately explain their causes." (I was not quite sure whether or not we were touching on that propaganda, so I took the vase without comment.)

"Yes, now examine this big jug, or vase," Sir Arthur continued. "It came down suddenly, inexplicably, on a seance table. This is what we call an *apport* — the French word for something brought. Apport phenomena are the bringing of objects — live birds and fish, fresh fruit, dew-laden flowers, coins — all manner of things! — from a distance, through walls, closed windows, locked doors, and so on, into the midst of a group of sitters. Darkness is not always essential, neither is a professional apport medium necessary. No one could say that the medium had this large jug hidden upon her person," Sir Arthur continued. "I happen to know a good deal about the medium. She was an amateur. It came down suddenly, inexplicably, on a seance table. The medium was an amateur, a poor woman, who gave away all the apports produced through her psychic powers. From first to last she

— or, rather, the spirits who used the psychic power she supplied — brought through about two thousand objects of various kinds — Chinese and Indian lamps, amulets, Tibetan pots — all manner of queer things — and among them all I do not think there was one that could have been got in England. This jug, for example, is Syrian ware. She was quite a poor woman, but she would not sell her apports. She just left them with the sitters. Of course, it is all very fantastic, but it is true."

Whether true or false, the Psychic Bookshop was costing Conan Doyle £1,500 a year and proved a disastrous undertaking. After five years the enterprise ceased trading in 1932.

SEE ALSO: *Strand Magazine* (p. 91), Major General Alfred Drayson (p. 131), Houdini (p. 133), Agatha Christie (p. 59), Albert Hall (p. 90).

Kensington Gore
Royal Albert Hall

Location of Conan Doyle's spiritualist memorial service

Lead, kindly Light, amid the encircling gloom,
Lead Thou me on;
The night is dark, and I am far from home;
Lead Thou me on;
Keep Thou my feet; I do not ask to see
The distant scene; one step enough for me.
— from "Lead, Kindly Light," by John
  Henry Newman (1801–90), favorite hymn
  of the Spiritualist movement

Conan Doyle died on the 11th of July, 1930. Two days later, on the 13th of July, a memorial service was organized for him by the Marylebone Spiritualist Association at London's prestigious Royal Albert Hall and was attended by a huge audience of around 6,000 people. Conan Doyle's family were seated on the stage: Lady Jean, her two sons Adrian and Denis, their sister, Jean, and half-sister, Mary, daughter of Conan Doyle's first wife, Louise (Touie) Hawkins. To the right of Lady Jean was an empty chair left vacant for spirit of the great man himself. The chairman of the proceedings was Mr. George Craze of the Marylebone Spiritualist Association, who opened the service by reading a statement on behalf of Lady Conan Doyle:

At every meeting all over the world, I have sat at my beloved husband's side, and at this great meeting, where people have come with respect and love in their hearts to do him honour, his chair is placed beside me, and I know that in the

spiritual presence he will be close to me. Although our earthly eyes cannot see beyond the earth's vibrations, those with the God-given extra sight called clairvoyance will be able to see the dear form in our midst. I want in my children's, and my own, and my beloved husband's name, to thank you all from my heart for the love for him which brought you here tonight.

The audience was then addressed by a few eminent spiritualist speakers, followed by the singing of the hymn, "Lead, Kindly Light." The audience were then asked to stand for two minutes of silence, after which Mr. Craze introduced Conan Doyle's favorite medium, Mrs. Estelle Roberts (1889–1970), considered by the Spiritualist movement to be one of the finest exponents of mediumship. Mrs. Roberts was the main event, and her task for the evening was to communicate and transmit messages from the spirit world. In her book, *Fifty Years a Medium*, she relates what happened that evening:

Many of those present hoped that Sir Arthur would dramatically come back and thus fulfill a promise he had made. He did return at this huge gathering, but not in the sensational manner hoped for by his audience.

Lady Doyle sat in the center of the platform. By her side there was a chair deliberately left empty as a symbol of his physical absence but an indication of his hoped for spirit presence. All around was a great concourse of spirit people anxious to communicate with their friends. For half an hour, by means of clairvoyance, I relayed their messages to individuals among the mass of people in the hall. But there was no sign of Sir Arthur. I kept looking about me, hoping he would appear. It was not until the audience stood for two minutes' silence as a tribute to him, that I suddenly became aware he was standing beside me. With this realization I became momentarily flustered. He saw it at once and quickly calmed me. "Carry on with your work. Go on, child," he said reassuringly. Then he went and sat in the "empty" chair by his wife.

I carried on transmitting spirit messages until Sir Arthur got to his feet and came over to my side. Slowly and deliberately he gave me a test message for Lady Doyle. It was an intimate one concerning another member of the family and referred to an event which had occurred only that morning. It convinced Lady Doyle that it must have come from her husband, as only she and the other member of the family were aware that the small incident described had happened.

After the memorial service Lady Jean claimed she received regular messages from her husband

The Royal Albert Hall, dedicated by Queen Victoria to her husband and consort, Prince Albert, in 1871.

Medium (Essex, UK: Psychic Press, 2008).

SEE ALSO: Emmeline Pankhurst (p. 85), Psychic Bookshop (p. 89), Major General Alfred Drayson (p. 131), Houdini (p. 133), Agatha Christie (p. 59), All Saints Churchyard (p. 139).

The Strand
Southampton St. and Exeter St.
Site of George Newnes Ltd., publishers of the Strand Magazine, *first magazine to publish the Sherlock Holmes short stories*

"The short story is one of the oldest forms of creative writing in the world. Compared with it formal poetry is a stripling and the novel a babe in arms."— Gerda Charles (1914–96)

through her automatic writing, proffering ideas, opinions, and helpful guidance in the running of the family affairs. Jean never doubted these messages from the spirit world and kept promoting the cause of the Spiritualist movement for the rest of her life. "I can look into my Beloved's dear face," she wrote, "when he meets me at the Gateway of Death, and say, 'I have tried to keep your Banner flying'—and we will part no more."

One of the stranger spirits who transmitted messages that day at the Albert Hall through Mrs. Roberts was Emily Wilding Davison, the suffragette who threw herself in front of King George V's horse at the Epsom Derby in 1913 and subsequently died from her injuries. Given Conan Doyle's passionate opposition to the women's suffrage movement, one has to wonder whether Miss Davidson was there that day in her role as a passive spirit or a militant out for revenge.

FURTHER INFORMATION: Mrs. Estelle Roberts was no stranger to the Royal Albert Hall and demonstrated her mediumistic gifts there on numerous occasions, usually accompanied by the spirit of her teacher and guide, the native American Indian known as Red Cloud. She was also influential in gaining government recognition for the Spiritualist movement during the 1950s after she demonstrated her talents before the Houses of Parliament.

FURTHER READING: E. Roberts, *Fifty Years a*

The short story has always been with us, but it was not always in fashion. It reached its zenith of popularity from around 1880 to the late 1920s, a time when the public actually purchased magazines to read the fiction printed in them! During these halcyon days short story writers were given favorable attention by publishers; and many of them, like Kipling and Conan Doyle, were paid vast sums for their stories. In short, it was a time of respect and admiration for the short story and their authors—glory days for the fiction periodical.

In 1881 George Newnes (1851–1910) began his career in publishing by launching *Tit-Bits from all the interesting Books, Periodicals, and Newspapers of the World.* Popularly known as *Tit-Bits*, it became a mass circulation publication which made him a fortune. Ten years later, in 1891, he published what was to become his best known publication, the *Strand Magazine*, a monthly magazine of fictional stories and factual articles. Its most memorable editor was Herbert Greenhough Smith (1855–1935), who edited the *Strand* from its beginnings until his retirement in 1930, a period of nearly forty years. Many writers passed through his hands over the years, but the most notable was Arthur Conan Doyle. One of his first stories to appear in the *Strand* was called "The Voice of Science," submitted by his new literary agent, A. P. Watt, and for which he received £4 per thousand words. It didn't set the world on fire, nor did it make much of an impact on Greenhough Smith, but the next stories of Conan Doyle's to be submitted by Watt, about a consulting detective in Baker Street, ignited a publishing phenomenon. "I at once realised that here was the greatest short story writer since Edgar Allan Poe," wrote Greenhough Smith. "I remember rushing into Mr. Newnes' room and thrusting the stories before his eyes.... Here, to an editor jaded with wading through reams of impossible stuff, comes a gift from Heaven, a godsend in the shape of the story that brought a gleam of happiness into the despairing life of this weary editor. Here was a new and gifted story-teller: there was no mistaking the ingenuity of the plot, the limpid clearness of the style, the perfect art of telling a story."

In July 1891 the *Strand* published its very first Sherlock Holmes story, "A Scandal in Bo-

The *Strand Magazine*, bound volume VII for January–June 1894, London.

hemia," subsequent stories followed, each one increasing the sales of the *Strand* and enthralling a public that couldn't get enough of the great sleuth. "Sherlock Holmes appears to have caught on," Conan Doyle informed his mother. He also had his own theory for Holmes's success. Most magazines ran with "disconnected stories," but a magazine which had a single character which appeared regularly throughout a series with "instalments complete in themselves" would inevitably unite its readers and their loyalty. Another reason for the *Strand* success was George Newnes' insistence that every page should carry an illustration, ensuring that much of the attraction of Holmes was due to the magazine's vivid drawings. The artist Sidney Paget (1860–1908) was commissioned to create the illustrations, and to this day it is his abiding images of the sleuth which are indelibly stamped on the public's consciousness. The spare frame, the hawk-like features, the intense pipe-smoking gaze, and of course, the deerstalker hat. Conan Doyle's own interpretation of Holmes didn't exactly match Paget's, but the partnership obviously worked, and he accepted it. In years to come it was a winning combination that would add over a 100,000 copies to the *Strand*'s monthly circulation figures, and as many zeros to Conan Doyle's bank balance.

FURTHER INFORMATION: The offices of George Newnes Ltd. were located at 8–11 Southampton Street, and Exeter Street, just off the Strand. The *Strand Magazine* ceased publication in 1950, but in 1998 the title was revived with a similar format to the original. www.strandmag.com

SEE ALSO: Tennison Road (p. 104), Ward, Lock & Company (p. 92), St. Bartholomew's Hospital (p. 94), Psychic Bookshop (p. 89).

The City

Salisbury Square
Warwick House

Former offices of Ward, Lock & Company, publishers of the first Sherlock Holmes novel, A Study in Scarlet

"The ring, man, the ring: that was what he came back for. If we have no other way of catching him, we can always bait our line with the ring. I shall have him, Doctor — I'll lay you two to one that I have him. I must thank you for it all. I might not have gone but for you, and so have missed the finest study I ever came across: a study in scarlet, eh? Why shouldn't we use a little art jargon. There's the scarlet thread of murder running through the colourless skein of life, and our duty is to unravel it, and isolate it, and expose every inch of it." — Arthur Conan Doyle, *A Study in Scarlet* (1887)

During the 1880s Conan Doyle was writing short stories in what was probably one its most receptive and fashionable periods in history, but what he really craved was to see his name on the spine of a novel. "It was about a year after my marriage," he wrote, "that I realized that I could go on doing short stories forever and never make headway. What is necessary is that your name should be on the back of a volume. Only so do you assert your individuality and get the full credit or discredit of your achievement." While in Southsea he completed a novel called *The Narrative of John Smith*. He posted it to a publisher, but it never arrived as the postal service lost it, and to this day it has never been seen again. His next effort was *The Firm of Girdlestone*, but that too fell on dead ground, and was returned from publishers with "the precision of a homing pigeon."

On 8 March 1886, Conan Doyle began writing *A Tangled Skein*, a story introducing the characters Sherringford Holmes and Ormond Sacker. He changed the title the following month to *A Study in Scarlet*, and the characters metamorphosed into Sherlock Holmes and Doctor Watson. Role models for Holmes included Poe's Auguste Dupin and Emile Gaboriau's Monsieur Lecoq, but Conan Doyle had another guiding light up his sleeve. He later wrote in his autobiography:

> I thought of my old teacher Joe Bell, of his eagle face, of his curious ways, of his eerie trick of spotting details. If he were a detective he would surely reduce this fascinating but organised business to something nearer to an exact science. I would try if I could get this effect. It was surely possible in real life, so why should I not make it plausible in fiction? It is all very well to say that a man is clever, but the reader wants examples of it — such examples as Bell gave us every day in the wards. The idea amused me.
>
> What should I call the fellow? I still possess the leaf of a notebook with various alternative names. One rebelled against the elementary art which

gives some inkling of character in the name and creates Mr. Sharps or Mr. Ferrets. First it was Sherringford Holmes; then it was Sherlock Holmes. He could not tell his own exploits, so he must have a commonplace comrade as a foil — an educated man of action who could both join in the exploits and narrate them. A drab, quiet name for this unostentatious man. Watson would do. and so I had my puppets and wrote my *Study in Scarlet*.

It was a story of unrequited love, murder and vengeance, set in Mormon Utah and Victorian London, and introduced one of Sherlock Holmes's favorite plot devices — the revenge mystery. The first three publishers it was submitted to rejected it, but the fourth publisher, Ward, Lock & Co., one of London's less prestigious publishers, made him an offer:

> Dear Sir
>
> We have read your story and are pleased with it. We could not publish it this year as the market is flooded at present with cheap fiction, but if you do not object to its being held over till next year, we will give you £25 for the copyright.
>
> Yours faithfully,
>
> Ward, Lock & Co.
>
> October 30, 1886

"It was not a very tempting offer," Conan Doyle declared, "and even I, poor as I was, hesitated to accept it. It was not merely the small sum offered, but it was the long delay, for this book might open a road for me. I was heart-sick, however, at repeated disappointments, and I felt that perhaps it was true wisdom to make sure of publicity, however late. Therefore I accepted, and the book became 'Beeton's Christmas Annual' of 1887. I never at any time received another penny for it."

And so Sherlock Holmes was born between the cheap pages of a pulp fiction magazine. The novel was later published as a "shilling shocker" book edition in July 1888 with a series of lackluster pen and ink drawings by Charles Doyle. Sherlock Holmes, however, didn't seize the public's reading appetite until the *Strand Magazine* published "A Scandal in Bohemia" in July 1891. By then it was obvious to everyone, including cheapskates Ward, Lock & Co., that Conan Doyle was a writer to be reckoned with. Ward, Lock & Co. later approached him to write a preface for *A Study in Scarlet* and to use

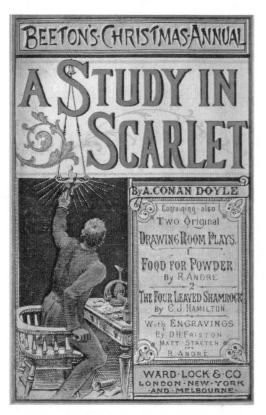

Sherlock Holmes's first appearance in print — *A Study in Scarlet* **in Beeton's Christmas Annual, 1887.**

West Smithfield
St. Bartholomew's Hospital

Location of the first meeting between Sherlock Holmes and Doctor Watson in 1881

"You have been in Afghanistan, I perceive."
— Arthur Conan Doyle, *A Study in Scarlet*

Standing at the Criterion Bar in Piccadilly Circus Watson meets by chance "young Stamford" who had been a dresser (assistant) under him at St. Bartholomew's Hospital (popularly known as Barts), his old medical school. Watson informs him of his search for cheaper lodgings and Stamford tells him of a "fellow" working at the chemical laboratory at Barts who was also looking to share lodgings. After lunch the two of them head for Barts and seek out Watson's prospective companion, whom Stamford describes as "a little queer in his ideas." Watson writes in *A Study in Scarlet*:

> We turned down a narrow lane and passed through a small side-door which opened into a wing of the great hospital. It was familiar ground to me, and I needed no guiding as we ascended the bleak stone staircase and made our way down the long corridor with its vista of whitewashed wall and dun-coloured doors. Near the farther end a low arched passage branched away from it and led to the chemical laboratory.
>
> This was a lofty chamber, lined and littered with countless bottles. Broad, low tables were scattered about, which bristled with retorts, test-tubes, and little Bunsen lamps with their blue flickering flames. There was only one student in the room, who was bending over a distant table absorbed in his work. At the sound of our steps he glanced round and sprang to his feet with a cry of pleasure. "I've found it! I've found it," he shouted to my companion, running towards us with a test-tube in his hand. "I have found a re-agent which is precipitated by haemoglobin, and by nothing else." Had he discovered a gold mine, greater delight could not have shone upon his features.
>
> "Dr. Watson, Mr. Sherlock Holmes," said Stamford, introducing us.
>
> "How are you?" he said cordially, gripping my hand with a strength for which I should hardly have given him credit. "You have been in Afghanistan, I perceive."
>
> "How on earth did you know that?" I asked in astonishment.
>
> "Never mind," said he, chuckling to himself. "The question now is about haemoglobin. No doubt you see the significance of this discovery of mine?"

the subtitle Sherlock Holmes. In a letter to his mother dated 14 October 1891, he stated his answer, "I refused…. So you see what a cantankerous son you have."

FURTHER INFORMATION: The nearest tube station to Salisbury Square is Blackfriars. Ebenezer Ward and George Lock founded their publishing house in 1854 on Fleet Street, but by the 1870s they had moved to larger premises at Warwick House in Salisbury Square. Famous for its tourist handbooks known as the *Red Guides*, they also published a number of literary works of note, including, Oscar Wilde's *The Picture of Dorian Gray*, and Thomas Hughes' *Tom Brown's School Days*.

FURTHER READING: E. Living, *Adventure in Publishing: The House of Ward Lock 1854–1954* (London, UK: Ward, Lock, 1954).

SEE ALSO: *Strand Magazine* (p. 91), St. Bartholomew's Hospital (p.94), St. Mary's Cathedral (p. 4).

"It is interesting, chemically, no doubt," I answered, "but practically—"

"Why, man, it is the most practical medico-legal discovery for years. Don't you see that it gives us an infallible test for blood stains. Come over here now!" He seized me by the coat-sleeve in his eagerness, and drew me over to the table at which he had been working. "Let us have some fresh blood," he said, digging a long bodkin into his finger, and drawing off the resulting drop of blood in a chemical pipette. "Now, I add this small quantity of blood to a litre of water. You perceive that the resulting mixture has the appearance of pure water. The proportion of blood cannot be more than one in a million. I have no doubt, however, that we shall be able to obtain the characteristic reaction." As he spoke, he threw into the vessel a few white crystals, and then added some drops of a transparent fluid. In an instant the contents assumed a dull mahogany colour, and a brownish dust was precipitated to the bottom of the glass jar.

"Ha! ha!" he cried, clapping his hands, and looking as delighted as a child with a new toy. "What do you think of that?"

"It seems to be a very delicate test," I remarked.

"Beautiful! beautiful! The old guaiacum test was very clumsy and uncertain. So is the microscopic examination for blood corpuscles. The latter is valueless if the stains are a few hours old. Now, this appears to act as well whether the blood is old or new. Had this test been invented, there are hundreds of men now walking the earth who would long ago have paid the penalty of their crimes."

"Indeed!" I murmured.

"Criminal cases are continually hinging upon that one point. A man is suspected of a crime months perhaps after it has been committed. His linen or clothes are examined and brownish stains discovered upon them. Are they blood stains, or mud stains, or rust stains, or fruit stains, or what are they? That is a question which has puzzled many an expert, and why? Because there was no reliable test. Now we have the Sherlock Holmes test, and there will no longer be any difficulty."

His eyes fairly glittered as he spoke, and he put his hand over his heart and bowed as if to some applauding crowd conjured up by his imagination.

"You are to be congratulated," I remarked, considerably surprised at his enthusiasm.

"There was the case of Von Bischoff at Frankfort last year. He would certainly have been hung had this test been in existence. Then there was Mason of Bradford, and the notorious Muller, and Lefevre of Montpellier, and Samson of New Orleans. I could name a score of cases in which it would have been decisive."

St. Barts—first meeting place between the two most famous characters in fiction.

"You seem to be a walking calendar of crime," said Stamford with a laugh. "You might start a paper on those lines. Call it the 'Police News of the Past.'"

"Very interesting reading it might be made, too," remarked Sherlock Holmes, sticking a small piece of plaster over the prick on his finger. "I have to be careful," he continued, turning to me with a smile, "for I dabble with poisons a good deal." He held out his hand as he spoke, and I noticed that it was mottled over with similar pieces of plaster, and discoloured with strong acids.

"We came here on business," said Stamford, sitting down on a high three-legged stool, and pushing another one in my direction with his foot. "My friend here wants to take diggings; and as you were complaining that you could get no one to go halves with you, I thought that I had better bring you together."

Sherlock Holmes seemed delighted at the idea of sharing his rooms with me. "I have my eye on a suite in Baker Street," he said, "which would suit us down to the ground. You don't mind the smell of strong tobacco, I hope?"

"I always smoke 'ship's' myself," I answered.

"That's good enough. I generally have chemicals about, and occasionally do experiments. Would that annoy you?"

"By no means."

"Let me see — what are my other shortcomings? I get in the dumps at times, and don't open my mouth for days on end. You must not think I am sulky when I do that. Just let me alone, and I'll soon be right. What have you to confess now? It's just as well for two fellows to know the worst of one another before they begin to live together."

I laughed at this cross-examination. "I keep a bull pup," I said, "and I object to row because my nerves are shaken, and I get up at all sorts of ungodly hours, and I am extremely lazy. I have another set of vices when I'm well, but those are the principal ones at present."

"Do you include violin playing in your category of rows?" he asked, anxiously.

"It depends on the player," I answered. "A well-played violin is a treat for the gods — a badly-played one —."

"Oh, that's all right," he cried, with a merry laugh. "I think we may consider the thing is settled — that is, if the rooms are agreeable to you."

"When shall we see them?"

"Call for me here at noon tomorrow, and we'll go together and settle everything," he answered.

"All right — noon exactly," said I, shaking his hand.

FURTHER INFORMATION: Located close to St. Paul's Cathedral, Barts was founded in 1123, and is said to be the oldest surviving hospital in England. The nearest tube is Chancery or St. Paul's (Central Line). The hospital museum is open to the public Tuesday to Friday from 10 A.M.–4 P.M. (closed bank holidays). Admission is free. Guided tours of the entrance hall and Great Hall of the hospital are conducted on Fridays at 2 P.M. Meet at the King Henry VIII gate on West Smithfield.

SEE ALSO: *Strand Magazine* (p. 91), Ward, Lock & Co. (p. 94), St. Mary's Cathedra (p. 4).

Tower Hamlets

Tower Hill

The Tower of London

Where Roger Casement (inspiration for Lord John Roxton in The Lost World*) awaited trial for high treason in 1916*

> I poked about a village church
> And found his family tomb
> And copied out what I could read
> In that religious gloom;
> Found many a famous man there;
> But fame and virtue rot.

> Draw round, beloved and bitter men,
> Draw round and raise a shout;
> The ghost of Roger Casement
> Is beating on the door.
> — William Butler Yeats, "The Ghost of Roger Casement"

In 1916 the Irish patriot and former British consular official, Sir Roger Casement (1864–1916), was arrested after landing in Ireland from a German submarine in an effort to take part in the Irish Nationalist revolt in Dublin, which became known as the Easter Rising. He was subsequently tried in England for high treason and hanged. His guilt was never queried, but it was the exposure of his private diaries — the so-called Black Diaries, which revealed his homosexual activities — that lay the British authorities open to accusations of foul play. Pleas for clemency could have saved him from the death penalty, but the exposure that he was a promiscuous homosexual made many sympathizers back away, and his execution went ahead virtually unopposed.

Conan Doyle, however, was not for turning and was one of the few who continued to campaign for Casement's reprieve until the very end, all be it convinced he had gone insane. "He was a man of fine character," Conan Doyle told the *Daily Chronicle*, "and that he should in full possession of his senses act as a traitor to the country which had employed and honoured him is inconceivable to anyone who knew him.... In all our discussions I have never heard him say a word which was disloyal to Great Britain. He was a sick man, however, worn by tropical hardships, and he complained often of pains in his head. Last May I had letters from him from Ireland which seemed to me so wild that I expressed fears at the time as to the state of his nerves. I have no doubt that he is not in a normal state of mind."

Conan Doyle first came in to contact with Casement through the Congo Reform Association. Casement, who had spent the best part of twenty years working in the consular service in the Congo, was determined to publicize the atrocities that were being committed against the natives under Belgium's administration, and prominent figures were approached to champion the cause. Conan Doyle gave Casement his full support and even went to the length of writing a book on the subject, titled *The Crime of the Congo* (1909), which he wrote in only eight days. The book pulled no punches and exposed the barbarism of the Congo's rubber harvest through Casement's reports and eyewitness accounts: "[Rubber] is collected by force," wrote Conan Doyle. "The soldiers drive the people into the bush; if they will not go they are shot down, their left hands being cut off and taken as trophies to the Commissary. The soldiers do not care whom they shoot down, and they most often shoot poor, helpless women and harmless children. These hands — the hands of men, women and children — are placed in rows before the Commissary, who counts them, to see the soldiers have not wasted the cartridges."

The River Thames water-gate entrance to the Tower of London, known as "Traitor's Gate," because of the number of prisoners accused of treason who have passed through it.

Casement retired from the consular service in 1913 and began to immerse himself in the struggle for Irish independence. With the outbreak of the First World War in 1914, he negotiated a declaration by Germany, which declared that under no circumstances would Germany invade Ireland. He even tried unsuccessfully to recruit an Irish Brigade from Irish prisoners-of-war. The Germans, although wary of Casement, could see the advantages a military uprising in Ireland might have on the course of the war; but their support in the end proved half-hearted and pathetic, and amounted to just a boatload of weapons sent to support the Easter Rising — a shipment that was intercepted by the Royal Navy and never reached the rebels. In a desperate bid to warn the rebels, whose cause he thought was doomed because of insufficient aid, Casement was put ashore in 1916 off the coast of County Kerry, where he was subsequently captured by the local police.

Before sentence was passed at his trial, he made an address to his countrymen: "I am being tried not by my peers of the live present, but by the peers of the dead past; not by the civilization of the twentieth century, but by the brutality of the

fourteenth; not even by a statute framed in the language of an enemy land — so antiquated is the law that must be sought today to slay an Irishman, whose offence is that he puts Ireland first."

Casement was hanged at Pentonville Prison and buried in quicklime in the prison cemetery. In 1965 his remains were taken to Ireland for a state funeral where he was buried with full military honors in the Republican plot in Glasnevin Cemetery in Dublin. In 1912 Conan Doyle based the explorer, sportsman and traveler, Lord John Roxton, on Roger Casement in *The Lost World*, who exclaims in chapter XIV: "By George! I wish I had fifty men with rifles. I'd clear out the whole infernal gang of them and leave this country a bit cleaner than we found it."

FURTHER INFORMATION: For many years the Casement Diaries were thought to be forgeries, but an independent forensic examination in 2002 carried out by Dr. Audrey Giles brought an end to years of controversy. The verdict was as follows: "The unequivocal and confident conclusion which the Giles Document Laboratory has reached is that each of the five documents collectively known as the

Black diaries is exclusively the work of Roger Casement's hand, without any reason to suspect either forgery or interpolation by any other hand. The Diaries are genuine throughout and in each instance." The Casement Diaries and the Giles Report can be viewed at The National Archives, Kew, Richmond, Surrey, TW9 4DU. Tel: +44(0)20 8876 3444. www.nationalarchives. gov.uk

The Tower of London is open to the public throughout the year. The nearest underground station is Tower Hill.

FURTHER READING: B. Inglis, *Roger Casement* (Belfast: Blackstaff, 1993); R. Sawyer, editor, *1910: The Black and the White—Roger Casement's Diaries* (New York: Random House, 1997); R. Sawyer, *Casement: The Flawed Hero* (London, UK: Routledge, 1984); R. R. Doerries, *Prelude to the Easter Rising: Sir Roger Casement in Imperial Germany* (Routledge, 1999); A. C. Doyle, *The Crime of the Congo* (Honolulu: University Press of the Pacific, 2004).

SEE ALSO: Salisbury Crags (p. 34).

Chelsea

146 Sloane Street

Former school of Edgar Allan Poe (1809–1849), a writer who greatly influenced Conan Doyle

"As modern writers learned to appreciate Poe's complexity and to take him more seriously, they explored and mined his fascinating and far-sighted works. George Eliot, Wilde and Stevenson borrowed his plots; Rossetti, Kipling and Joyce adopted his themes; Pater and Conrad utilized his theories; Conan Doyle recreated his characters."—Jeffrey Meyers, *Edgar Allan Poe: His Life and Legacy* (1992)

On 8 March 1886 Conan Doyle began writing a story called *A Tangled Skein*, which introduced the characters Sherringford Holmes and Ormond Sacker. By April the title had changed to *A Study in Scarlet*, and fortunately for literary history, the characters names were changed to Sherlock Holmes and Doctor Watson. The detective genre in 1886 had only been around for 40 years, and among the role models which were the inspiration for the Holmes character was Edgar Allan Poe's Auguste Dupin. The Sherlock Holmes stories are littered with examples

of this influence. Dupin, like Holmes, has a taste for enigmas, conundrums and hieroglyphics. Both their exploits are recorded by loyal, but intellectually sluggish friends. Both are bachelors, and both have extraordinary powers of observation. In "The Murders in the Rue

Edgar Allan Poe c1830s.

Morgue" Dupin, through a process of calculated reasoning, deduces the murderer is an orangutan; in *The Sign of Four* Holmes deduces the killer, who is "larger than a child and as agile as a monkey," to be a pygmy. The subject of ciphers appeared in Poe's "The Gold-Bug" and reappears in "The Musgrave Ritual" and "The Dancing Men" by Conan Doyle.

Conan Doyle never disguised his debt to Poe and was always generous in acknowledging his appreciation. In 1907 he paid homage to his mentor in the book *Through the Magic Door*, an affectionate ramble through Doyle's favorite literature:

Poe is, to my mind, the supreme original short story writer of all time. His brain was like a seed-pod full of seeds which flew carelessly around, and from which have sprung nearly all our modern types of story. Just think of what he did in his offhand, prodigal fashion, seldom troubling to repeat a success, but pushing on to some new achievement. To him must be ascribed the monstrous progeny of writers on the detection of crime—; "quorum pars parva fui!" Each may find some little development of his own, but his main art must trace back to those admirable stories of Monsieur Dupin, so wonderful in their masterful force, their reticence, their quick dramatic point. After all, mental acuteness is the one quality which can be ascribed to the ideal detective, and when that has once been admirably done, succeeding writers must necessarily be content for all time to follow in the same main track. But not only is Poe the originator of the detective story; all treasure-hunting, cryptogram-solving yarns trace back to his "Gold Bug," just as all pseudo-scientific Verne-and-Wells stories have their prototypes in the "Voyage to the Moon," and the "Case of Monsieur Valdemar." If every man who receives a cheque for a story which owes its springs to Poe were to pay tithe to a monument for the master, he would have a pyramid as big as that of Cheops.

And yet I could only give him two places in my team. One would be for the "Gold Bug," the other for the "Murder in the Rue Morgue." I do not see how either of those could be bettered. But I would not admit *perfect* excellence to any other of his stories. These two have a proportion and a perspective which are lacking in the others, the horror or weirdness of the idea intensified by the coolness of the narrator and of the principal actor, Dupin in the one case and Le Grand in the other.

And all this didactic talk comes from looking at that old green cover of Poe. I am sure that if I had to name the few books which have really influenced my own life I should have to put this one second only to Macaulay's Essays. I read it young when my mind was plastic. It stimulated my imagination and set before me a supreme example of dignity and force in the methods of telling a story. It is not altogether a healthy influence, perhaps. It turns the thoughts too forcibly to the morbid and the strange.

He was a saturnine creature, devoid of humour and geniality, with a love for the grotesque and the terrible. The reader must himself furnish the counteracting qualities or Poe may become a dangerous comrade. We know along what perilous tracks and into what deadly quagmires his strange mind led him, down to that grey October Sunday morning when he was picked up, a dying man, on the side-walk at Baltimore, at an age which should have seen him at the very prime of his strength and his manhood.

FURTHER INFORMATION: Edgar Allan Poe's parents died before he reached his third birthday, and he was fostered, but never adopted, by John and Francis Allan from Richmond, Virginia. John Allan was partners in a merchant company, and in 1815 he embarked on a business trip with his family to England. On their arrival in London they took lodgings at 47 Southampton Street in Bloomsbury; and a few months later young Edgar entered a boarding school run by the Misses Dubourg—a name he later used for the laundress-witness in "The Murders in the Rue Morgue"—at 146 Sloane Street. In 1818 he entered a boarding school in Stoke Newington. After five years in England his family returned to America in 1820.

Corner of Chelsea Bridge Road and Chelsea Bridge
The Boer War Memorial

Memorial to a conflict Conan Doyle participated in as part of the medical staff of the Langman hospital unit

Take a community of Dutchmen of the type of those who defended themselves for fifty years against all the power of Spain at a time when Spain was the greatest power in the world. Intermix with them a strain of those inflexible French Huguenots who gave up home and fortune and left their country for ever at the time of the revocation of the Edict of Nantes. The product must obviously be one of the most rugged, virile, unconquerable races ever seen upon earth. Take this formidable people and train them for seven generations in constant warfare against savage men and ferocious beasts, in circumstances under which no weakling could survive, place them so that they acquire exceptional skill with weapons and in horsemanship, give them a country which is eminently suited to the tactics of the huntsman, the marksman, and the rider. Then, finally, put a finer temper upon their military qualities by a dour fatalistic Old Testament religion and an ardent and consuming patriotism. Combine all these qualities and all these impulses in one individual, and you have the modern Boer—the most formidable antagonist who ever crossed the path of Imperial Britain. Our military history has largely consisted in our conflicts with France, but Napoleon and all his veterans have never treated us so roughly as these hard-bitten farmers with their ancient theology and their inconveniently modern rifles.—Arthur Conan Doyle, *The Great Boer War* (1900)

Conan Doyle was never one to turn his back on the rallying call to war, and in 1899 he walked into a London recruitment center and attempted to enlist in the Middlesex Yeomanry who were then fighting in the Boer War. A portly 40 year old, however, was not the army's idea of prime cannon fodder, and when asked what his military experience was, he inflated his slender experiences as a war correspondent with the army in Egypt in 1896. When holidaying with his wife there, the Sudanese dervishes rose up against the British-controlled Egyptian Army; and Conan Doyle, in true Richard Hannay fashion, wired for an honorary post as a war correspondent with the *Westminster Gazette*. Leaving his wife in Cairo, he bought a revolver and headed for the war zone. He saw plenty of camels and even met Lord Kitchener, but saw no action. The recruiting officer was not convinced and put him on the reserve list. "Two white lies are permitted to a gentleman," he later remarked, "to screen a woman, or to get into a fight when the fight was a rightful one. So I trust I may be forgiven." One person who didn't forgive his actions was his mother, who raged in a letter to him, "How dare you! What do you mean by it? Why, your very height and breadth would make you a simple and sure target!... There are hundreds of thousands who can fight for one who can make a Sherlock Holmes or a Waterloo.... For God's sake listen to me; even at your age.... I am coming down if you leave me in uncertainty. This is altogether too dreadful." When it came to a man's patriotic duty, however, Conan Doyle could not be swayed. When his friend John Langman offered him a place on the medical staff of a fifty-bed, privately funded hospital unit about to leave for South Africa, he jumped at the chance. And on 28 February 1900, Conan Doyle sailed off to war.

The Langman Hospital was sent to the recently captured Boer capital of Bloemfontein, in the Orange Free State, where "wagons of sick and wounded began to disgorge at our doors," wrote Conan Doyle. The front line was only twenty miles away and the Boers had cut off the town's water supply forcing strict rationing on the townspeople and British troops. Many were forced to drink water from the contami- nated local river and an overwhelming typhoid epidemic ensued killing around forty people a day. The epidemic lasted a month. "Four weeks may seem a short time in comfort," Conan Doyle commented, "but it is a very long one under conditions such as those, amid horrible sights and sounds and smells, while a haze of flies spreads over everything, covering your food and trying to force themselves into your mouth — every one of them a focus of disease." The water pumps were eventually recaptured by British forces on 24 April. Longing for some front line experience, Conan Doyle accompanied the troops as an observer. The Boers, much to his regret, retreated without a fight. He did see action, however, at Vet River, when the troops came under heavy artillery fire during their advance on Pretoria, capital of the South African Republic.

Throughout his short sojourn in South Africa (March to July 1899) Conan Doyle was continually taking notes and conducting interviews for a history he wanted to write about the war, a book which became *The Great Boer War*, published in 1900. "So much for the Empire," he wrote in his concluding paragraph. "But what of South Africa? There in the end we must reap as we sow. If we are worthy of the trust, it will be left to us. If we are unworthy of it, it will be taken away. Kruger's downfall should teach us that it is not rifles but Justice which is the title-deed of a nation. The British flag under our best administrators will mean clean government, honest laws, liberty and equality to all men. So long as it continues to do so, we shall hold South Africa. When, out of fear or out or greed, we fall from that ideal, we may know that we are stricken with that disease which has killed every great empire before us."

FURTHER INFORMATION: The Chelsea Boer War Memorial to the 6th Dragoon Guards (The

Soldier-doctor Conan Doyle in the Boer War (Phillip Bergem).

Carabiniers) was created by English sculptor
Adrian Jones (1845–1938). His best known
work is the sculpture "Peace in her Quadrige,"
which surmounts the Wellington Arch at Hyde
Park Corner, London.

SEE ALSO: Undershaw (p.000).

Cheyne Row
Statue of Thomas Carlyle (1795–1881)

"He was an intelligent cabman too, for having
heard Frank say 'Thomas Carlyle's house' after
giving the address 5 Cheyne Row, he pulled up
on the Thames Embankment. Right ahead of
them was Chelsea Bridge, seen through a dim,
soft London haze — monstrous, Cyclopean, giant
arches springing over a vague river of molten
metal, the whole daintily blurred, as though out
of focus. The glamour of the London haze, what
is there upon earth so beautiful? But it was not
to admire it that the cabman had halted.

'I beg your pardin', sir,' said he, in the softly
insinuating way of the Cockney, 'but I thought
that maybe the lidy would like to see Mr. Carlyle's statue. That's 'im, sir, a-sittin' in the overcoat with the book in 'is 'and.'

Frank and Maude got out and entered the
small railed garden, in the centre of which the
pedestal rose. It was very simple and plain — an
old man in a dressing-gown, with homely worn-
out boots, a book upon his knee, his eyes and
thoughts far away. No more simple statue in all
London, but human to a surprising degree. They
stood for five minutes and stared at it." — Arthur
Conan Doyle, *A Duet with an Occasional Chorus*
(1899)

Conan Doyle was greatly influenced by the
historian and essayist Thomas Carlyle, so much
so, that he confessed to his mother that he had
"started a fermentation in his soul." On his voy-
ages to the Arctic and West Africa, the works of
this high Victorian thinker were always within
reach of his bunk, and he once presented a lecture to the Southsea Literary Society on his hero.
Doctor Watson, however, informs us in *A Study
in Scarlet* that Sherlock Holmes was remarkably
ignorant of Carlyle and "enquired in the naivest
way who he might be and what he had done."

Thomas Carlyle was born in Ecclefechan,
Dumfriesshire, the son of a stonemason. He arrived in Edinburgh in 1809, barely 14 years of
age, to study at the university for a general arts
degree. He left in 1813, without taking his degree, and took up teaching. He returned to Ed-

inburgh again in 1817 to begin theological training, but religious doubts and disaffection with
the church put an end to his intended career in
divinity. He met Jane Welsh, and after a fre-
netic courtship, they married in 1826. He was
31, careerless, suffering from chronic dyspepsia,
possibly impotent, and would not achieve fame
until middle age.

Carlyle's early efforts at trying to make a living from his pen included writing entries for
Brewster's Encyclopaedia. He also tutored and
began penning magazine articles. As a writer
and historian he became influenced by German
philosophy and literature, and in 1824 he published a translation of Goethe's *Wilhelm Meister*.
In 1833–4, *Sartor Resartus*, his first major work
on social philosophy, was published in install-
ments in *Fraser's Magazine*. His best-known
work remains his *History of the French Revolution* (3 volumes, 1837), the first of which had
to be rewritten after a servant accidentally burnt
the draft. Described by Charles Dickens as "that
wonderful book" — which he claimed in a letter
in 1851 to be reading "for the 500th time" — it
was, no doubt, a major influence on his own *A
Tale of Two Cities* (1859).

The Carlyles settled in Chelsea at 5 Cheyne
Row in June 1834, where they lived together
for 32 years until Jane's death. In 1848 William
Thackeray told his mother, "Tom Carlyle lives
in perfect dignity" in a little house in Chelsea,
"with a snuffy Scotch maid to open the door,
and the best company in England ringing at it."

FURTHER INFORMATION: Carlyle's statue was
sculpted by Joseph Edgar Boehm and cast in
bronze. It was unveiled in 1882.

The Carlyle's house at 5 Cheyne Row (re-
numbered 24) is now owned by the National
Trust and is open to the public (Tel: +44 (0)20
7352 5108) www.nationaltrust.org.uk

The largest collection of letters, journals and
related material of the Carlyles is in the National
Library of Scotland in Edinburgh. The second
largest collection is in the Houghton Library,
Harvard University.

SEE ALSO: George Square (p. 107).

FURTHER READING: J. A. Froude, Thomas
Carlyle: *A History of the First Forty Years of his
Life* (Honolulu: University Press of the Pacific,
2002); R. Ashton, *Thomas and Jane Carlyle*:

Portrait of a Marriage (London, UK: Pimlico, 2003).

Camden

Lincoln's Inn Fields
Hunterian Museum at the Royal College of Surgeons

Location of Jonathan Wild's skeleton, possible role model for Professor Moriarty

"Have you ever read of Jonathan Wild?"

"Well, the name has a familiar sound. Someone in a novel, was he not? I don't take much stock of detectives in novels — chaps that do things and never let you see how they do them. That's just inspiration, not business."

"Jonathan Wild wasn't a detective, and he wasn't in a novel. He was a master criminal, and he lived last century — 1750 or thereabouts."

"Then he's no use to me. I'm a practical man."

"Mr. Mac, the most practical thing that ever you did in your life would be to shut yourself up for three months and read twelve hours a day at the annals of crime. Everything comes in circles, even Professor Moriarty. Jonathan Wild was the hidden force of the London criminals, to whom he sold his brains and his organisation on a fifteen per cent commission. The old wheel turns and the same spoke comes up. It's all been done before and will be again"

— Arthur Conan Doyle, Sherlock Holmes attempting to explain the roots of Professor Moriarty to Scotland Yard's Inspector McDonald, *The Valley of Fear* (1915)

Conan Doyle described his fictional creation, Professor Moriarty, as "the Napoleon of Crime" — the arch enemy and greatest adversary of Sherlock Holmes. He was also, "a man of good birth and excellent education," Holmes informs us in "The Final Problem," "endowed by nature with a phenomenal mathematical faculty. At the age of twenty-one he wrote A Treatise on the Binomial Theorem, which has had a European vogue. On the strength of it he won the mathematical chair at one of our smaller universities, and had, to all appearances, a most brilliant career before him. But the man had hereditary tendencies of the most diabolical kind. A criminal strain ran in his blood, which, instead of being modified, was increased and rendered infinitely more dangerous by his extraordinary mental powers. Dark rumours gathered round

him in the University town, and eventually he was compelled to resign his chair and come down to London."

Moriarty only makes an appearance in one Sherlock Holmes story, "The Final Problem," where the two of them reputedly plunged to their deaths over the Reichenbach Falls, but he is mentioned in others. Conan Doyle's inspiration for the character, however, has been the subject of much conjecture over the years. Suggested role models have included, master criminal Adam Worth, astronomer Simon Newcomb, and mathematician and philosopher George Boole. My candidate though, has to be the notorious lawbreaker Jonathan Wild (1683–1725), mentioned by Conan Doyle in *The Valley of Fear*.

In the early 18th century Jonathan Wild was the godfather of crime in London, controlling most of the city's criminal underworld, calling himself by the self-styled title of "Thief-taker General." He was the son of a wigmaker from Wolverhampton who made his way to London only to end up in debtor's prison. Here he met the thieves and con men who would mold his future, and on his release he set himself up as a receiver of stolen goods. Before long he hatched a master plan — that of returning the stolen goods to their rightful owners for an agreed reward. So successful was his scheme that he developed a vast network of warehouses full of stolen loot, involving most of the low life of London as his "agents." All criminals had to give Wild a share of their spoils. If they refused they were informed on to the police. The authorities, who were heavily bribed by Wild, apparently viewed his organization as a kind of private police force, who could retrieve stolen property and catch criminals with ease. Over sixty thieves were brought to justice and hanged because of his testimony. The Privy Council, the body that advised the government, actually consulted him for advice on controlling crime.

The law finally caught up with him when he was convicted of receiving a reward for returning stolen lace and condemned to death by hanging. He tried to evade the hangman's noose by swallowing an overdose of laudanum, but his stomach was pumped, and he kept his appointment with the gallows. Wild's body was buried

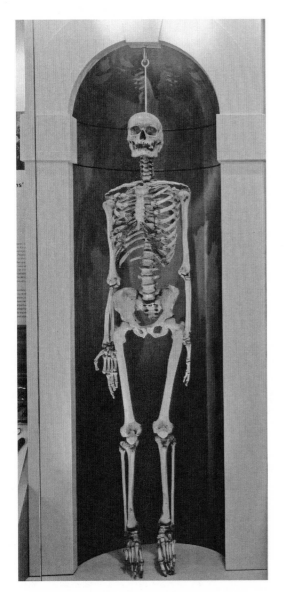

The skeleton of Jonathan Wild at The Hunterian Museum.

in secret, but was exhumed shortly afterwards and sold to the Royal College of Surgeons for dissection, where his skeleton still remains on public view.

Since his death he has become the subject of novels, plays and operas, none less than from the pen of Henry Fielding in *The History of the Life of the Late Mr. Jonathan Wild the Great* (1743), where he describes Wild's last moments on the scaffold with the skills and license that only a great satirist can: "Wild, in the midst of

the shower of stones, &c., which played upon him, applied his hands to the parson's pocket, and emptied it of his bottle-screw, which he carried out of the world in his hand. The ordinary being now descended from the cart, Wild had just opportunity to cast his eyes around the crowd, and to give them a hearty curse, when immediately the horses moved on, and with universal applause our hero swung out of this world."

FURTHER INFORMATION: Hunterian Museum, The Royal College of Surgeons of England, 35–43 Lincoln's Inn Fields, London WC2A 3PE. Tel: +44(0)20 7869 6560. www.rcseng.ac.uk/museums.

The Hunterian Museum is free of charge and is open Tuesday to Saturday 10–5 pm. It is situated on the first floor. The nearest underground station is Holborn (Central and Piccadilly Lines), approximately 5–10 minutes' walk away. Temple (Circle and District Lines) is 10–15 minutes' walk. Multi story car parking is available in Drury Lane and Bloomsbury Square.

FURTHER READING: G. Howson, *It Takes a thief: Life and Times of Jonathan Wild* (London, UK: Ebury Press, 1987); H. Fielding, *The History of the Life of the Late Mr. Jonathan Wild the Great* (Gloucestershire, UK: Echo Library, 2007); D. Defoe, *Defoe on Sheppard and Wild: The True and Genuine Account of the Life and Actions of the Late Jonathan Wild* (London, UK: Harper Perennial, 2004).

Greenwich

Romney Road
National Maritime Museum
Relics of HMS Foudroyant

> "You hucksters, have you still to learn the things that money will not buy?"— Extract from a letter by Conan Doyle to the Admiralty in 1891.

Conan Doyle always had a penchant for a military relic and his houses were strewn with medieval armor and napoleonic weaponry. The history of warfare was a subject close to his heart, and any desecration of the Empire's glorious past was sure to engage his wrath. In 1891, when he heard that the Lords Commissioners of the Admiralty were selling off Nelson's flagship HMS *Foudroyant* for scrap, he penned a stern letter to them. He was so incensed he even composed a poem about the affair. It's not Milton, but the following extract does get across his patriotic point. No comment from the Admiralty was recorded:

> Who says the Nation's purse is lean,
> Who fears for claim or bond or debt,
> When all the glories that have been
> Are scheduled as a cash asset?
> If times are bleak and trade is slack,
> If coal and cotton fail at last,
> We've something left to barter yet
> Our glorious past.
> There's many a crypt in which lies hid
> The dust of statesman or of king;
> There's Shakespeare's home to raise a bid,
> And Milton's house its price would bring.
> What for the sword that Cromwell drew?
> What for Prince Edward's coat of mail?
> What for our Saxon Alfred's tomb?
> They're all for sale!
> Go barter to the knacker's yard
> The steed that has outlived its time!
> Send hungry to the pauper ward
> The man who served you in his prime!
> But when you touch the Nation's store,
> Be broad your mind and tight your grip.
> Take heed! And bring us back once more
> Our Nelson's ship.
> And if no mooring can be found
> In all our harbours near or far,
> Then tow the old three-decker round
> To where the deep-sea soundings are;
> There, with her pennon flying clear,
> And with her ensign lashed peak high,
> Sink her a thousand fathoms sheer.
> There let her lie!

Nelson's flagship HMS *Foudroyant* (French for "thunder and lightning") was named after a French battleship which was captured by the British in 1758, broken up in 1787. The second HMS *Foudroyant*, a battleship with eighty guns, was launched in 1798. She became Nelson's flagship in the Mediterranean in 1799–1800 and fought in the recapture of Naples from the French, the recapture of Malta, and the Egyptian campaign. In 1862, towards the end of her service life, she was converted to a training ship. In 1892 the Admiralty sold her off for breaking up to a German company, despite strong public disapproval. At the eleventh hour she was reprieved when George Wheatley Cobb bought

her back for the nation at a cost of £20,000. To offset the restoration costs, she was exhibited at seaside resorts around the coast. In 1897 she was moored off Blackpool, and during a violent storm she was wrecked on Blackpool Sands. The ship was unsalvageable, but the salvage company recovered expenses by producing souvenirs from the wreck, including hundreds of medallions and coins from her copper bottom and furniture from her timbers.

FURTHER INFORMATION: The National Maritime is located in Greenwich, just a short walk from the Cutty Sark, and has archived 354 items relating to HMS *Foudroyant*.

Croydon
South Norwood
12 Tennison Road

Home of Conan Doyle from 1891 to 1894 and where he killed off Sherlock Holmes

"A few words may suffice to tell the little that remains. An examination by experts leaves little doubt that a personal contest between the two men ended, as it could hardly fail to end in such a situation, in their reeling over, locked in each other's arms. Any attempt at recovering the bodies was absolutely hopeless, and there, deep down in that dreadful caldron of swirling water and seething foam, will lie for all time the most dangerous criminal and the foremost champion of the law of their generation. The Swiss youth was never found again, and there can be no doubt that he was one of the numerous agents whom Moriarty kept in this employ. As to the gang, it will be within the memory of the public how completely the evidence which Holmes had accumulated exposed their organization, and how heavily the hand of the dead man weighed upon them. Of their terrible chief few details came out during the proceedings, and if I have now been compelled to make a clear statement of his career it is due to those injudicious champions who have endeavoured to clear his memory by attacks upon him whom I shall ever regard as the best and the wisest man whom I have ever known."—Arthur Conan Doyle, "The Adventure of the Final Problem" (1893)

In the spring of 1891 Conan Doyle probably made the biggest decision of his life when he decided to turn his back on a struggling medical practice and devote his life to writing. Literature promised freedom, fame, and hopefully fortune,

Death in suburbia—12 Tennison Road (Phillip Bergem).

a potential his medical career was never going achieve. The first thing he had to do was extricate himself from the throngs of city center London and find a more relaxed suburb where his writing could be conducted without any disturbance. He found a house south of the River Thames in the middle-class suburb of South Norwood, a short train ride from central London. No. 12 Tennison Road was a spacious, sixteen-room house built in the red-brick Victorian style, the perfect place to get down to

the serious business of writing, free once and for all from the treadmill of medicine. "I should at last be my own master," he wrote.

He began a regular routine of writing most mornings. Afternoons were for recreation and family, and in the evening he took up his pen once more. He was now at the most prolific period of his writing life, creating inventive, energetic, and most importantly, profitable stories, from Sherlock Holmes to historical fiction. The first series of Sherlock Holmes stories was still being published in the *Strand* during his early days at South Norwood, and probably around a third of all Holmes stories were written here. But the real reason future generations will remember No. 12 Tennison Road is that this was the house where Conan Doyle killed off the great sleuth in the story 'The Adventure of the Final Problem.' In December 1893 it was published in the *Strand* and its readers struggled to cope with the loss of their hero. Conan Doyle had closed the door once and for all—or so he believed—on what he described as "a lower stratum of literary achievement." His pulp fiction days were over and the great historical novel waited in the wings.

SEE ALSO: Upper Wimpole Street (p. 73), *Strand Magazine* (p. 91).

FURTHER INFORMATION: 12 Tennison Road is marked by an English Heritage Blue Plaque erected in 1973. It is not open to the public. Conan Doyle's son Kingsley was born here on 15 November 1892 and was baptized at nearby St. Mark's Church in Albert Road.

BERKSHIRE

Reading
Forbury Gardens
The Maiwand Lion

A memorial commemorating the Battle of Maiwand where Doctor Watson was wounded during the Second Afghan War

"In the year 1878 I took my degree of Doctor of Medicine of the University of London, and proceeded to Netley to go through the course prescribed for surgeons in the army. Having completed my studies there, I was duly attached to the Fifth Northumberland Fusiliers as Assistant Surgeon. The regiment was stationed in India at the time, and before I could join it, the second Afghan war had broken out. On landing at Bombay, I learned that my corps had advanced through the passes, and was already deep in the enemy's country. I followed, however, with many other officers who were in the same situation as myself, and succeeded in reaching Candahar in safety, where I found my regiment, and at once entered upon my new duties.

The campaign brought honours and promotion to many, but for me it had nothing but misfortune and disaster. I was removed from my brigade and attached to the Berkshires, with whom I served at the fatal battle of Maiwand. There I was struck on the shoulder by a Jezail bullet, which shattered the bone and grazed the subclavian artery. I should have fallen into the hands of the murderous Ghazis had it not been for the devotion and courage shown by Murray, my orderly, who threw me across a packhorse, and succeeded in bringing me safely to the British lines." — Arthur Conan Doyle, *A Study in Scarlet*

The British Empire waged three wars with Afghanistan between 1838 and 1919 to counter Russian expansionism, a strategic rivalry which became known as The Great Game. During the Second Afghan War (1878–80), Doctor Watson was struck by a bullet from a Jezail, the long-barrelled Afghan matchlock or flintlock musket. Conan Doyle sets the scene at the Battle of Maiwand (1880) where a British brigade of about 2,500 suffered a catastrophic defeat when they faced the Afghan forces of Ayub Khan, brother of Afghanistan's deposed ruler. His army was a massive 40,000 strong, and also included bands of what Doctor Watson described as "murderous Ghazis," warriors who wage a holy war, the 19th century counterpart of today's Mujahideen. The British force, led by General Burroughs, had orders to secure the Maiwand Pass and halt Ayub's advance on Kabul. Overwhelmed and outflanked, the 66th (Berkshire) Regiment fought on until the remnants of their regiment, around 120 men, were forced to withdraw to a walled garden. With only two officers and nine other ranks left, they broke out of the garden, formed a back-to-back square until the last man of the 66th fell. The overall battle resulted in the deaths of over 900 British and Indian soldiers and over 2,000 Afghans, with the British retreating in disarray to Kandahar. The carnage at Maiwand was described in detail in the letters of Major John T. Ready, a survivor of the 66th (Berkshire) Regiment (now the 1st Battalion, the Rifles). In these letters Major Ready mentions the wounded "Dr. Preston," the battalion's Medical Officer, Surgeon Major A. F. Preston, who is believed to have been Conan Doyle's inspiration for the military exploits of Doctor Watson.

SEE ALSO: Sir Patrick Heron Watson (p. 28), The Criterion (p. 78).

FURTHER INFORMATION: The enormous Maiwand Lion memorial was erected in 1886 to commemorate the annihilation of the 66th (Berkshire) Regiment at the Battle of Maiwand and is located in Forbury Park off Forbury Road, Reading. The letters of Major Ready can be viewed at the National Library of Scotland in Edinburgh (MS. 2544). www.nls.uk. Memorabilia from the Battle of Maiwand can be seen at The Wardrobe, The Rifles (Berkshire and Wiltshire) Museum, 58 The Close, Salisbury, Wiltshire, SP1 2EX. Tel: +44(0) 1722 419419. www.thewardrobe.org.uk.

The term "The Great Game" is usually attributed to the British Intelligence officer Arthur Conolly, captain of the Sixth Bengal

The Maiwand Lion — memorial to the 66th (Berkshire) Regiment's annihilation at the Battle of Maiwand in 1880.

Light Cavalry, who introduced the phrase which best described the British and Russian Empires ongoing battle to dominate Central Asia. Conolly was also an explorer, a writer and a spy, who penetrated deep into Russia, often in disguise. In 1842 he was captured by the Emir of Bukhara and executed on charges of spying for the British Empire. Rudyard Kipling introduced the phrase into popular culture in his novel "Kim" (1901).

FURTHER READING: R. J. Stacpoole-Ryding, Maiwand: The Last Stand of the 66th (Berkshire) Regiment in Afghanistan, 1880 (Gloucestershire, UK: The History Press, 2008).

SURREY

Hindhead
Portsmouth Road
Undershaw

Home of Conan Doyle from 1897 to 1907 and where he wrote The Hound of the Baskervilles

"But at last the house took recognizable shape: a long, barn-like structure, red-bricked, tile-hung, heavy-gabled, lying across the neck of the valley. Arthur stood on his newly laid terrace and cast an inspecting eye on the broad lawn, recently rolled and seeded.... He decided to call it Undershaw, after the hanging grove of trees beneath which it lay. The name would give this modern construction a fine old Anglo-Saxon resonance."
— Julian Barnes, *Arthur & George*, (2005)

In 1893 Conan Doyle's first wife, Louise, was diagnosed with pulmonary tuberculosis and given only a few months to live. In the fall of that year the Doyles escaped the damp English climate and journeyed to Davos in the Swiss Alps, renowned for its beneficial climate towards consumptives. Robert Louis Stevenson had wintered there, and Thomas Mann set his novel *The Magic Mountain* in a local sanatorium. Davos was a place of pilgrimage for the consumptive where the pure air was said to cleanse and regenerate infected lungs. And true to form, Louise's health improved, and she returned to England, via Egypt, in April 1896, with more strength and hope than when she had left.

The previous year, in October 1895, Conan Doyle had met the writer and consumptive, Grant Allen (1848–99), who had cured himself not by traveling abroad in search of a pure climate, but by living in the clarified air of the Surrey hills in the village of Hindhead. And it was his opinion that Louise could safely return to England providing she lived there cocooned by its propitious climate. "It was quite a new idea to me that we might actually live with impunity in England once more," Conan Doyle wrote, "and it was a pleasant thought after resigning oneself to a life which was unnatural to both of us at foreign health resorts." Suitably convinced, Conan Doyle promptly investigated the area and bought a plot of land in the village. He sold his house in South Norwood and instructed an architect to design and build him another one at this newfound Utopia.

In October 1897 the Doyles moved into their new home which they named Undershaw — after the Anglo-Saxon word "shaw" meaning a thicket or a small wood. The imposing red brick building was set in four acres and was reached by a meandering drive. Stained glass windows displayed the family's coat of arms. Electric light, still a rarity in the countryside, illuminated its interiors, which included a thirty-seat dining room, guest bedrooms, a billiards room, and a wood-panelled drawing room hung with hunting trophies and antique weaponry. A large house needs a large domestic staff, so cooks, parlor maids, gardeners and a butler were hired. A passenger-carrying monorail was built in the garden, where there were croquet courts, tennis courts and stables for the horses. With their peripatetic life now at an end, Conan Doyle, Louise and their two young children could settle into their earthly paradise, a Shangri-La which they sincerely hoped had the power to prolong a consumptive's life.

Conan Doyle wrote a number stories at Undershaw, including "The Tragedy of Korosko"

(1898) and *A Duet with an Occasional Chorus* (1899); but the most memorable was the classic, *The Hound of the Baskervilles* (1902). It was from Undershaw that Conan Doyle left for the Boer War in 1900 as part of the medical staff of the Langman hospital unit, which resulted in him writing *The Great Boer War* (1900) and *The War in South Africa—Its Cause and Conduct* (1902). He also took up the new sport of motoring and had many a mishap, once overturning his Wolsley when he slammed into Undershaw's gateposts. The car landed on top of him and he was lucky to escape with his life.

The healthy air of Hindhead did help to prolong Louise's life. In 1893 the prognosis was only a few months, which she outlived by thirteen years, dying on 4 July 1906, aged forty-nine. Conan Doyle was at her bedside: "She told me that she had no pain and was easy in her mind," he wrote. "I was much in her room after her death and standing by her body I felt that I had done my best." She was buried in the churchyard of St. Lukes at nearby Grayshott. A year later Conan Doyle married his second wife, Jean Leckie, and moved into their new home at Windlesham in Crowborough, East Sussex.

SEE ALSO: High Moorland Visitor Centre (p. 111), Fletcher Robinson (p. 114), The Boer War Memorial (p. 99), Churchyard of St. Lukes (p. 138), Windlesham (p. 123), Bush House (p. 128).

FURTHER INFORMATION: Undershaw became a hotel in the 1940s, closing its doors over sixty years later in 2004. In recent years there have been several unsuccessful attempts to subdivide Undershaw and build in its grounds. To date the house is in a considerable state of neglect and its fate remains in abeyance. In 1859 a new railway line was built linking London to Portsmouth on the south coast of England. The line carved its way through the highlands of Surrey and the station at Haslemere (about a 2 miles from Hindhead and about fifty miles

Fate in the balance—a bedraggled and boarded up Undershaw in 2010 (The Victorian Society)

southwest of London), meant that the hilltops of Surrey; and its invigorating, pure air, was within easy reach of the metropolis. Many writers fled from the city to what was now an accessible wilderness and settled there. They became know as "The Hilltop Writers," and included such illustrious names as Alfred Tennyson, Christina Rossetti, George Eliot, Richard Le Gallienne, Margaret Oliphant, Mrs. Humphry Ward, H. G. Wells, and George Bernard Shaw.

Frensham
Frensham Pond

Where Conan Doyle turned his rifle into a howitzer

Conan Doyle always immersed himself in the British war effort, whether it was the Boer War, the First World War, or just a skirmish on the fringes of the Empire. War seemed to mesmerize him, and he was usually one of the first in the queue to offer support. He was always dreaming up ideas and inventions which would assist the armed forces, ranging from body armor to redesigning sea mines. One of his wackier ideas was how to convert a rifle into a howitzer, a short field gun for firing shells on high trajectories at low velocities. One day, a few miles from his home at Hindhead, he experimented at Frensham Pond. He wrote:

> I had spent a good deal of thought over the problem how best to attack men who lay concealed behind cover. My conclusions were that it was useless to fire at them direct, since, if they knew their business, very little of them would be vulnerable. On the other hand, if one could turn a rifle into a portable howitzer and drop a bullet with any sort of rough general accuracy within a given area, then it seemed to me that life would hardly be possible within that area. If, for example, the position was twenty thousand square yards in size, and twenty thousand rifles were dropping bullets upon it, each square yard would sooner or later be searched and your mark would be a whole prostrate or crouching body.... But the crux was to discover the exact ranges. To do this I went down to Frensham Pond and, standing among the reeds and tilting the gun very slightly forward, I pulled the trigger. The bullet very nearly fell upon my own head. I could not locate it, but I heard quite a loud thud.... My idea was to mark the bullet splashes on the calm water of the lake, but though I fired and fired at various angles not a splash could I see. Finally a little man who may have been an artist broke in upon my solitude.
>
> "Do you want to know where your bullets are going?"
>
> "Yes, sir, I do."

"Then I can tell you, sir, for they have been dropping all round me."

I felt that unless my howitzer was to claim its first victim on the spot I had better stop. As I was convinced that the idea was both practical and much needed I communicated full particulars to the War Office. Here is the letter I had in reply.

> "War Office
>
> February 16, 1900
>
> Sir — With reference to your letter concerning an appliance for adapting rifles to high-angle fire I am directed by the Secretary of State for War to inform you that he will not trouble you in the matter.
>
> I am sir, your obedient servant,
>
> (signature illegible)
>
> Director General of Ordnance"

FURTHER INFORMATION: Ironically, it was the lowland heath and ponds of Frensham Common which doubled for Dartmoor in Hammer's 1958 production of *The Hound of the Baskervilles*; and I feel sure, had the studio known of Conan Doyle's "appliance for adapting rifles to high-angle fire," they would have featured it in the film's finale as the perfect way to finish off the great hound.

KENT

Chatham
The Historic Dockyard
Kent Police Museum
Testament to the Victorian policeman

"I am the last and highest court of appeal in detection. When Gregson, or Lestrade, or Athelney Jones are out of their depths — which, by the way, is their normal state — the matter is laid before me. I examine the data, as an expert, and pronounce a specialist's opinion." — Arthur Conan Doyle, Sherlock Holmes pontificating about his skills to Doctor Watson, *The Sign of Four* (1890)

Holmes and Watson frequently came into contact with police forces around the country. Most of the time it was the Metropolitan Police force of London, based at Scotland Yard, but they also worked with other constabularies, including Kent. Watson observes in "The Man with the Twisted Lip" that the "silence" was "broken only by the heavy, regular footfall of the policeman." Today it would be the wail of the police siren, but in Victorian Britain the clack of a constable's hobnail boots was a familiar and reassuring sound on the streets. With his bull's eye lantern and truncheon hooked onto his belt, and a wooden rattle to whirl around his head to summon assistance, the uniformed police constable was ready for anything. He has now all but disappeared; and today's media usually caricatures him as a naive, working class, and often blundering instrument of the law, a view often perpetuated by the Sherlock Holmes stories. The Victorian policeman, however, was a lot more sophisticated than the media would lead us to believe; and had they not been, Sherlock Holmes would have had a lot more than Professor Moriarty to worry about. Evidence of this can be found in abundance in the archives and memorabilia of the Kent Police Museum, one of the few places left in Britain where the public can explore the life of the Victorian copper.

It was after the Peterloo Massacre in Manchester in 1819, when cavalry charged into a crowd of protesters demanding parliamentary reform, that Home Secretary, Sir Robert Peel, set up a uniformed police force for London. The terms "bobbies" and "peelers" come from his name. In 1856 the County and Borough Police Act made it compulsory for all counties to have a uniformed police force. Their uniform was a frock coat and high hat (later a kepi), accompanied by a truncheon and a rattle (replaced in 1884 by the whistle), and in the late 1800s the force adopted the helmet. In the Victorian era, police officers were working seven days a week. In 1912, however, everything in the garden got rosy, and they were allowed one day off in every fourteen. Gregson, Lestrade and Athelney Jones, therefore, were probably not "out of their depths," as described by Holmes in *The Sign of Four*, but more likely suffering from stress and exhaustion.

SEE ALSO: Scotland Yard (p. 84).

FURTHER INFORMATION: The Kent Police Museum, The Historic Dockyard, Chatham, Kent, ME4 4TE. Tel: +44(0)1634 403260. www.kent-police-museum. co.uk. For opening hours consult Web site. Parking is not a problem and there is easy access for wheelchairs.

FURTHER READING: C. Emsley, *The Great British Bobby: A History of British Policing from the 18th Century to the Present* (London, UK: Quercus, 2009).

Maidstone
Mill Street
Maidstone Carriage Museum

A collection of Victorian horse-drawn vehicles from the era of Holmes and Watson

"In the morning you will send for a hansom, desiring your man to take neither the first nor the second which may present itself. Into this hansom you will jump, and you will drive to the Strand end of the Lowther Arcade, handing the address to the cabman upon a slip of paper, with a request that he will not throw it away. Have your fare ready, and the instant that your cab stops, dash through the Arcade, timing yourself to reach the other side at a quarter-past nine. You will find a small brougham waiting close to the kerb, driven by a fellow with a heavy black cloak tipped at the collar with red. Into this you will step, and you will reach Victoria in time for the Continental express."—Arthur Conan Doyle, "The Final Problem," *The Memoirs of Sherlock Holmes* (1894)

For many of us, the Sherlock Holmes stories were our first literary introduction to the horse-drawn carriages of the Victorian era. One of the timeless images of Holmes and Watson is

A Bow-fronted Brougham.

of the two of them hurtling through foggy London streets in a horse-drawn cab, bouncing over gaslit cobbles in pursuit of a villain. Victorian streets and country lanes, blissfully free of the motor car, were a jumble of rattling carriages of all shapes and sizes — traps, dogcarts, hansoms, and broughams — all designed for a specific purpose.

The hansom cab would have been chosen essentially for speed, and was, therefore, one of the preferred modes of transport for Holmes and Watson. Patented by Yorkshireman, Joseph Aloysius Hansom, in 1836, this two-wheeled "safety cab" became enormously popular around the world. It was fast, light, extremely maneuverable, and cheap, needing only a single horse to pull it. It also had a low center of gravity, making it safer on the road, especially when cornering. It seated only two (three at a push), with the driver perched up behind the roof, who would communicate through a trapdoor with his passengers. Londoners often carried a cab-whistle; one shrill blow would summon a growler (a four-wheeled cab), two shrill blows a hansom.

The Holmes stories not only immortalized the hansom, but they also gave us our first encounter with the ubiquitous cabbie, a man who comes into contact hourly with the world at large and has an opinion on everything, just waiting for your ears only. "Bless you," says the cabbie in Doyle's "The Cabman's Story." "If I was to tell you all the thieves and burglars, and even murderers, as have been in my growler one time or another, you'd think I'd given the whole Newgate Calendar [a monthly bulletin of executions] a lift."

Situated in the 14th century stables of the Archbishop's Palace, Maidstone Carriage Museum is home to the largest British collection of horse-drawn vehicles, including Royal and state carriages. The collection was started by local benefactor and former Mayor, Sir Garrard Tyrwhitt-Drake, and was opened in 1946. Most of the carriages featured in Conan Doyle's fiction can be seen here; but if you whistle for one, expect a long wait, and sadly, no cockney cabbie is around to bend your ear.

FURTHER INFORMATION: Maidstone Carriage Museum, Mill Street, Maidstone, ME15 6YE. Tel: +44(0)1622 602838. www.maidstone.gov. uk. London's Hansom Cab pub, at 84–86 Earls Court Road opened in 1810 and was named in honor of Joseph Aloysius Hansom who lived nearby. www.hansomcabkensington.com

DEVON

Princetown
Tavistock Road
The High Moorland Visitor Centre
Where Conan Doyle stayed when researching and writing The Hound of the Baskervilles

"The moon was shining bright upon the clearing, and there in the centre lay the unhappy maid where she had fallen, dead of fear and of fatigue. But it was not the sight of her body, nor yet was it that of the body of Hugo Baskerville lying near her, which raised the hair upon the heads of these three dare-devil roysterers, but it was that, standing over Hugo, and plucking at his throat, there stood a foul thing, a great, black beast, shaped like a hound, yet larger than any hound that ever mortal eye has rested upon. And even as they looked the thing tore the throat out of Hugo Baskerville, on which, as it turned its blazing eyes and dripping jaws upon them, the three shrieked with fear and rode for dear life, still screaming, across the moor. One, it is said, died that very night of what he had seen, and the other twain were but broken men for the rest of their days."— Arthur Conan Doyle, The Hound of the Baskervilles (1902)

There are many hound legends in West Country folklore, and one which Conan Doyle may have woven into his plot was that of the iniquitous 17th century squire, Richard Cabell, on whose death a pack of hounds are alleged to have gathered and howled around his house. His tomb can be seen in a small sepulcher near the remains of Holy Trinity Church, Buckfast Leigh, where he was buried in 1672. Fearing that he might rise from the grave, anxious locals supposedly drove an iron stake through his heart and covered his tomb with a large granite slab. Until recently, the stonemason's guiding marks for cutting the name on the tomb were visible, and these showed that the proposed cutting of his surname was never completed, implying that something happened to unnerve the stonemason!

His friend and collaborator, Fletcher Robinson, lived near Dartmoor at Park Hill House, about four miles from Newton Abbot; and it was here that Conan Doyle stayed in early 1901 to research and write at least part of the book. Using the house as a base, they explored the surrounding countryside for locations in the company of Robinson's young carriage driver, William Henry Baskerville, known as Harry, who always claimed he donated his name to the story. Harry lived in the small lodge house called Park Lodge on the corner of Park Hill Crossroads, and it was here that the Robinson family carriage was kept for excursions on the moor. "I had to drive him [Conan Doyle] and Bertie [Fletcher Robinson] about the moors," he recalled. "I used to watch them in the billiards room in the old house, sometimes they stayed long into the night, writing and talking together."

Conan Doyle also stayed at the Rowe's Duchy Hotel (now The High Moorland Visitor Center) in Princetown in 1901, again using it as a base to explore parts of the moor unreachable by carriage. Many Holmesian scholars have attempted to determine the whereabouts of all the real-life locations in *The Hound of the Baskervilles*, and to date, all have failed. The main reasons for this failure can be attributed to Conan Doyle's atmospheric merging of fact with fiction — for example by increasing and decreasing distances and by combining the components of various locations into one, making it almost impossible to identify them, even though the area has changed very little since the time of Conan Doyle's visit. Originally he used many of the real names of places on the moor, but subsequently he changed some of these, thus making the search for the exact spot of many of the locations difficult to identify. Some of the most important sites, arrived at by the calculated guesswork of Holmesian scholars, are detailed on the map. When venturing onto the moor, make sure someone knows your itinerary and your estimated return time. Take great care if deviating from the beaten track and always take

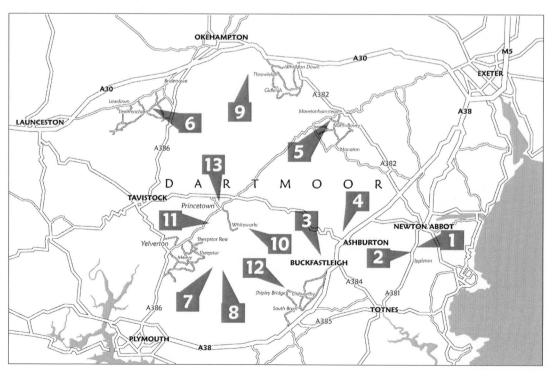

warm and waterproof clothing with you, as the weather can change dramatically within a matter of minutes. Large areas are used as artillery firing ranges. Do not pick up anything that looks suspicious. When in use these ranges have red flags flying on their boundaries. The best map for locational exploration is the OS Map No. 28 — Dartmoor —1:25000 scale.

MAP KEY:

1. Fletcher Robinson's House: Park Hill is the large house slightly up the hill from the Harry Baskerville lodge (see below) in the direction of Newton Abbot.

2. Harry Baskerville's House: This small lodge house, called "Park Lodge" is located on the corner of the Park Hill crossroads, the junction between the Newton Abbot to Totnes main road and the lane leading to Ipplepen. It is a private residence, but it can be seen from the main road.

3. The Cabell Sepulchre: The tomb of Richard Cabell (1622?–1672), who, it is claimed, was the original Hugo Baskerville, is located in a sepulcher in the churchyard of the Church of

Harry (Henry) Baskerville's grave in the churchyard of St. Andrew's in Ashburton (Brian W. Pugh Collection).

the Holy Trinity on the hill overlooking Buckfastleigh.

4. Harry Baskerville's Grave: Harry is buried in the upper section of the churchyard of the parish church of St. Andrew in Ashburton, under his formal name of Henry Baskerville.

5. Manor House Hotel (Baskerville Hall): Near Moretonhampstead, this hotel was used in the 1931 Gainsborough Pictures version, starring Robert Rendel, who was born on Lustleigh on Dartmoor, where the "Baskerville" railway scenes were filmed. Unfortunately, the building was not built until 1907, so it could not have been used by Conan Doyle as a location, who completed his book in 1902.

6. Lewtrenchard (Baskerville Hall): This location was strongly recommended by one of the greatest ever Holmesian scholars, William S. Baring-Gould, but then this was his family's ancestral home. It is now a hotel.

7. Giant's Basin (MR: 595670)

8. Deadman's Bottom (MR: 608668) Hugo's Death Site: Hugo chased the young maiden across the moor before meeting the hound of death. His death took place in a goyal, or deep dip, and there are two standing stones shaped like fangs nearby. The two candidates for this site can be reached on a seven mile circuit around Higher Hartor Tor, but this route should only be followed by experienced Moor navigators.

9. Raybarrow Pool (MR: 640902)

10. Fox Tor Mires (MR: 618707) Grimpen Mire: These are the only two realistic candidates for the location where Stapleton kept the hound. A mire is an area of swampy ground, but it is usually taken to indicate an area where a person or creature can actually sink beneath the surface. Even in these two areas it would be extremely difficult for a person to become fully submerged, as the depths of these mires have decreased greatly with drier weather conditions and the introduction of drainage systems on the moor. Care is still needed, however, in the area of the mire.

11. Black Tor (Meavy) (MR: 573718)

12. Black Tor (Avon) (MR: 681635) Black Tor: This is the Tor upon which Holmes was seen when Watson and Sir Henry chased Selden, and Watson later walks to it in the rain. There are four Black Tors on the Moor, but

Fox Tor.

only these two are candidates because they are within reasonable distance of the candidates for Baskerville Hall.

13. Princetown Prison: There is no doubt about Doyle's prison location. It has been where it is now since the Napoleonic Wars, and there is no other major prison on the Moor. The main

gate of the prison can be seen from the road, but be warned that photography is not permitted in this area.

SEE ALSO: Cromer Hall (p. 70), Fletcher Robinson (p. 114), Lopes Arms (p. 116), Undershaw (p. 107).

FURTHER INFORMATION: The High Moorland Visitor Centre, Tavistock Road, Princetown, Yelverton, Devon, PL20 6QF. Tel: +44 (0)1822 890414. Open daily except Christmas Day. Admission free. For an insight into prison life throughout history, Dartmoor Prison has a museum which is open to the public all year round. For details consult www.dartmoor-prison.co.uk.

FURTHER READING: P. Weller, *The Hound of the Baskervilles: Hunting the Dartmoor Legend* (Twellington, UK: Halsgrove, 2001); B. W. Pugh and P. R. Spiring, *On the Trail of Arthur Conan Doyle: An Illustrated Devon Tour* (East Sussex, UK: Book Guild, 2008); B. W. Pugh and P. R. Spiring, *Bertram Fletcher Robinson: A Footnote to The Hound of the Baskervilles* (London, UK: MX Publishing, 2008).

Ipplepen
Paternoster Lane
Parish Church of St Andrew's

Grave of Bertram Fletcher Robinson (1870–1907), journalist and editor who assisted Conan Doyle in researching The Hound of the Baskervilles *(1902)*

"Except for the various dedications of 'The Hound of the Baskervilles,' Fletcher Robinson appears to be virtually unknown. One hunts in vain for any mention of him in 'The Oxford Companion to English Literature,' 'The Reader's Encyclopedia,' 'The Encyclopedia Britannica' and 'The Columbia Encyclopedia,' and he apparently said nothing worthy of note on record, as he is not mentioned in either Bartlett's 'Familiar Quotations' or 'The Oxford Dictionary of Quotations.' So he was a literary non-entitiy,

The grim visage of Dartmoor Prison, home to some of the most dangerous and notorious criminals in English penal history.

except for the single fact that he was the inspiration for the best Sherlock Holmes story ever written, which entitles him, it seems to me to be posthumously knighted (if, indeed, he is dead) beatified, and later on, if things go well, canonized."

— Extract from Toronto magistrate, S. Tupper Bigelow's article, "The Singular Case of Fletcher Robinson," published in *The Baker Street Gasogene* (1961).

Ever since its publication in 1902, Fletcher Robinson's involvement with the creation of *The Hound of the Baskervilles* has been the subject of endless and passionate debate. Did he just plant the seed of the idea, or did he collaborate in the actual writing of the story? It seems unlikely that we will ever know the truth, but what is certain is that Fletcher Robinson was a talented writer whose work is now largely forgotten.

He first met Conan Doyle in July 1900 on the voyage home from Capetown when they were both returning from the Boer War. Conan Doyle had been on the medical staff of a volunteer hospital unit, and Fletcher Robinson a war correspondent for the *Daily Express*. The two of them became friends and shared a "very joyous voyage." No one knows for certain what they talked about during the long voyage, but Robinson's old college friend, Harold Michelmore (1871–1957), who later became the Robinson family solicitor, claimed in a letter published in *The Western Morning News* (a regional Cornwall and Devon newspaper) in 1949 that "Fletcher Robinson told Doyle the plot of the story which he intended writing about Dartmoor, and Conan Doyle was so intrigued by it that he asked Fletcher Robinson if he would object to their writing it together."

Whether the story contained the plot of what finally became *The Hound of the Baskervilles* is open to debate, but it seems more than likely that during the long voyage the two men would have thrown around their different ideas and opinions, and the Dartmoor hound legends could well have been discussed. Their liner docked at Southampton in July 1900, and the following March both men took a short golfing holiday in Norfolk together. It was here they agreed to collaborate on a book. By the end of the month, Conan Doyle was visiting Robinson

at his home in Dartmoor, and both men became immersed in the folklore and landscape of the moor.

In 1905 *The New York Tribune* published an article in which Fletcher Robinson recounted his time with Conan Doyle on Dartmoor:

One of the most interesting weeks that I ever spent was with Doyle on Dartmoor. He made the journey in my company shortly after I told him, and he accepted from me, a plot which eventuated in 'The Hound of the Baskervilles.' Dartmoor, the great wilderness of bog and rock that cuts Devonshire at this point, appealed to his imagination. He listened eagerly to my stories of the ghost hounds, of the headless riders and of the devils that lurk in the hollows — legends upon which I have been reared, for my home lay on the borders of the moor. How well he turned to account his impressions will remembered by all readers of 'The Hound.'

Two incidents come especially to my recollection. In the center of the moor lies the famous convict prison of Princetown. In the great granite buildings, swept by the rains and clouded in the mists, are lodged over a thousand criminals, convicted on the more serious offences. A tiny village clusters at the foot of the slope on which they stand, and a comfortable old-fashioned inn affords accommodation to travellers.

The morning after our arrival Doyle and I were sitting in the smoking-room when a cheery-cheeked maid opened the door and announced "Visitors to see you, gentlemen." In marched four men, who solemnly sat down and began to talk about the weather, the fishing in the moor streams and other general subjects. Who they might be I had not the slightest idea. As they left I followed them into the hall of the inn. On the table were their four cards. The governor of the prison, the deputy governor, the chaplain and the doctor had come, as a pencil note explained, "to call on Mr. Sherlock Holmes."

One morning I took Doyle to see the mighty bog [Fox Tor Mires], a thousand acres of quaking slime, at any part of which a horse and rider might disappear, which figured so prominently in 'The Hound.' He was amused at the story I told him of the moor man who on one occasion saw a hat near the edge of the morass and poked at it with a long pole he carried. "You leave my hat alone!" came a voice from beneath it. "Whoi! Be there a man under 'at?" cried the startled rustic. "Yes, you fool, and a horse under the man."

From the bog we tramped eastward to the stone fort of Grimspound, which the savages of the Stone Age in Britain, the aborigines who were earlier settlers than Saxons or Danes or Norsemen, raised with enormous labour to act as a haven of refuge from marauding tribes to the South. The good preservation in which the Grimspound fort still remains is marvellous. The twenty-feet slabs of granite — how they were ever hauled to their places is a mystery to historian and engineer — still encircle the stone huts where the tribe lived. Into one of these Doyle and I walked, and sitting down on the stone which probably served the three thousand year-old chief as a bed we talked of the races of the past. It was one of the loneliest spots in Great Britain. No road came within a long distance of the place. Strange legends of lights and figures are told concerning it. Add thereto that it was a gloomy day overcast with heavy cloud.

Suddenly we heard a boot strike against a stone without and rose together. It was only a lonely tourist on a walking excursion, but at site of our heads suddenly emerging from the hut he let out a yell and bolted. Our subsequent disappearance was due to the fact the we both sat down and rocked with laughter, and as he did not return I have small doubt Mr. Doyle and I added yet another proof of the supernatural to tellers of ghost stories concerning Dartmoor.

Fletcher Robinson's "mighty bog" appeared in the final story as "the great Grimpen Mire" along with the stone hut and "the great convict prison of Princetown." And although Conan Doyle had killed off Sherlock Holmes eight years previously, he shrewdly revived him as the central character by predating the story to before his supposed death at the Reichenbach Falls. By doing so not only restored the great sleuth

The grave of Bertram Fletcher Robinson in the churchyard of St. Andrew's, Ipplepen (Brian W. Pugh Collection).

back to life, but also restored his bank balance. *The Hound of the Baskervilles* was first serialized in the *Strand* in August 1901, for which Conan Doyle negotiated a fee of £100 per thousand words. The British edition's circulation doubled to 300,000 copies, and Fletcher Robinson's input was acknowledged by a footnote which read: "This story owes its inception to my friend, Mr. Fletcher Robinson, who has helped me both in the general plot and in the local details." The following year the book was published and went on to become a best-seller. Conan Doyle's later expressions of gratitude for Robinson, although somewhat variable in their obligation, were also stated in succeeding editions of the book. Robinson did receive occasional payments from Conan Doyle, including one for £500 in 1901, but the real depth of his participation remains an enigma.

Fletcher Robinson died aged only 36 on 21 January 1907 from enteric fever (typhoid) and peritonitis. In 1902 a parody of *The Hound of the Baskervilles* was published in *The Bookman* entitled "The Bound of the Astorbilts," written by American writer Charlton Andrews. His final paragraph read as follows: "As I gazed, from far out upon the moor there came the deep, unearthly baying of a gigantic hound. Weirdly it rose and fell in bloodcurdling intensity until the inarticulate sound gradually shaped itself into this perfectly distinguishable wail: 'I wonder how much of it Robinson wrote?'"

SEE ALSO: The Athenaeum (p. 80), The High Moorland Visitor Centre (p. 111), Cromer Hall (p. 70), Undershaw (p. 107).

FURTHER INFORMATION: St. Andrew's Church, Paternoster Lane, Ipplepen, Newton Abbot, Devon TQ12 5RY. Tel: +44(0)1803 812215.

FURTHER READING: B. W. Pugh and P. R. Spiring, *Bertram Fletcher Robinson, A Footnote to The Hound of The Baskervilles* (London, UK: MX Publishing, 2008).

Roborough
Tavistock Road
The Lopes Arms

An old English inn which provided lodgings for Conan Doyle and friends in 1882

"Not a living creature did we meet upon our solitary walk, save a few scraggy Devonshire sheep, who looked at us wistfully, and followed us for

some distance, as if curious as to what could possibly have induced us to trespass on their domain.... Strangers have been found dead on it before now.... They lose themselves, and then wander in a circle until they fall from fatigue."
— Arthur Conan Doyle, "The Winning Shot" (1883)

There was nothing Conan Doyle loved better than a photographic expedition, combining the exploration of unknown countryside with his love of the camera. On one of these expeditions he headed for Dartmoor, with a couple of friends, to whom he gave the soubriquets "Commodore" and "Genius." He later recounted the experience in an article titled "Dry Plates on a Wet Moor" for *The British Journal of Photography*, in which he describes a journey from Plymouth to Tavistock. This may well have been his first contact with the Moor, which would eventually become the setting for "The Winning Shot," "The Adventure of Silver Blaze" and *The Hound of the Baskervilles*:

The Lopez Arms, with "a kitchen door left artfully open to waft a savoury odour into the street."

Stifling the unworthy temptation to return to our luxurious hotel, we strode sturdily northwards in the direction of the Moor. As we advanced the character of the scenery began to change. Rugged 'tors' and tangled masses of half-withered vegetation shut us in, and the narrow road wound through a wilderness in which the only living creatures seem to be a few half-starved Devonshire sheep, who eyed us curiously, as if speculating upon our motives for intruding upon their domains. Wild and stern as was the scene there was a certain rough beauty in it all, and several charming little nooks and corners were secured by our ever watchful cameras. The enormous number of white signposts fixed at the angle where every sheep path departed from the main track told a grim story of the byegone dangers of the Moor — where men had wandered in circles until they had dropped dead of hunger and fatigue. Indeed, with all these precautions, during the last twelve months there have been at least three cases of individuals having met with a similar fate.

The long summer evening was drawing to a close before we trudged into the pretty little village of Roborough, where we had determined to put up for the night. The old English inn — with its signpost of Admiral Vernon and a kitchen door left artfully open to waft a savoury odour into the street — was so irresistible that it was for-

tunate we had pre-arranged to make it our headquarters. There with cameras stacked in the corner, and discarded plate-carriers and knapsacks, we indulged in all the luxury of a lounge and well-earned smoke while a substantial tea-dinner was in process of preparation. There was something in the old-world flavour of the whole place which was so congenial to the tastes of the conservative Commodore that I quite expected to hear him propose that our expedition should terminate there and then, and the remainder of the holiday be spent in this luxurious little wayside tavern. However, he rose superior to the temptation, and sketched out our programme for the morrow with the air of a man suffering for conscience sake...

There are disadvantages even in old-fashioned inns and antiquated four-post beds, as we found to our cost during the watches of the night. As the Genius expressed it — "We felt a bit 'crowded' at first, but there was more room when we had given the sheets a shaking." However, the healthy exercise which we had taken triumphed eventually over every obstacle, and we strode forth in the morning like giants refreshed, bearing away in our knapsacks a goodly bottle of milk and a plentiful store of bread for our luncheon on the moor.

Leaving Roborough behind us, we pushed steadily northward through a waste even more delicate than that which we traversed the day before. For ten miles neither house nor inhabitant met our eyes — nothing but a long, undulating plain covered with scanty vegetation; and intersected by innumerable peaty brooks.

SEE ALSO: High Moorland Visitor Centre (p. 111), Fletcher Robinson (p. 114).

FURTHER INFORMATION: Roborough is situated on the northern outskirts of Plymouth just off the A386. The Admiral Vernon is now The Lopes Inn, 27–29 Tavistock Road, Roborough, Plymouth. Tel: +44(0)1752 301411. www.lopesarms.co.uk.

FURTHER READING: J. M. Gibson and R. L. Green, *Essays on Photography* (London, UK: Secker & Warburg, 1982).

Plymouth
1 Durnford Street

Site of Dr. Budd's surgery, where Conan Doyle practiced briefly in 1882

> "I have no doubt he did a great deal of good, for there was reason and knowledge behind all that he did, but his manner of doing it was unorthodox in the extreme." — Conan Doyle reflecting on George Budd.

While a student at Edinburgh University, Conan Doyle befriended a classmate named George Turnavine Budd, an unpredictable, moody and high-strung character, whom he once described as "half genius and half quack," who no doubt brightened up many a dull lecture at Old College with his horseplay. His antics were amusingly described by Conan Doyle in his 1895 semi-autobiographical novel, *The Stark Munro Letters*. He wrote:

> I remember, that an address which was being given to us by an eminent London specialist was much interrupted by a man in the front row, who amused himself by interjecting remarks. The lecturer appealed to his audience at last. "These interruptions are insufferable, gentlemen," said he; "will no one free me from this annoyance?" "Hold your tongue — you, sir, on the front bench," cried Cullingworth [Budd], in his bull's bellow. "Perhaps you'll make me," said the fellow, turning a contemptuous face over his shoulder. Cullingworth closed his note-book, and began to walk down on the tops of the desks to the delight of the three hundred spectators. It was fine to see the deliberate way in which he picked his way among the ink bottles. As he sprang down from the last bench on to the floor, his opponent struck him a smashing blow full in the face. Cullingworth got his bulldog grip on him, however, and rushed him backwards out of the class-room. What he did with him I don't know, but there was a noise like the delivery of a ton of coals; and the champion of law and order returned, with the sedate air of a man who had done his work. One of his eyes looked like an over-ripe damson, but

> we gave him three cheers as he made his way back to his seat. Then we went on with the dangers of Placenta Praevia.... He never seemed to work, and yet he took the anatomy prize over the heads of all the ten-hour-a-day men. That might not count for much, for he was quite capable of idling ostentatiously all day and then reading desperately all night; but start a subject of your own for him, and then see his originality and strength.... He was fond of rough horse-play; but it was better to avoid it with him, for you could never tell what it might lead to. His temper was nothing less than infernal.

After graduating Budd set up a practice in Bristol where his late father had been an eminent physician. He set his sights high, pursuing wealthy patients and projecting a pseudo affluence which he could ill afford for bait. The business soon collapsed, and Budd wrote to Conan Doyle asking his advice on how to extricate himself from financial ruin. Doyle's advice was direct, perhaps too direct for a sociopath like Budd — meet with your creditors, ask them to postpone your debts, and make a fresh start. Budd took the advice and was granted a deferment of his debts, and headed for Plymouth where new pastures awaited.

In Plymouth he set up a practice in Durnford Street, a working-class area near the naval dockyard, which was the antithesis to his Bristol one. His scheme, or more likely, scam, was a simple one. Offer consultations for free, but charge a handsome fee for prescriptions, which, according to Conan Doyle, he dispensed in a "heroic and indiscriminate manner." Business became so lucrative that he invited Conan Doyle to join the practice, promising a salary of three hundred pounds, boasting that thirty thousand patients had consulted him in a year. "This looked like business," wrote Conan Doyle, "so off I went," despite the misgivings of his mother, who had never liked Budd.

Conan Doyle found that Budd's practice was indeed thriving, but resembled "something more like a cattle market than a medical practice. He roared and shouted, scolded them, joked them, pushed them about, and pursued them sometimes into the street, or addressed them collectively from the landing." Although now earning decent money, it wasn't long before Conan Doyle's conscience began to weigh heavily and guiltily on his mind, and his mother was continually reproaching him for his association with Budd in her letters. One of these letters fell into Budd's hands, and predictably he flew off the handle, wrenching his partner's brass plate from the wall, effectively dismissing him from the practice, claiming a fall in profits since Conan Doyle's arrival. Budd suggested he set up on his own and offered him a loan of one pound a week until he became established — an agreement he later reneged upon. Conan Doyle, no doubt wishing he had listened to his mother's premonitions, left Plymouth at the end of June 1882, where he boarded a steamer for Southsea to try his luck further along the English coast.

Budd did not live long after their break-up, dying in his early thirties in 1889, leaving his wife and four children in impoverished circumstances. Conan Doyle later contributed to their support. "He was a remarkable man and narrowly escaped being a great one," wrote Conan Doyle. "I understand that an autopsy revealed some cerebral abnormality."

FURTHER INFORMATION: A plaque marking Conan Doyle's brief stay in Plymouth was erected on the former Renwick's Garage building at the junction of Durnford Street and Emma Place. This building, along with the plaque, have since disappeared, and a block of flats now stands on the site. Sherlockian quotes can be seen along Durnford Street set into the pavement. Conan Doyle's lodgings were at 6 Elliot Terrace, home of the Budd family.

SEE ALSO: Bush House (p. 128).

FURTHER READING: Arthur Conan Doyle, *The Stark Munro Letters* (London, UK: Longmans Green, 1895).

CORNWALL

Mullion
Craig-a-Bella-Sherlock
Poldhu Cove

The "whitewashed house" mentioned in "The Adventure of the Devil's Foot"

"Thus it was that in the early spring of that year we found ourselves together in a small cottage near Poldhu Bay, at the further extremity of the Cornish peninsula. It was a singular spot, and one peculiarly well suited to the grim humour of my patient. From the windows of our little whitewashed house, which stood high upon a grassy headland, we looked down upon the whole sinister semicircle of Mounts Bay, that old death trap of sailing vessels, with its fringe of black cliffs and surge-swept reefs on which innumerable seamen have met their end. With a northerly breeze it lies placid and sheltered, inviting the storm-tossed craft to tack into it for rest and protection.

Then come the sudden swirl round of the wind, the blistering gale from the south-west, the dragging anchor, the lee shore, and the last battle in the creaming breakers. The wise mariner stands far out from that evil place."

— Arthur Conan Doyle, "The Adventure of the Devil's Foot," *His Last Bow* (1917)

Conan Doyle vacationed several times in the area around Poldhu Cove, where he was inspired to make it the setting for the Sherlock Holmes story "The Adventure of the Devil's Foot." Situated on the Lizard Peninsula about a mile along the coast from the village of Mul-

Poldhu Cove (Phillip Bergem).

lion, the peninsula is the most southerly point of mainland Cornwall. Throughout history its coast has proved treacherous for shipping, and many vessels have foundered on its rock-strewn beaches. The Cornish language translation of Poldhu is "black pool," and Conan Doyle warns "the wise mariner" to keep his distance from this "evil place." A spectacular setting, however, does not always make for spectacular story, and "The Adventure of the Devil's Foot" is a plodding and predictable tale, written by a creator weary of

his creation, and one of the least memorable Holmes stories. Poldhu's real claim to fame is its association with Guglielmo Marconi who set up a Wireless Station there, and on 12 December 1901, transmitted the first transatlantic radio message to a receiving station in Newfoundland.

FURTHER INFORMATION: Craig-a-Bella-Sherlock and its neighbor, Craig-a-Bella-Mycroft, are available for holiday rental through Cornish Cottages. www.cornishcottagesonline.com.

EAST SUSSEX

Groombridge
Groombridge Place

Inspiration for the Manor House in The Valley of Fear

"The Manor House, with its many gables and its small diamond-paned windows, was still much as the builder had left it in the early seventeenth century.... The only approach to the house was over a drawbridge, the chains and windlass of which had long been rusted and broken. The latest tenants of the Manor House had, however, with characteristic energy, set this right, and the drawbridge was not only capable of being raised, but actually was raised every evening and lowered every morning. By thus renewing the custom of the old feudal days the Manor House was converted into an island during the night — a fact which had a very direct bearing upon the mystery which was soon to engage the attention of all England." — Arthur Conan Doyle, *The Valley of Fear* (1915)

The Valley of Fear, like *A Study in Scarlet*, is a novel in two distinct parts. In the first half Holmes and Watson are deep in rural England investigating a mysterious murder, while the second half is told in flashback set in the coal mining communities of Pennsylvania and follows the ex-

ploits of Pinkerton detective Birdy Edwards. The plot revolves around one of Conan Doyle's favorite themes — the revenge mystery. But because Holmes and Watson are removed from the action of the second half, it was not hugely popular with his readers.

Conan Doyle set the opening mystery at Birlstone Manor, based on Groombridge Place, an ancient Jacobean moated manor house, only 4 miles from his home at Windlesham in Crowborough, where he was a frequent guest at Groombridge's regular séances. The murder Holmes investigates is a classic locked-room mystery, where the lord of the manor has had most of his head blown away by a sawn-off

Groombridge Place (Brian W. Pugh Collection).

The Drunken Garden, Groombridge Place, mentioned in *The Valley of Fear* (Brian W. Pugh Collection).

shotgun. In the garden at Groombridge plaques have been erected at relevant spots detailing passages from the novel. One reads, "I took a walk in the curious old-world garden which flanked the house.... In that deeply peaceful atmosphere one could forget or remember only as some fantastic nightmare that darkened study, with the sprawling, bloodstained figure upon the floor." Another, beside a stone seat shaded by a flowering trellis reads, "Concealed from the eyes of anyone approaching from the house, there was a stone seat ... my eyes lit upon Mrs. Douglas and the man Barker (wife and closest friend of the deceased) before they were aware of my presence. Her appearance gave me a shock ... she had been demure and discreet. Now all pretence of grief had passed away from her."

FURTHER INFORMATION: Groombridge Place is open to the public and is located in the village of Groombridge, 4 miles south west of Tunbridge Wells on the B2110. Parking is plentiful and free. There is a train station at Tunbridge Wells where the bus service to Groombridge is hourly, except on Sundays. You can also take the Spa Valley Railway steam train from Tunbridge Wells West station, but this train does not run every day. For details consult www.spavalleyrailway.co.uk. Groombridge Place is open daily from 10:00 A.M. till 5:30 P.M. (or dusk if earlier) from late March to early November. For precise

opening times consult www.groombridge.co.uk or phone +44(0)1892 861444.

SEE ALSO: Allan Pinkerton (p. 54), Spa Valley Railway (p. 121).

Station Road
Groombridge Station and the Spa Valley Railway
Used by Holmes and Watson in The Valley of Fear

"'We have, I think, just time to catch our train at Paddington, and I will go further into the matter upon our journey. You would oblige me by bringing with you your very excellent field glass.'

And so it happened that an hour or so later I found myself in the corner of a first-class carriage, flying along, en route for Exeter, while Sherlock Holmes, with his sharp, eager face framed in his earflapped travelling cap, dipped rapidly into the bundle of fresh papers which he had procured at Paddington. We had left Reading far behind us before he thrust the last of them under the seat, and offered me his cigar-case.

'We are going well,' said he, looking out of the window, and glancing at his watch. 'Our rate at present is fifty-three and a half miles an hour.'

'I have not observed the quarter-mile posts,' said I.

'Nor have I. But the telegraph posts upon this line are sixty yards apart, and the calculation is a simple one.'" — Arthur Conan Doyle, "Silver Blaze," *Memoirs of Sherlock Holmes* (1893)

The ultimate symbol of American transport is the highway, stretching across the vast continent from coast to coast, offering the freedom to go just about anywhere. The British iconic counterpart, however, has always been the train, especially the steam trains of yesteryear; and the crime writer has always had a deep affection for them, none more so than Conan Doyle. His stories are littered with the trappings associated with them, from the humble railway porter to the luxuries of the Pullman car. Sherlock Holmes frequents most of the great London railway stations in his adventures and Bradshaw's Railway Guide sits comfortably on his bookshelf at Baker Street.

Although the British rail network today no

Groombridge Railway Station — an English idyll from the golden age of steam.

Piltdown
Barkham Manor

Where "Piltdown Man" was discovered, a famous paleontological hoax Conan Doyle is often suspected of engineering

"My dear chap, things don't happen like that in real life. People don't stumble across enormous discoveries.... Leave that to the novelists. The fellow is as full of tricks as the monkey-house at the Zoo. It's all absolute bosh.... If you are clever and know your business you can fake a bone as easily as you can a photograph."
—Arthur Conan Doyle, *The Lost World* (1912)

longer uses steam, the heritage railway scene is very much alive and kicking in the UK, and one of the best places to experience it is on the Spa Valley Railway. Not just because many of its locos and rolling stock belong to the Victorian era, but because Holmes and Watson actually used this line in *The Valley of Fear* (1915) en route to Birlstone Manor to investigate a mysterious murder. Birlstone was based on the manor house of Groombridge Place, and the train route from Tunbridge Wells actually stops at the village of Groombridge, just a 10 minute walk from the old Jacobean mansion which is open to the public. The Spa Valley Railway runs between Tunbridge Wells, High Rocks, Groombridge, and Birchden; crossing the Kent and East Sussex border, a distance of 4 miles, along the former Three Bridges to Tunbridge Wells Central Line, also affectionately known as The Cuckoo Line.

SEE ALSO: Groombridge Place (p. 120), Allan Pinkerton (p. 54).

FURTHER INFORMATION: Spa Valley Railway, West Station, Neville Terrace, Tunbridge Wells, TN2 5QY. Tel: +44(0)1892 537715. www.spa valleyrailway.co.uk. Trains run throughout the year, but not on a regular basis. For a current timetable consult the Web site.

Seven miles south of Crowborough, just off the A272, lies the village of Piltdown, where, in 1912, at a gravel pit on Barkham Manor, the remains of a skull were unearthed by workmen. They were shown to local amateur palaeontologist, Charles Dawson, who later discovered further remains. Piecing the fragments together he created a skull which appeared to resemble a half-human and half-ape ancestor. Dawson consulted British Museum expert, Arthur Smith Woodward, and both of them later presented their groundbreaking findings to a packed audience of the Geological Society as Eoanthropus Dawsoni (Dawson's Dawn Man), popularly known as Piltdown Man. They argued that the skull was a million years old and the "missing link" between apes and humans. Conan Doyle believed firmly in the skull's validity, but many were convinced it was a fake.

The skull remained the subject of controversy for many years until it was revealed to be a hoax in 1953 when scientists from Oxford University and the British Museum subjected the skull to chemical testing and proved it to be a forgery. Radiocarbon dating showed that the skull was less than 1,000 years old, and the jaw bone belonged to a female orangutan. The bone fragments had also been stained to make them look fossilized. Who the perpetrator of the hoax was still remains a mystery. Candidates include

The Piltdown Man pub. "Free House" in the UK does not, alas, mean free drinks, but refers to the pub's independent status as opposed to brewery owned pubs.

Dawson, Woodward, and numerous others connected to them, including Arthur Conan Doyle.

Fossils had always fascinated Conan Doyle and the earth around Crowborough was rich with the bones of prehistory. He first met Smith Woodward in 1909 when he came to inspect the tracks of a huge lizard and other fossils he had discovered in a local quarry, a meeting which later led to his acquaintance with Dawson. In a letter to Woodward, Dawson wrote, "Conan Doyle has written and seems excited about the skull. He has kindly offered to drive me in his motor anywhere."

The arguments for Conan Doyle being the perpetrator of the hoax are all circumstantial. He was an amateur in the world of palaeontology. He enjoyed going on digs. He was a neighbor of Dawson. He had a grudge against established science because it exposed one his revered psychics, and he sought to discredit the scientific establishment by falsifying fossil evidence and turn scientific analyses on its head. My favorite is the one which argues that *The*

Lost World explains the entire Piltdown hoax, including the exact location of the skull fragments, as a hidden puzzle. The game's not afoot Watson — it's a skull!

FURTHER INFORMATION: Barkham Manor is not open to the public. A stone commemorating Dawson's Piltdown discovery was unveiled at the dig site in 1938. The Piltdown Man pub stands close to the site for thirsty amateur sleuths still on the scent.

FURTHER READING: J. S. Weiner and C. Stringer, *The Piltdown Forgery* (UK: Oxford University Press, 2003).

Crowborough
Hurtis Hill
Windlesham Manor

Home of the Conan Doyle family from 1907 to 1930

> "Light green of grass and richer green of bush
> Slope upwards to the darkest green of fir.
> How still! How deathly still! And yet the hush
> Shivers and trembles with some subtle stir,
> Some far-off throbbing like a muffled drum,
> Beaten in broken rhythm oversea,
> To play the last funeral march of some
> Who die today that Europe may be free."
> — Arthur Conan Doyle, "The Guns in Sussex," describing the guns of Flanders, which could be heard at Windlesham during the First World War.

In November 1907, after their Mediterranean honeymoon, Conan Doyle and his second wife, Jean Leckie, settled into their new home named Windlesham at Crowborough in the heart of the High Weald. In 1913 Conan Doyle described the magnificent view from his first floor study in *The Poison Belt*:

> The road in its gentle curves had really brought us to a considerable elevation — seven hundred feet, as we afterwards discovered. Challenger's house was on the very edge of the hill, and from its southern face, in which was the study window, one looked across the vast stretch of the weald to where the gentle curves of the South Downs formed an undulating horizon. In a cleft of the hills a haze of smoke marked the position of Lewes. Immediately at our feet there lay a rolling plain of heather, with the long, vivid green stretches of the Crowborough golf course, all dotted with the players. A little to the south, through an opening in the woods, we could see a section of the main line from London to Brighton. In the

immediate foreground, under our very noses, was a small enclosed yard, in which stood the car which had brought us from the station.

Formerly known as Little Windlesham, the house was named after a school near Brighton, where the late husband of the former owner had been headmaster of a pre-prep school of the same name. The Doyle's, however, ditched the diminutive adjective "Little" and started expanding. Two extensive wings and six gables were added. A large billiards room, which doubled as a ballroom, was built to house Jean's grand piano and a full-size billiards table. Conan Doyle's typically male relics were proudly displayed, including Napoleonic and medieval weaponry, and animal heads and rugs, watched over by Sidney Paget's portrait in oils of Conan Doyle. Garages, tennis courts, and a summerhouse, known as "the hut," were built in the newly landscaped garden. The house, now a residential care home, has since been renamed Windlesham Manor, a highborn suffix the Doyles would have been delighted with.

The books Conan Doyle wrote here, either in his first floor study or in "the hut," included *The Lost World*, *The Poison Belt*, *The Land of Mist*, *Sir Nigel*, and numerous Sherlock Holmes stories. Guests who visited included politicians, generals, writers, and stars of stage and screen, but not everyone called to pay homage to the famous wordsmith. In 1913 outraged suffragettes poured acid into a Royal Mail post box at his front gate in protest against his views on female suffrage, a cause which he publicly opposed.

Conan Doyle had three children with Jean, all them born at Windlesham: Denis Stewart Percy (1909–55), Adrian Malcolm (1910–70) and Lena Jean Annette (1912–97). Windlesham was also earmarked to be Conan Doyle's final resting place, and after suffering a heart attack which caused his death on 7 July 1930, he was buried under a copper beech in the garden close to "the hut." His family and friends in the spiritual community, did their utmost to avoid a funeral of black-garbed grief. Bright and breezy dress was the order of the day. "The funeral was unlike any other," the *Daily News Chronicle* informed its readers. "There were no tears, no anguish, and hardly anything that savoured death."

On her death in 1940 Conan Doyle's wife Jean was buried beside him at Windlesham. In 1955 the Windlesham estate was sold and the remains of the Doyle's were reinterred in the New Forest at All Saints Church, Minstead.

SEE ALSO: St. Margaret's Church (p. 88), Cloke's Corner (p. 125), Professor William Rutherford (p. 39), Albert Hall (p.90), Churchyard of All Saints (p. 139).

FURTHER INFORMATION: Windlesham is now a residential care home and is not open to the public, but it can be viewed from the courtyard. Conan Doyle's study at Windlesham looked over towards Crowborough Beacon Golf Club, where he often played a few rounds with Rudyard Kipling. Local legend has it that Conan Doyle made a pact with his son Kingsley to meet him on what is now the fourth green exactly one year after his death should he die in battle during World War I. Kingsley did die, but whether the pact was carried out is not known.

Behind Windlesham, in Lordswell Lane, stands Monkstown (since renamed Monkswell), former home of the Leckie family. The original oak grave markers which stood in the garden at Windlesham can be seen at All Saints Church in Minstead. After the death of Jean in 1940, Windlesham was leased to the Home Office for military use. A Canadian regiment — the Lincoln and Welland — were the last soldiers to be garrisoned

Windlesham.

Conan Doyle's funeral in 1930 at Windlesham — "no tears, no anguish, and hardly anything that savoured death."

there. Shortly before D-Day they vacated the house for a bivouac to the southwest, next to Crowborough golf course. Tragically, a flying bomb exploded over their campsite killing nine and seriously injuring others. A memorial was erected on the spot, and an annual ceremony pays tribute to those who lost their lives.

Cloke's Corner
Statue of Sir Arthur Conan Doyle

"Pay no attention to what the critics say. A statue has never been erected in honor of a critic." — Jean Sibelius (1865–1957)

Conan Doyle was a resident of Crowborough for over twenty years, from 1907 until 1930, and the town's proud homage to him was a life-size statue unveiled on 14 April 2001. Unlike other statues around the globe, this one is not predictably of Sherlock Holmes, but of the great man himself, all 6 foot 4 inches of him. The statue was sculpted locally by David Cornell and erected at the crossroads known as Cloke's Corner, named after a local architect who refurbished the area in the 1960s. Across the street can be seen The NatWest Bank, formerly the London and County Bank, and local bank of Conan Doyle. In 1947, his son Denis, while searching for some documents in the bank vaults, unearthed an unknown manuscript for a stage play featuring Sherlock Holmes, titled *The Crown Diamond*. A short distance at 6 The Broadway stands Café Baskerville, a pleasant watering hole dedicated

to the great sleuth. In nearby Church Road lies All Saints Church where vicar, Samuel Fisher Akroyd, baptized all three of Conan Doyle's Crowborough-born children — Denis (1909), Adrian (1911) and Jean (1913). Beside the church stands the town's war memorial; and among the names inscribed are Lieutenant A. A. K. C. Doyle (Kingsley), Conan Doyle's son from his first marriage, and Captain M. Leckie, brother of Conan Doyle's wife Jean. Kingsley died of pneumonia in 1918 at St. Thomas's Hospital, London, weakened by injuries received on the Somme. Malcolm Leckie was killed at Mons in 1914.

SEE ALSO: Windlesham (p. 123).

Corner of Luxford Lane and Luxford Road
Former site of Wesley Poultry Farm
Scene of the "Chicken Run Murder"

All his life Conan Doyle was a crusader against injustice. If he thought a miscarriage of justice had taken place, he did not hesitate to offer his services to the victim. His two most sensational cases were that of George Edalji and

Legend in bronze — Conan Doyle's statue at Cloke's Corner.

Oscar Slater, who, through Conan Doyle's efforts, were both acquitted of their crimes. One of the lesser known cases he became interested in was that of Norman Thorne who was hanged for the murder of his girlfriend, Elsie Cameron, in 1925, on circumstantial evidence. The case became known as the Chicken Run Murder.

In 1917, Norman Thorne, an unemployed engineer, met typist Elsie Cameron in London. In 1922, on money borrowed from his father, Thorne moved to Crowborough and started a chicken farm. The farm was a rough and ready affair and Thorne lived in a small shed on the farm struggling to make ends meet. Elsie, who was still residing in London, informed Thorne that she was pregnant by him. Meanwhile, Thorne had fallen for a local girl named Bessie Coldicott and wrote to Elsie stating, "I am between two fires." On 9 December 1924, Elsie, deceived and heartbroken, boarded the train for Crowborough. Thorne claimed she never arrived.

The resulting police investigation turned up three witnesses who claimed they saw a young woman walking towards the farm around the time of Elsie's disappearance. Thorne was arrested and a search was made of the farm revealing Elsie's suitcase and clothes. Thorne had no option but to change his original statement:

> When I opened the hut door I saw Miss Cameron hanging from a beam that supports the roof, by a piece of cord as used for the washing line. I cut the cord and laid her on the bed. She was dead. I then put out the lights. She had her frock off and her hair was down. I lay across the table for about an hour. I was about to go to Dr. Turle and knock up someone to go for the police and I realised the position I was in, and decided not to do so. I then went down to the workshop.... I got my hacksaw and some sacks and took them back to the hut. I took off Miss Cameron's clothes and burned them in the fireplace in the hut. I then laid the sacks on the floor and sawed off her legs and the head by the glow of the fire. I put them in sacks, intending to carry them away, but my nerve failed me and I took them down to the workshop and I left them there. I went back to the hut and sat in the chair all night. Next morning, just as it got light, I buried the sacks and a tin containing the remains in a chicken run. It is the Leghorn chicken run, the first pen from the gate.

Thorne was subsequently charged with murder. The defense pleaded suicide, but the jury returned a verdict of guilty, and Thorne was hanged at London's Wandsworth Prison on 22 April 1925. Conan Doyle, who attended the trial, claimed that there was probably only one chance in a hundred that Thorne had not committed the murder, but while that chance existed he would willingly partake in a campaign for a reprieve. "I am against capital punishment except in very extreme cases," he said, "and to justify it I think the evidence should be stronger than it was in this case."

SEE ALSO: George Edalji (p. 67), Oscar Slater (p. 51).

ISLE OF WIGHT

Shanklin
Shanklin Chine

Chine Hill, Visited by Conan Doyle on his trip to "The Island"

> "Where have I been for the last three or four days? Down at the Island.... The Island is where? No matter. It is the most splendid domain that any man looks upon in these latitudes."— Oliver Wendell Holmes *The Autocrat at the Breakfast-Table* (1858)

One of Conan Doyle's many excursions, fueled by his passion for outdoor photography, included a day trip to the Isle of Wight in the spring of 1884. Together with a friend in a hired horse and trap, he roamed across the island via Ryde, the Roman villa at Brading, past the famous Shanklin Chine and onto Ventnor; a trip he recalled in an article titled "A Day on 'The Island'" for a photographic journal:

> Perhaps there is no tract of land in the world, which compresses into such a small space so many diversities of configuration as the Isle of Wight. It is a miniature of the great country from which it

has been separated. There are moors and fells as bleak as those of Cumberland or the West Riding; chalk downs which recall Kent and Sussex; wooded undulating plains like those of Hampshire; and great stretches of rich arable land as fertile and as cultivated as any in Leicestershire.

The journey to Portsmouth [from London] occupies about two hours and a-half, and the traveller is eventually deposited upon the harbour pier, alongside which the fine, roomy 'Victoria' is snorting impatiently out of its two funnels, and in full readiness for its short voyage. 'All aboard!' shouts the captain. The warps are thrown off, and the vessel steams slowly out of harbour.

The solent is five miles broad between Portsmouth and Ryde, so that twenty-five minutes of steaming brings the travellers across. The first move after getting into the town of Ryde is to repair to a large horse-and-trap agency there, and to engage an open carriage for the day — a matter which is not a very expensive one. Thus provided, the whole island is at their command.

As you plunge into the heart of the country the sea disappears entirely, and you might imagine yourself in one of the midland counties of England. About three miles from Ventnor there is a large inn on one side of the road and a wicket gate on the other. Here the coachman pulls up with decision. At first, knowing the habits and customs of coachmen, our travellers imagine the inn to be the reason of this peremptory halt; but the landlord quickly sets them right, and they learn that the wicket gate is the attraction. Passing through it, camera in hand, they pick their way down a winding path and then across a brawling torrent. From there the path runs down a thickly wooded valley, the trees meeting overhead so as to hide the sky, and the stream gurgling among the bracken far beneath. This is the famous Shanklin Chine, and certainly a more beautiful or fairy-like scene could hardly be conceived.

Leaving the Chine behind, the carriage rolled over a tolerably level road a couple of miles in length, terminating in a steep hill, which was rather a pull for the tired horse. Up to this, as I have said, there were no signs of the sea, but on reaching the crest of the hill a wonderful view lay before the party. Almost directly beneath was the ocean, stretching right away in every direction to the horizon. Coming so unexpectedly I know of no view in the world which gives such an idea of an infinite expanse. Here and there one looks straight down on the deck of some steamer or sailing ship, ploughing across to St. Malo or tacking along to Southampton.

They look like toy vessels — mere specks in the enormous stretch of water around them. It is needless to say that cameras were once more in requisition, and this magnificent seascape packed away in our plate carriers.

When one leaves Ryde he fancies that he has seen the steepest town in the world, but his mind broadens when he comes to Ventnor. It is very much steeper, and gives the impression of being a little more than perpendicular. It is the fact of being on the side of this hill that gives the place its great reputation as a resort for consumptives. No wind but the balmy south one can get hear it. Still there are draw-backs, and when a consumptive falls out of his front door down the High-street and into the sea his language is just as virulent as that of any healthy man.

Commend me to the 'Crab and Lobster' Hotel at Ventnor. Its situation is charming, its fare excellent, and its charges moderate; or, at least, moderate for the island, which is never at any time an economical spot. At one of the open windows which line the elegant coffee-room, and through which the summer breeze wafts the perfume of many a flower unknown in higher latitudes, there sat that day two pampered and enervated photographers who had solemnly packed away their cameras and delivered their whole minds up to the one idea of a comfortable dinner with a soothing pipe to follow. After all they had a right then to indulge in a little dolce far niente, since they had accumulated a finer variety of picturesque effects and interesting views than could have been taken in a week in a less-favoured locality.

Ventnor High Street.

FURTHER INFORMATION: There are over 350 ferry crossings a day from Portsmouth to the Isle of Wight connecting with all major road and rail links. For opening times and admission prices to Shanklin Chine consult www.shanklinchine.co.uk. Tel: +44(0)1983 866432. There is no parking at the Chine, but parking is available at Vernon Meadow car park in the Old Village and along Shanklin Esplanade. The former Crab and Lobster Hotel building still stands in Grove Road, Ventnor, but has since been converted into flats. Adjacent to this building sits a row of cottages which was once the Crab and Lobster Inn, considered to have been one of the island's oldest inns, dating from around 1760.

FURTHER READING: J. M. Gibson and R. L. Green, *Essays on Photography* (London, UK: Secker & Warburg, 1982).

HAMPSHIRE

Southsea
Bush House
Elm Grove

Former site of No. 1 Bush Villas, where Conan
Doyle practiced from 1882 to 1890

"...and so I found myself in the heart of Birchespool [Southsea] with a base of operations secured. I looked out of the little window of my lodgings at the reeking pots and grey sloping roofs, with a spire or two spurting up among them, and I shook my teaspoon defiantly at them. 'You've got to conquer me,' said I, 'or else I'm man enough to conquer you.'" — Arthur Conan Doyle, *The Stark Munro Letters* (1895)

Conan Doyle arrived in Southsea in June 1882, following the failure of his brief but action-packed partnership in the Plymouth practice of his "half genius and half quack" friend Dr. George Budd. Southsea was a stab in the dark for him, but it was a suburb of Portsmouth, which, like Plymouth, had a large naval garrison, and therefore had many similarities. A successful practice established here could prove remunerative; but with no capital, and with little more than £10 in his wallet, it would be no easy task.

He arrived by steamer, stepping ashore at Southsea's Clarence Pier. In his semi-autobiographical novel, *The Stark Munro Letters*, Conan Doyle describes his arrival in detail. Southsea in the story is depicted as the fictional town of Birchespool, and his arrival is not by steamer, but by train:

When I turned out with my brass plate, my trunk, and my hat-box upon the Birchespool

platform, I sat down and wondered what my first move should be. Every penny was going to be of the most vital importance to me, and I must plan things within the compass of that tiny purse. As I sat pondering, there came a sight of interest, for I heard a burst of cheering with the blare of a band upon the other side of the station, and then the pioneers and leading files of a regiment came

No. 1 Bush Villas in the early 1900s, wedged between the Baptist Church and Madame Lee's corset shop.

swinging on to the platform. They wore white sun-hats, and were leaving for Malta, in anticipation of war in Egypt. They were young soldiers — English by the white facings — with a colonel whose moustache reached his shoulders, and a number of fresh-faced long-legged subalterns. I chiefly remember one of the colour-sergeants, a man of immense size and ferocious face, who leaned upon his Martini, with two little white kittens peeping over either shoulder from the flaps of his knapsack. I was so moved at the sight of these youngsters going out to do their best for the dear old country, that I sprang up on my box, took off my hat, and gave them three cheers. At first the folk on my side looked at me in their bovine fashion — like a row of cows over a wall. At the second a good many joined, and at the third my own voice was entirely lost. So I turned to go my way, and the soldier laddies to go theirs; and I wondered which of us had the stiffest and longest fight before us.

I left my baggage at the office, and jumped into a tramcar which was passing the station, with the intention of looking for lodgings, as I judged that they would be cheaper than an hotel.

From his temporary lodgings Conan Doyle searched in earnest for a base to start his practice. In *The Stark Munro Letters* he describes pinning "a large shilling map of the town" on the wall of his lodgings and systematically studying the lay of the land. Finally he found what he wanted. "There was one villa to let," he wrote, "which undoubtedly was far the most suitable for my purpose. In the first place it was fairly cheap — forty pounds, or fifty with taxes. The front looked well. It had no garden. It stood with the well-to-do quarter upon the one side, and the poorer upon the other. Finally, it was almost at the intersection of four roads, one of which was a main artery of the town. Altogether, if I had ordered a house for my purpose I could hardly have got anything better."

Although describing the novel's fictitious address, it is an accurate description of Conan Doyle's first surgery at 1 Bush Villas, Elm Grove, Southsea. Bush Villas was a three-story, eight-roomed unfurnished house, wedged between a hotel and a church, with a rent of £40 a year. With the bare bones required to set up a practice now in place, Conan Doyle then went shopping for the icing on the cake and returned with "three pounds" worth of furniture for the consulting room, a bed, a tin of corned beef and two enormous brass plates. "He also placed an ad

in the local newspaper under "Miscellaneous Wants," which read: "Dr Doyle begs to notify that he has removed to 1, Bush villas, Elm Grove, next the Bush Hotel." All he had to do now was await the arrival of his patients — a waiting game he describes in detail in his 1894 book of medical tales, *Round the Red Lamp*, the lamp that traditionally hung outside a doctor's surgery:

> Dr. Wilkinson rearranged his room, as was his habit a dozen times in the day. He laid out his large Quain's Dictionary of Medicine in the forefront of the table so as to impress the casual patient that he had ever the best authorities at his elbow. Then he cleared all the little instruments out of his pocket-case — the scissors, the forceps, the bistouries, the lancets — and he laid them all out beside the stethoscope, to make as good a show as possible. His ledger, day-book, and visiting-book were spread in front of him. There was no entry in any of them yet, but it would not look well to have the covers too glossy and new, so he rubbed them together and daubed ink over them. Neither would it be well that any patient should observe that his name was the first in the book, so he filled up the first page of each with notes of imaginary visits paid to nameless patients during the last three weeks. Having done all this, he rested his head upon his hands and relapsed into the terrible occupation of waiting.
>
> Terrible enough at any time to the young professional man, but most of all to one who knows that the weeks, and even the days during which he can hold out are numbered. Economise as he would, the money would still slip away in the countless little claims which a man never understands until he lives under a rooftree of his own. Dr. Wilkinson could not deny, as he sat at his desk and looked at the little heap of silver and coppers, that his chances of being a successful practitioner were rapidly vanishing away.

Slowly his practice began to grow and strengthen and his ledger filled up with the names of patients, but sitting behind a desk in anticipation was not the only way to gather in the multitude. If the mountain won't come to Mohammed, thought Conan Doyle, Mohammed must go to the mountain.

"Do not think that practice will come to you," he wrote in *The Stark Munro Letters*. "You must go to it. You may sit upon your consulting room chair until it breaks under you, but without purchase or partnership you will make little or no progress. The way to do it is to go out, to mix everywhere with men, to let them know you.

You will come back many a time and be told by a reproachful housekeeper that some one has been for you in your absence. Never mind! Go out again. A noisy smoking concert where you will meet eighty men is better for you than the patient or two whom you might have seen at home. It took me some time to realise, but I speak now as one who knows."

And so Conan Doyle built his practice. And slowly, but surely, after a shaky start, things began to improve as more names were written into the register. During the first year his annual earnings were £154, rising to £300 by his third. It wasn't a fortune, but it was a gaining of ground and the foundations were now getting firmer. Gradually the newcomer was becoming part of the Southsea community. He joined the Portsmouth Literary and Scientific Society and presented a talk on "The Arctic Seas." A doctor at his local bowling club began to refer patients to him. It was also through a club contact that he became an adviser for an insurance company.

His mother sent his ten-year-old brother, Innes, to live with him, an odd accoutrement for a grown man to be saddled with while trying to carve his niche in life, but no doubt Conan Doyle appreciated the company. Innes was enrolled at the local school and fit well into the everyday tasks of a doctor's surgery by polishing the brass plate, general tidying up, and even taking his big brother's watch to the pawn shop.

During this early period Conan Doyle was also writing articles for *The British Journal of Photography*, and he also published various short stories, including, "My Friend the Murderer" (1882), which he sold to London Society for £10.

For "The Captain of the Pole-star" (1883), he received ten guineas, and Cornhill Magazine paid him around £30 for "J. Habakuk Jephson's Statement" (1883).

In March 1885 a local doctor sought a second opinion from him. A young man named Jack Hawkins, who was living in lodgings with his widowed mother and sister, was suffering from violent fits. Conan Doyle confirmed the doctor's diagnosis of cerebral meningitis. The hotel, however, wanted him removed; and in sympathy, Conan Doyle offered Jack a room at Bush Villa, where he died a few days later. This sad occurrence led to a relationship developing between Conan Doyle and Jack's sister Louise, whom he called "Touie." Six months later, in August 1885, they were married. Also that month Conan Doyle obtained his doctorate from Edinburgh University, making his social respectability in Southsea complete.

With an expanding practice, finding the time to write became increasingly difficult. In his early days he had plenty of empty interludes to jot down a yarn, but now things were changing, and which activity would suffer most? Writing or medicine? He also wanted to escape from the erratic and often unattributed treadmill of short-story writing. "What is necessary," he wrote, "is that your name should be on the back of a volume. Only so do you assert your individuality, and get the full credit of your achievement." His initial attempt ended in disaster when the manuscript for a novel titled, *The Narrative of John Smith* was lost in the post. In January 1884 he began work on the novel, *The Firm of Girdlestone*, which took two years to complete. The finished manuscript, however, was persistently returned by publishers and was temporarily abandoned. It would eventually be published in 1890. During March 1886 he began writing a novel featuring a character which would in due course make the recurring rejection slip a rarity and secure Conan Doyle's place in the annals of literary history. *A Tangled Skein*, introduced the characters Sherringford Holmes and Ormond Sacker. A few weeks later the title changed to *A Study in Scarlet* and the names Sherringford and Ormond Sacker were dropped in favor of Sherlock Holmes and Doctor Watson. The literary world, however, was not quite ready for Holmes and Watson yet. The best offer was £25 for the copyright of *A Study in Scarlet*, which Conan Doyle reluctantly accepted. Also during his time at Bush Villas he wrote the historical novels *Micah Clarke* (1889) and *The White Company* (1890). *The Sign of Four* followed in 1890.

Conan Doyle was now making his name as a writer, but it was still a name that couldn't survive on its own without the income of A. Conan Doyle, MD. The Doyle's first child, Mary Louise, was born in 1889, and two years later, in March 1891, the family left Southsea for London, where Conan Doyle set himself up as an ophthalmologist in search of the lucrative income of the private specialist.

SEE ALSO: Dr. Budd (p. 118), Undershaw (p. 107), Upper Wimpole Street (p. 73).

FURTHER INFORMATION: Bush Villas were destroyed during a bombing raid in January 1941. A block of flats, named Bush House, now stands on the site where a memorial plaque marks the spot. Clarence Pier was also destroyed during the same bombing raid. The Hawkins family lived in lodgings at 2 Queens Gate at the bottom of Osborne Road, Southsea.

FURTHER READING: G. Start, *A Study in Southsea* (Ronan, MT: Milestone, 1987).

Kingston Cross
The Blue Anchor Pub

Birthplace of Portsmouth Football Club for which Conan Doyle played goalkeeper

> "With your natural advantages, Watson, every lady is your helper and accomplice.... I can picture you whispering sweet nothings with the young lady at the Blue Anchor, and receiving hard somethings in exchange."— Arthur Conan Doyle, "The Adventure of a Retired Colourman," *The Casebook of Sherlock Holmes* (1927)

As a young and ambitious doctor, Conan Doyle needed patients to visit and register with him if he was going to survive. To publicize his meager practice he immersed himself in the social life of Southsea, joining various societies and clubs to meet the locals he hoped would become the lifeblood of his profession. Sport was always high on his agenda, and he joined the local bowling and cricket clubs. On the evening of 14 October 1884, he became a founding member and player of what became Portsmouth Football Club. The interested parties met at the Blue Anchor pub and decided on a "uniform" consisting of a dark blue jersey, white knickerbockers, dark blue stockings and peaked cap. All the players played under their real names, but strangely, Conan Doyle, who frequently played in goal, used the pseudonym "A. C. Smith." Perhaps it was a private joke, or perhaps he was distancing himself from a game usually associated with the working classes. More likely it was the aspiring writer in him relishing in the mystique of the nom de plume.

FURTHER INFORMATION: On the night of 11 July 1940, Luftwaffe bombers overshot their dockyard targets and dropped them on the Blue Anchor. Today's Blue Anchor was later erected on the site and contains some of the furnishings from the original pub. The football club formed in 1890 at the pub was an amateur team. Today's professional Portsmouth Football Club was founded in 1898 by John Brickwood, a local brewer.

20 Ashburton Road

Former home of Major-General Alfred Drayson, an early influence on Conan Doyle's spiritualist beliefs

> "You don't know what plague has fallen on the practitioners of theology? I will tell you, then. It is Spiritualism. While some are crying out against it as a delusion of the Devil, and some are laughing at it as an hysteric folly, and some are getting angry with it as a mere trick of interested or mischievous persons, Spiritualism is quietly undermining the traditional ideas of the future state which have been and are still accepted,— not merely in those who believe in it, but in the general sentiment of the community, to a larger extent than most good people seem to be aware of."— Oliver Wendell Holmes "The Professor at the Breakfast-Table" (1860)

Conan Doyle was attracted to spiritualism at an early age. In 1881, aged only twenty-one, he attended a Birmingham lecture with the deliberately enigmatic title, "Does Death End All?" It didn't make much of an impression on him, and in later life he wrote, "I had at that time the usual contempt which the young educated man feels towards the whole subject which has been covered by the clumsy name of spiritualism." He remained inclined to question or doubt until his arrival in Southsea where he began to dabble with mental telepathy and local séances. He claimed to have transmitted thoughts between himself and a friend named Henry Ball. "Again and again," he wrote, "sitting behind him, I have drawn diagrams, and he in turn has made approximately the same figure. I showed beyond any doubt whatever that I could convey my thoughts without words." Local séances were less rewarding, and seemed to consist of tedious sittings around swaying, leg-tapping dining-room tables. "I was interested," he wrote, "but very sceptical." At this point in time Conan

Doyle was probably ready to cut himself adrift from the crude table-turning antics of the seance room, but the influence of a fellow member of the Portsmouth Literary and Scientific Society seemed set to alter his bearings.

Major General Alfred Drayson had had a distinguished army career as a surveyor in the Royal Artillery, serving in South Africa, India and Canada, and had recently retired to Southsea. He was also a writer, whose books ranged from military textbooks to adventure stories for boys. He had a passion for amateur astronomy and a was a fervent believer in spiritualism. In fact Drayson's commitment to the psychic world was so unwavering that he claimed he received through an apport — the materialization of solid objects during a seance — regular deliveries of fruit and vegetables from Brooklyn, New York, and "none had to be bought for the household." One has to stop here and question Conan Doyle's judgment in his dealings with Drayson. Here is a man who not long before was enthralled by the deductive reasoning of Dr. Joseph Bell now associating himself with a man who receives fruit and vegetables through the ether from Long Island. But Conan Doyle was now on the cusp of being sucked headlong into the psychic movement and nothing, not even fruit and vegetables, was going to sway him. Conan Doyle and his wife Louise attended psychic sessions at Drayson's house, but they were hit or miss affairs, and not experiences designed to convert the sceptic. One seance, however, did kindle his belief, when he attended a demonstration by an experienced medium of "considerable mediumistic power." He later described his experience in a letter he wrote to the psychic periodical "Light" in 1887:

> Last week I was invited by two friends to join them in a sitting with an old gentleman who was reputed to have considerable mediumistic power. It was the first time I had ever had the opportunity of sitting with anyone who was not a novice and inquirer like myself.... On sitting, our medium came quickly under control, and delivered a trance address, containing much interesting and elevating material. He then became clairvoyant, describing one or two scenes which we had no opportunity of testing.... We then proposed writing. The medium took up a pencil, and after a few convulsive moments, he wrote a message to each of us.

Mine ran: "This gentleman is a healer. Tell him from me not to read Leigh Hunt's book" [Conan Doyle had been contemplating reading Hunt's 'Comic Dramatists of the Restoration' — a notion he hadn't shared with anyone].... I can only say that if I had had to devise a test message I could not have hit upon one which was so absolutely inexplicable on any hypothesis except that held by Spiritualists.

Conan Doyle may have seen this demonstration as a groundbreaking example of the wonders of spiritualist phenomena, but had the master observer, Dr. Joseph Bell, been sitting round that table a lot more would have been revealed by using the simple powers of perception. But Conan Doyle was now slowly moving towards the launch of a lifelong spiritualist crusade, and nothing, or no one, could stop him. He was well and truly hooked.

SEE ALSO: Psychic Bookshop (p. 89), *Strand Magazine* (p. 91), Houdini (p. 133), Agatha Christie (p. 59), Albert Hall (p. 90).

70 Palmerston Road

Site of the former medical practice of Dr. James Watson and possible origin for the name of Holmes's faithful accomplice

"The singular fact about 'the dog in the night,' as we all know, was that it didn't bark; and the singular fact about Holmes in the night is that he is never seen going to bed. The writer of the tales, the Watson person, describes over and over again, in detail, all the other minutia of that famous household — suppers, breakfasts, arrangement of furniture, rainy evenings at home — but not once are we shown either Holmes or Watson going to bed. I wondered why not? I got suspicious. The uglier possibilities that occurred to me was that Holmes had false teeth or that Watson wore a toupee, I rejected as preposterous. They were much too obvious, and shall I say unsinister.... And right at the very start, on page 9 of 'A Study in Scarlet,' I found this: '...it was rare for him to be up after ten at night, and he had invariably breakfasted and gone out before I rose in the morning.' I was indescribably shocked. How had so patent a clue escaped so many millions of readers through the years? That was, that could only be, a woman speaking of a man. Read it over. The true authentic speech of a wife telling of her husband's — but wait. I was not indulging in idle speculation, but seeking evidence to establish a fact. It was unquestionably a woman speaking of a man, yes, but whether a wife of a husband, or a mistress of a lover, ... I admit I blushed. I blushed for Sherlock Holmes, and I closed the book."— Rex Stout, "Watson Was a Woman" *The Art of the Mystery Story*, (New York: Simon and Schuster, 1946).

There has been much conjecture over the years about the origins of the name Watson. American crime writer Rex Stout (1886–1975) was not even convinced he was a man in his hilarious lark of an essay, "Watson Was a Woman," but there are only two Doctor Watsons, as far as we know, that Conan Doyle had any close contact with throughout his life — and neither was a woman! The first was the Scottish surgeon and forensic expert, Dr. Patrick Heron Watson (1832–1907), whom he encountered as a young medical student at Edinburgh University, and the other was Dr. James Watson, a practitioner in Southsea.

Conan Doyle first met Dr. James Watson as a fellow member of Southsea's Literary and Scientific Society. Watson, like Doyle, was born in Edinburgh and studied medicine at Edinburgh University; and although nine years older, he would have been taught by many of Conan Doyle's contemporaries. He became a junior houseman at Edinburgh's Royal Infirmary and was later appointed medical officer for the Foreign Service in Manchuria. After eighteen years in the Orient he returned with his family and settled down to the life of a general practitioner in Southsea's Palmerston Road. The last we hear of him is in December 1890, when he presided over a farewell dinner to Conan Doyle, at the Grosvenor Hotel, Southsea before his departure for London,

Personally, my own choice for Watson, would be Dr. Patrick Heron Watson, as he had many of the inherent qualities of his fictional counterpart. But perhaps Conan Doyle wasn't exactly sure himself. Maybe it was just a name plucked out of the ether. Even Watson's wife seemed bewildered. In "The Man with the Twisted Lip" she calls her husband "James" when his name was "John."

SEE ALSO: Patrick Heron Watson (p. 28), Royal Infirmary (p. 12), Maiwand Lion (p. 105), The Criterion (p. 78).

PORTSMOUTH

Guildhall Walk
Hippodrome House

Site of the Hippodrome Theatre where Conan Doyle first saw Houdini perform in 1920

"Tell the people that all I am trying to do is to save them from being tricked in their grief and sorrows, and to persuade them to leave Spiritualism alone and take up some genuine religion."— Harry Houdini

The unlikely friendship between Conan Doyle, disciple of the psychic crusade, and the famous escapologist and antispiritualist, Harry Houdini began in March 1920, when Houdini mailed Doyle a copy of his book, *The Unmasking of Robert-Houdin* during his UK tour. Jean Eugène Robert-Houdin (1805–71) was a French magician regarded as the father of modern conjuring. Harry Houdini (born Ehrich Weiss) was so much in awe of Robert-Houdin that he actually assumed the stage name of Houdini in his honor, wrongly believing that the "i" on the end meant "like" in French. The book also exposed American stage mediums, the Davenport Brothers, whom Conan Doyle implicitly believed in.

A friendly correspondence sprang up between Houdini and Conan Doyle which eventually led to a meeting in April,1920 at the Hippodrome Theatre in Portsmouth, where Houdini was performing. Later that month, when Houdini was appearing in Brighton, Conan Doyle invited the great showman to lunch at Windlesham, his house in nearby Crowborough. And so began an implausible friendship.

Houdini was, of course, a great self-publicist; and ingratiating himself with one of the world's most famous authors was a way of sharing his limelight. But he also questioned the very roots of his Spiritualism. "You will note that I am still a sceptic," he told Conan Doyle, "but a seeker after the Truth. I am willing to believe, if I can find a Medium who, as you suggest, will not resort to 'manipulation' when the Power does not 'arrive.'" Houdini knew all the tricks, many of which he used in his acts, and he was a master at spotting the fraud. He was notorious for attending séances in disguise, often with a policeman and reporter, where, at the end, he would dramatically expose the charlatan.

Conan Doyle probably wanted more than anything to convert this famous agnostic, but he was also determined to ferret out the quacks, and he introduced Houdini to some of his Spiritualist circle. Houdini was not convinced. As their peculiar friendship developed, Conan Doyle described him as "far and away the most curious character I have ever encountered. I have met better men, and I have certainly met very many worse ones, but I have never met a man who had such strange contrasts in his nature, and whose actions and motives it was more difficult to foresee or to reconcile."

The world's greatest escape artist, Harry Houdini, shakes hands with the world's greatest crime writer, Arthur Conan Doyle (Brian W. Pugh Collection).

Despite trying to remain friends over the years, they were continually at loggerheads with each other and ended up attacking each other in the press and threatening lawsuits. Although this was a predictable finale to their precarious friendship, Conan Doyle later wrote to Houdini's widow saying that he was "sorry that shadows grew up between us."

Houdini was without a doubt the world's greatest escape artist, staging endless death-defying feats which had no equal. Conan Doyle, however, became convinced that many of these stunts were not achieved by trickery, but because Houdini himself was a powerful Spiritualist medium. "If his powers were to be drawn from that [psychic] source," he wrote, "then his first and fundamental law must be that it be camouflaged in every possible way, and that no one at all should know his secret. If this be granted, a great many disconnected points become at once a connected whole.... We can even imagine that a campaign against mediums, fortified by the knowledge that false mediums do exist, would be an excellent smoke-screen."

FURTHER INFORMATION: Houdini died of peritonitis from a ruptured appendix on October 31, 1926. It was always rumored that he had been poisoned by Spiritualists, and 80 years after his death it was proposed that his body be exhumed for tests. It was, of course, a publicity stunt for a new Houdini biography, but one in which Houdini would have revelled. Had it actually gone ahead, I'm sure, when opened, the coffin would have been empty. The Portsmouth Hippodrome was destroyed by the Luftwaffe during the Second World War. An office block named Hippodrome House now stands on the site.

FURTHER READING: Harry Houdini, *A Magician Among the Spirits* (Fredonra, NY: Fredonia Books, 2002); Arthur Conan Doyle, *The Edge of the Unknown* (Dodo Press, 2008).

Museum Road
City Museum & Records Office
The Arthur Conan Doyle Collection

Bequeathed to the city of Portsmouth by Richard Lancelyn Green (1953–2004), The Arthur Conan Doyle Collection is one of the largest collections of Doylean memorabilia in the world. It includes hundreds of books, many of them first editions, Doyle family papers and photographs, Sherlock Holmes ephemera, archives on Doyle's spiritualism quest and psychic investigations, film and TV memorabilia, articles of Doyle's clothing, and even a Snoopy Detective lamp. But the pièce de résistance of the collection has to be Richard Lancelyn Green's recreation of Sherlock Holmes's study at 221B Baker Street. The Collection's patron is the British actor, writer and comedian, Stephen Fry. Fry says:

> Conan Doyle remains one of those writers so intensely stitched into our culture that it's easy not to notice him. The immense talent, passion and literary brilliance that he brought to his work gives him a unique place in English letters. His Holmes stories introduced the wider reading public to more than just the principles of observation and deduction, close reasoning and cunning detective work, for which they're celebrated. It was through the blazingly well written pages that the wider reading public became aware of such things as Mormonism, the Ku Klux Klan, corrupt unions, the mafia, cocaine and opium use, and much else besides from the bloody and macabre underside of Victorian grandeur and empire. He is unique in simultaneously bringing down the curtain on one era and raising one on another, ushering in a genre of writing, that while, imitated and expanded, has never been surpassed. His own life as footballer, cricketer, eye surgeon, champion of injustice, investigator of the paranormal, is itself the stuff of legend. Personally, I'd walk a mile in tight boots just to read his letters to the milkman.

> Richard Lancelyn Green himself was born into a world of literary fantasy. His father was a children's novelist and a friend of such writers as Tolkien and C.S. Lewis, and encouraged the love of reading in his son from an early age. Richard started his Sherlockian collecting at the age of five, a passion which continued until his death forty five years later. In his lifetime he became one the foremost Conan Doyle experts in the world, as well as one of the leading international collectors of Conan Doyle memorabilia. His bequest, containing in excess of 16,000 items, is the most wide-ranging Conan Doyle collection in the world. It is more priceless than The Mazarin Stone, The Blue Carbuncle, the fabulous black pearl of the Borgias, The Naval Treaty, The Bruce-Partington Plans, the Duke of Holdernesse's cheque, and the Beryl Coronet, all combined.

SEE ALSO: Marylebone Library (p. 78).
FURTHER INFORMATION: City Museum and Records Office, Museum Road, Portsmouth, PO1 2LJ. Tel: +44(0)23 9282 7261. www.conandoylecollection.co.uk

Admission to the Conan Doyle Collection is free and there is also free car parking in the grounds of the museum. Open daily 10 A.M.–5 P.M.

Cosham
Portsdown Hill
Where Conan Doyle observed and photographed the Volunteer Review of 1884

"To understand anything about the manoeuvres it was necessary to have a highly-trained imagination. To grasp them thoroughly argued an immense power of fancy, only to be obtained, as one of my companions declared, by the aid of stimulants." — Conan Doyle

On 14 April 1884 over 20,000 soldiers, most of them volunteers, took part in a military exercise on Portsdown Hill on the outskirts of Portsmouth. The occasion was very much a celebration of military might and boastful swagger, with many a dashing feat in the face of a sea of blank cartridges. Flags and bunting hung from public buildings. Triumphal arches were erected, and Conan Doyle, along with his two sisters and a friend, joined the thousands of excited spectators on Portsdown Hill. Dragging along his camera and accessories he became a fledging war photographer for a day, an experience he later recounted for the readers of a photographic journal:

> The battle was to begin at twelve o'clock, and as we were anxious not to miss any of the slaughter we made a forced march so as to get on the ridge before that hour. There is not a finer natural theatre in the world than the Portsdown Hill and the country around it, nor any place where such a large number of spectators can follow operations upon a large scale and grasp the drift of them. On one side beneath you is the village of Cosham and the little town of Portchester, with its historical castle, and on each side the broad stretches of Portsmouth harbour and Langstone harbour. In the background lies the great Hampshire seaport itself, and beyond it the silver streak of the Solent, bounded on the horizon by the long, well-wooded shores of the Isle of Wight. On the other side the declivity is as sharp, and the spectator looks down on an undulating, fairly open country, rolling away for some twelve miles to Buster Hill and the Petersfield district. The

main roads stand out like lines of chalk — as, indeed, many of them are — upon the landscape.
Both views, to the north and to the south, make
splendid photographs, but we had already done
them justice and were in quest of rarer game.

To understand anything about the manoeuvres
it was necessary to have a highly-trained imagination. To grasp them thoroughly argued an immense power of fancy, only to be obtained, as one
of my companions declared, by the aid of stimulants. The great forts which line the summit of
the ridge, and command the country round for
mile, are to be supposed not to exist. This is out
of consideration for the wives and families of the
invading army, then the sea is also abolished and
put out of the question. For the day Portsmouth
was an inland town, defended by a garrison of
some two thousand men. A reinforcement of four
thousand or so are on their march from the west-
ward to strengthen the place. An enemy, however, numbering ten thousand or so, comes down
from the north in a highly-reprehensible and vin-
dictive manner, and interposes itself between the
town and the relieving column, and endeavours
to prevent its getting into the town. This was the
cause of all the trouble.

There was a glitter of arms away to the eastward, and column after column of troops — black,
grey, and red — appeared in sight marching up
the valley, with a double line of skirmishers in
front of the leading brigade. This was the attacking force. Their advance was directed towards the
relieving or western army, but a rattle of mus-
ketry in the distance showed that the garrison had
made a sortie and were engaging the flank of the
invaders. At the same moment the head of the
western force began to appear near Fort Southwick, and very shortly the skirmishers of both
sides were hard at work. The sight in the valley
was now a pretty one. Two long lines of smoke
showed the position of the hostile skirmishers.
Behind these on both sides were regiments hurry-
ing up in open order to join the fray; behind that
again was the main body coming up in columns
of companies, while the cavalry, finding the situation becoming somewhat warm, were slowly re-
tiring. Occasionally a regiment would rise and
make a rush forward or backward in a way which
would have entailed a premature interview with
their Creator had it been done in actual warfare.
The reckless hardihood of these men was almost
incredible. They were too brave to lie down, so
they strutted about regardless of rifles and Nor-
denfeldts [guns], with a cool contempt of danger
which came like a revelation upon one of my
companions, who had seen some real hard fighting in his lifetime, and who bore in his waistcoat
pocket a certain piece of bronze called the Victoria Cross — as honestly as ever a decoration was.

"Why," he remarked, "there wouldn't have been
any of them left at all. They would have been ut-
terly annihilated;" and we forthwith began plan-
ning out graveyards and arranging for the decent
internment of the belligerents.

FURTHER INFORMATION: Portsdown Hill (430
ft.) is a chalk escarpment overlooking Portsmouth, and you can drive, cycle, or walk up the
hill from Cosham. As a result of the 1859 Royal
Commission, a series of forts were built on the
hill to protect the town and its naval dockyard
from an inland invasion. It is now a conservation area. The north side of Portsdown Hill
overlooks the village of Southwick and its
manor house, Southwick House, where, in the
months leading up to D-Day it became the
headquarters of General Eisenhower and the
Allied Expeditionary Force.

FURTHER READING: J. M. Gibson and R. L.
Green, *Essays on Photography* (London, UK:
Secker & Warburg, 1982).

Beaulieu
Beaulieu Abbey
Setting for the opening of The White Company

"The great bell of Beaulieu was ringing. Far
away through the forest might be heard its musical clangor and swell. Peat-cutters on Black-
down and fishers upon the Exe heard the distant
throbbing rising and falling upon the sultry summer air. It was a common sound in those parts —
as common as the chatter of the jays and the
booming of the bittern. Yet the fishers and the
peasants raised their heads and looked questions
at each other, for the angelus had already gone
and vespers was still far off. Why should the great
bell of Beaulieu toll when the shadows were neither short nor long?

All round the Abbey the monks were troop-
ing in. Under the long green-paved avenues of
gnarled oaks and of lichened beeches the white-
robed brothers gathered to the sound. From
the vine-yard and the vine-press, from the bou-
vary or ox-farm, from the marl-pits and salterns,
even from the distant iron-works of Sowley and
the outlying grange of St. Leonard's, they had
all turned their steps homewards. It had been no
sudden call. A swift messenger had the night
before sped round to the outlying dependen-
cies of the Abbey, and had left the summons for
every monk to be back in the cloisters by the
third hour after noontide. So urgent a message
had not been issued within the memory of old
lay-brother Athanasius, who had cleaned the

Abbey knocker since the year after the Battle of Bannockburn." — Arthur Conan Doyle, *The White Company* (1891)

Built in the heart of the New Forest, Beaulieu was a Cistercian abbey founded by King John in 1203–04, and is the starting point for Conan Doyle's historical novel, *The White Company*. Set against the backdrop of the Hundred Years War — a succession of separate wars lasting from 1337 to 1453 between the royal households of Valois and Plantagenet — the "White Company" is a band of mercenary archers led by Sir Nigel Loring who join the army of the Black Prince. One of Sir Nigel's followers is Alleyne Edricson, a young man in his twenties who was raised by the monks of Beaulieu, and who is eventually knighted for his bravery and wins the hand of Maude, Sir Nigel's beautiful daughter.

The White Company was Conan Doyle's second historical novel, which he considered "bolder and more ambitious" than his first effort, *Micah Clarke*, written in 1889. The seeds for setting the opening of *The White Company* in Hampshire were sown during a short holiday when he was staying with friends at a house on Emery Down in the New Forest for Easter of 1889. The house was only seven miles from Beaulieu Abbey, and within easy walking distance through the forest. Other nearby locations also featured in the story, including Hatchet Pond and Denny Wood. During the summer of that year, he again spent several weeks at a cottage in the New Forest immersing himself in the folklore of the 14th century, surrounded by books of myths and legends of English chivalry.

"I devoted two years to the study of four-teenth-century life in England," he told a journalist after the book's publication. "The period has hardly been treated in fiction at all, and I had to go back to early authorities for everything. I set myself to reconstruct the archer, who has always seemed to me to be the most striking figure in English history.... He was primarily a soldier, one of the finest that the world has ever seen — rough, hard-drinking, hard-swearing, but full of pluck and animal spirits." The novel was obviously a labor of love for Conan Doyle, for many years later, when in his sixties, he told a journalist that when he wrote it he "was young and full of the first joy of life and action, and I think I got some of it into my pages. When I wrote the last line, I remember that I cried: 'Well, I'll never beat that,' and threw the inky pen at the opposite wall, which was papered with duck's-egg green. The black smudge was there for many a day."

Much to Conan Doyle's delight, the book became a best-seller. Many of the critics, however, were not convinced and the book received lackluster reviews. The truth of the matter was that the time of the epic historical novel was well and truly over, and no novel, good, bad or indifferent, could change that — a fact Conan Doyle refused to accept. No doubt he looked forward to continuing the legacy of his mentor, Sir Walter Scott; but the dazzling success of Sherlock Holmes was about derail everything.

FURTHER INFORMATION: The ruins of Beaulieu Abbey are located within the grounds of Beaulieu Palace, a 13th century house which was formerly the Great Gatehouse of Beaulieu Abbey and is now the ancestral home of Lord and Lady Montague. Admission

The Domus seen through the ruined arches of Beaulieu Abbey.

price covers entrance to Beaulieu Abbey, the Palace House and Gardens, and the National Motor Museum, founded by the Montague in 1952. Open every day of the year except Christmas Day. By Road take the M27 and exit at junction 2. Follow the brown and white tourist signs for Beaulieu. The nearest main line rail station is Brockenhurst. Tel: +44(0)1590 612345. www.beaulieu.co.uk.

Grayshott
Headley Road
Churchyard of St. Lukes
Grave of Mary Doyle (1837–1920)

"Youth fades; love droops, the leaves of friendship fall;
A mother's secret hope outlives them all."
— Oliver Wendell Holmes (1809–1894)

Mary Doyle, née Foley, was a force to be reckoned with, who exercised her influence and guidance over her famous son until the day she died. "The Ma'am," as she was affectionately known, was married when she was seventeen years old to Charles Doyle, with whom she had nine children — seven girls and two boys — two of whom died in infancy. She was well educated and came from Anglo-Irish stock, an ancestry which she romanticized and wove into tales of chivalry for her children. She took up the role of single parent early in her marriage, when her husband, although a talented artist and draughtsman, descended into alcoholism and made life insufferable for his family until he was eventually institutionalized. Conan Doyle escaped much of the horror and violence of home life when he was packed off to boarding school, but an impregnable bond always existed between mother and son. In later life he consulted her on just about everything, from manuscripts to wives. The best description we have of her is in Conan Doyle's 1895 autobiographical novel, *The Stark Munro Letters*:

Now, with my mother — ah, but my mother must have a paragraph to herself. You met her, Bertie! You must remember her sweet face, her sensitive mouth, her peering, short-sighted eyes, her general suggestion of a plump little hen, who is still on the alert about her chickens. But you cannot realise all that she is to me in our domestic life. Those helpful fingers! That sympathetic brain!

Ever since I can remember her she has been the quaintest mixture of the housewife and the woman of letters, with the highbred spirited lady as a basis for either character. Always a lady, whether she was bargaining with the butcher, or breaking in a skittish charwoman, or stirring the porridge, which I can see her doing with the porridge-stick in one hand, and the other holding her Revue des deux Mondes within two inches of her dear nose. That was always her favourite reading, and I can never think of her without the association of its browny-yellow cover.

She is a very well-read woman is the mother; she keeps up to date in French literature as well as in English, and can talk by the hour about the Goncourts, and Flaubert, and Gautier. Yet she is always hard at work; and how she imbibes all her knowledge is a mystery. She reads when she knits, she reads when she scrubs, she even reads when she feeds her babies. We have a little joke against her, that at an interesting passage she deposited a spoonful of rusk and milk into my little sister's ear-hole, the child having turned her head at the critical instant. Her hands are worn with work, and yet where is the idle woman who has read as much?

Then, there is her family pride. That is a very vital portion of the mother. You know how little I think of such things. If the Esquire were to be snipped once and for ever from the tail of my name I should be the lighter for it. But, ma foi! — to use her own favourite expletive — it would not do to say this to her. On the Packenham side (she is a Packenham) the family can boast of some fairly good men — I mean on the direct line — but when we get on the side branches there is not a monarch upon earth who does not roost on that huge family tree. Not once, nor twice, but thrice did the Plantagenets intermarry with us, the Dukes of Brittany courted our alliance, and the Percies of Northumberland intertwined themselves with our whole illustrious record. So in my boyhood she would expound the matter, with hearthbrush in one hand and a glove full of cinders in the other, while I would sit swinging my knickerbockered legs, swelling with pride until my waistcoat was as tight as a sausage skin, as I contemplated the gulf which separated me from all other little boys who swang their legs upon tables. To this day if I chance to do anything of which she strongly approves, the dear heart can say no more than that I am a thorough Packenham; while if I fall away from the straight path, she says with a sigh that there are points in which I take after the Munros.

She is broad-minded and intensely practical in her ordinary moods, though open to attacks of romance. I can recollect her coming to see me at

The grave of Mary Doyle — "young-looking and comely to be the mother of about thirty-five feet of humanity" (Brian Tapp).

a junction through which my train passed, with a six months' absence on either side of the incident. We had five minutes' conversation, my head out of the carriage window. "Wear flannel next your skin, my dear boy, and never believe in eternal punishment," was her last item of advice as we rolled out of the station. Then to finish her portrait I need not tell you, who have seen her, that she is young-looking and comely to be the mother of about thirty-five feet of humanity. She was in the railway carriage and I on the platform the other day. "Your husband had better get in or we'll go without him," said the guard. As we went off, the mother was fumbling furiously in her pocket, and I know that she was looking for a shilling.

SEE ALSO: Masongill (p. 57).

FURTHER INFORMATION: Mary Doyle left Edinburgh in 1882 for Masongill in Yorkshire where she lived until June 1917, when she moved to Bowshot Cottage, West Grinstead, in Sussex, to be near her daughter Connie. She died aged eighty-three on 30 December 1920. Her Celtic cross headstone is inscribed with the words "To know her was to love her." Conan Doyle was

unable to attend her funeral as he was lecturing in Australia. Conan Doyle's first wife, Louise Hawkins (1857–1906), their son, Kingsley (1892–1918), and their daughter, Mary Louise (1889–1976), are also buried in the churchyard of St. Lukes. All the Doyle graves are in Section 2 of the churchyard, to the north of the church.

Minstead
Churchyard of All Saints
Grave of Arthur and Jean Conan Doyle

> "Trusty, dusky, vivid, true
> With eyes of gold and bramble-dew
> Steel-true and blade-straight
> The great artificer
> Made my mate.
> Honour, anger, valour, fire;
> A love that life could never tire;
> Death quench or evil stir,
> The mighty master
> Gave to her.
> Teacher, tender, comrade, wife,
> A fellow-farer true through life,
> Heart-whole and soul-free
> The august father
> Gave to me."
> — Robert Louis Stevenson, "My Wife"
>   *Songs of Travel* (1895)

The edge of the unknown — grave of Arthur and Jean Conan Doyle (Brian W. Pugh Collection).

Conan Doyle and his wife Jean were originally buried in the grounds of Windlesham, their home at Crowborough. But following the sale of the estate in 1955, their bodies were exhumed and reinterred in All Saints churchyard in Minstead. Conan Doyle would certainly have approved, as the heritage of this ancient village stretches back to the *Domesday Book*, where it is referred to as Mintestede (mint place) because of the profusion of wild mint that grew around the village. Conan Doyle mentions it in his novel *The White Company*, and his country retreat at Bignell Wood was only about three miles away. It was an area he knew well and a fitting resting place for a man who steeped much of his life in the traditions of merry olde England. His epitaph, the first two lines of which come from Robert Louis Stevenson's poem "My Wife," reads as follows:

> STEEL TRUE
> BLADE STRAIGHT
> ARTHUR CONAN DOYLE
> KNIGHT
> PATRIOT, PHYSICIAN & MAN
>   OF LETTERS

22 MAY 1859 — 7 JULY 1930
AND HIS BELOVED, HIS WIFE
JEAN CONAN DOYLE
REUNITED 27 JUNE 1940

A narrow lane links the church to the village, and the Conan Doyles lie buried beneath an oak tree to the rear of the church. Parts of All Saints church date from as early as 1272, and the pulpit is made from New Forest oak. The most ancient stone in the church is the font which lies in front of the pulpit. It lay buried for over two hundred years until discovered by an Abbott who was digging in the Rectory garden in the late 19th century. Reputedly made during Saxon times, legend has it that it was hidden to safeguard it from the grasp of the Puritans. In the bell tower, which was rebuilt in 1774, there hang five bells, one of which predates the Reformation. On the north side of the church lies the grave of Thomas White, whose epitaph has had a word (probably "faithful") removed, reputedly by his widow who discovered his infidelity after his death.

SEE ALSO: Windlesham (p. 123), Albert Hall (p. 90).

Appendix 1.
A Select Chronology

1794–95

ACD's paternal grandmother, Marianne Conan, born.

1797

ACD's paternal grandfather, John Doyle (as an artist, known as H.B.), born.

1809

ACD's maternal grandparents, William Foley and Catherine Pack, born.

1820

February 13
John Doyle married Marianne Conan at St. Andrews Church, Dublin.

1822

John and Marianne Doyle arrived in London from Ireland and resided at 60 Berners St.

1832

March 25
ACD's father, Charles Altamont Doyle, born in Bayswater, London.

1835

April 24
William Foley married Catherine Pack.

1837

June 4 or July 8
ACD's mother, Mary Josephine Elizabeth Foley, born.

December 2
Joseph Bell born at 22 St Andrew Square, Edinburgh.

1840

Death of William Foley.

1847

April
Catherine Foley, together with her two daughters, Mary and Catherine, arrive in Edinburgh from Ireland and reside at 27 Clyde St.

1849

Charles Doyle moves to Edinburgh from London to take up the post of clerk in the Office of Works and lodges with Catherine Foley.

1854–59

Joseph Bell studies medicine at the University of Edinburgh.

1855

July 31
Charles Doyle marries his landlady's daughter, Mary Foley, at St. Mary's RC Cathedral, York Place, Edinburgh.

1856

July 22
ACD' sister Anne Mary Francis Conan Doyle (Annette) born at 1 South Nelson St., Edinburgh.

1857

April 10
ACD's first wife, Louise Hawkins (Touie), born in Dixton, Monmouthshire.

1858

April 22
ACD's sister Catherine Amelia Angela Doyle born at 5 Nelson St., Edinburgh. Died six months later of hydrocephalus.

1859

Joseph Bell graduates with MD from University of

Edinburgh and becomes House Surgeon to James Syme.

May 22
Arthur Conan Doyle born at 11 Picardy Place, Edinburgh, at 4:55 A.M.

May 24
ACD baptized Arthur Ignatius Conan Doyle at St. Mary's RC Cathedral.

1860

October 4
Birth of Sherlockian illustrator Sidney Paget.

1861

May 4
ACD's sister Mary Helena Monica Harriet Doyle born at 11 Picardy Place.

1861–2

The Doyle family reside at 3 Tower Bank, Portobello, Edinburgh.

1862

June 3
Death of Mary Helena Monica Harriet Doyle from laryngitis.

June 7
Death of Catherine Foley.

1866

ACD lives with Mary Burton at Liberton Bank House, Edinburgh, and attends Newington Academy at Salisbury Place.

February 22
ACD's sister Caroline Mary Burton Doyle (Lottie) born at Liberton Bank.

1868

The Doyle family reside at 3 Sciennes Hill Place, Edinburgh.

January 2
Death of ACD's grandfather John Doyle (HB).

March 4
ACD's sister Constance Amelia Monica Doyle born at Sciennes Hill Place.

September 15
ACD attends Jesuit run Hodder Preparatory School, Lancashire.

1870

ACD attends Stonyhurst Jesuit College, Lancashire.

1871

October 20
Joseph Bell appointed Full Surgeon to Royal Infirmary of Edinburgh.

1873

March 31
ACD's brother John Francis Innes Hay Doyle born at 3 Sciennes Hill Place.

1875

Birth of Jean Leckie, ACD's second wife.

March 16
ACD's sister Jane Adelaide Rose (Ida) Doyle born at 2 Argyle Park Terrace, Edinburgh.

September
ACD attends Stella Matutina (Stonyhurst branch school) Feldkirch, Austria, until 28 June 1876.

1876

June
Charles Doyle admitted to Blairerno, an institution for alcoholics in Kincardineshire.

October 25
ACD enters the Faculty of Medicine at the University of Edinburgh.

1877

March 2
ACD's sister Bryan Mary Julia Josephine Doyle (Dodo) born at 2 Argyle Park Terrace, Edinburgh.

August
The Doyle family reside at 23 George Square, Edinburgh.

1878

Joseph Bell appoints ACD as his out patient clerk.

April
ACD assistant to Dr. Charles Richardson in Sheffield.

July
ACD assistant to Dr. H. F. Elliot in Ruyton-XI-Towns, Shropshire.

1879

Summer
ACD assistant to Dr. R. R. Hoare in Birmingham.

September 6
First fictional story, "The Mystery of Sasassa Valley," published in *Chamber's Journal*.

1880

February 28
Sails on an Arctic whaler as ship's surgeon for seven months.

1881

The Doyle family reside at 15 Lonsdale Terrace, Edinburgh.

August 1
ACD graduated as Bachelor of Medicine (MB) and Master of Surgery (CM) at the University of Edinburgh.

October 22
Serves as ship's surgeon on board the SS Mayumba for a three month voyage to West Africa.

1882

Renounces Roman Catholic faith.

Summer
Joins the medical practice of Dr. Budd in Plymouth.

June 24
Arrives in Southsea.

July 1
Sets up his own practice at 1 Bush Villas, Southsea.

1885

May
Charles Doyle committed to Montrose Royal Lunatic Asylum.

July
ACD graduates with MD from University of Edinburgh.

August 6
Marries Louisa (Touie) Hawkins.

1886

Begins attending psychic meetings in Southsea.

1887

November
A Study in Scarlet published in *Beeton's Christmas Annual*.

1889

January 23
Birth of Mary Louise Conan Doyle, daughter of ACD and Louise.

February
Micah Clarke published.

August 30
Attends a dinner with J. M. Stoddart, editor of *Lippincott's Monthly Magazine*, Oscar Wilde, and Irish MP, T. P. Gill, the outcome of which results in ACD writing *The Sign of Four* and Wilde writing *The Picture of Dorian Gray*.

1890

The White Company published.

February
The Sign of Four published in *Lippincott's Monthly Magazine*.

December
First issue of the *Strand Magazine* magazine published.

1891

March
ACD and family move to London, residing at 23 Montague Place, Bloomsbury, with consulting rooms at 2 Upper Wimpole St, where he hoped to practice as an ophthalmologist.

April
ACD's new literary agent, A. P. Watt, sends "A Scandal in Bohemia" to the editor of the *Strand Magazine*.

June
ACD moves to 12 Tennison Rd., South Norwood, Surrey, having given up medicine to become a full-time writer.

July
Sherlock Holmes stories begin appearing in the *Strand Magazine*.

August
The White Company published in America.

October 26
The White Company published in London.

1892

May
Charles Doyle transferred to The Crichton Royal Asylum, Dumfries.

October 14
The Adventures of Sherlock Holmes published by George Newnes, Ltd., London.

November 16
Birth of Arthur Alleyne Kingsley Conan Doyle, son of ACD and Louise.

1893

ACD becomes a member the Society of Psychical Research.

Summer
ACD and Louise on tour in Switzerland and visit the Reichenbach Falls near Meiringen.
Louise diagnosed with pulmonary tuberculosis.

October 10
Charles Doyle dies at The Crichton Royal Asylum, Dumfries, age 61.

Autumn
ACD and Louise return to Switzerland where the climate was said to be beneficial to consumptives.

December
ACD kills off Sherlock Holmes when "The Final Problem" appears in the *Strand*.

December 13
The Memoirs of Sherlock Holmes published by George Newnes, Ltd., London.

1894

September 23
ACD, accompanied by his brother Innes, sails for a lecture tour of America, returning on December 15.

December
ACD joins his family in Davos, Switzerland.

1895

ACD and Louise spend most of the year in Switzerland.

November
They both travel to Egypt.

1896

April
Returned from Egypt.

May
The Doyles reside at Grayswood Beeches, Haslemere, while their new house, Undershaw, is being built.

1897

March
ACD meets Jean Leckie whom he later marries.

Autumn
ACD and family move into their new home, Undershaw, at Hindhead.

1898

Actor and playwright William Gillette begins performing as Sherlock Holmes.

October 11
Start of the Boer War.

December
ACD volunteers for active service, but is rejected due to his age.

1900

February
ACD sails for South Africa with private field hospital.

September 24
ACD nominated Central Edinburgh's candidate for the Liberal Unionist Party.

1901

August
The Hound of the Baskervilles is serialized in the *Strand Magazine*.

September 9
William Gillette performs *Sherlock Holmes* at London's Lyceum Theatre.

1902

ACD awarded knighthood at Buckingham Palace.

1905

December 30
ACD nominated Unionist candidate for the Border Burghs.

1906

July 4
ACD's wife, Louise, dies, age 49.

December
ACD defends George Edalji.

1907

September 18
ACD marries Jean Leckie.

November 30
ACD and Jean settle in Crowborough, Sussex.

1908

January 28
Death of Sidney Paget, age 47.

1909

March 17
Birth of Denis Percy Stewart Conan Doyle, son of ACD and Jean.

1910

November 19
Birth of Adrian Malcolm Conan Doyle, son of ACD and Jean.

1911

October 4
Death of Joseph Bell age 73.

1912

August
ACD attacks the conviction of Oscar Slater with the publication of a booklet condemning the justice of the verdict.

December 21
Birth of Lena Jean Annette Conan Doyle, daughter of ACD and Jean.

1914

May 27
ACD and Jean embark for a lecture tour of the USA and Canada.

August 4
Outbreak of World War I.

1916

ACD announces conversion to Spiritualism.

1918

October 28
ACD's son Kingsley dies of pneumonia.

1919

February 19
ACD's brother Innes dies of pneumonia.

1920

June
ACD becomes fascinated with the Cottingley fairy photographs.

September 17
ACD and family depart for a lecture tour of Australia.

December 30
ACD's mother dies, age 83.

1922

April 9
ACD and family embark for a lecture tour of the USA and Canada.

1923

April 3
ACD and family embark for a further lecture tour of the USA and Canada.

October
ACD's autobiography *Memories and Adventures* serialized in the *Strand Magazine*.

1925

ACD opens the Psychic Bookshop in London.

1927

April
The last Sherlock Holmes story, *The Adventure of Shoscombe Old Place* is published.

1928

November 12
ACD and family embark for a lecture tour of South Africa, Rhodesia and Kenya.

October
ACD lectures in the Netherlands, Denmark, Sweden and Norway.

1930

June
His final work, *The Edge of the Unknown*, published.

July 7
ACD suffers a heart attack and dies, age 71.

Appendix 2.
Residences of Arthur Conan Doyle

Edinburgh

11 Picardy Place

Birthplace of Arthur Conan Doyle on 22 May 1859. Built in 1809, Picardy Place was named after a colony of French Huguenots who settled in the area in the late 17th century. The north side of Picardy Place, including Conan Doyle's birthplace, was demolished in 1969 to make way for a major traffic junction.

Tower Bank House

Also known as 3 Tower Bank, the Doyle family moved here in c1861–62. The house has since been demolished and the street name changed to Figgate Bank in 1966. The area, known as Portobello, was a popular Edinburgh seaside resort.

Liberton Bank House

In 1865 Conan Doyle was sent to stay with his mother's friend Mary Burton at Liberton Bank, probably to distance him from his alcoholic father. Built c1780, the house is now part of a school teaching children with special needs. From here he attended school at Newington Academy at 8 Salisbury Place.

3 Sciennes Gardens

The Doyle family moved into this tenement flat in c1867–8. Conan Doyle was still attending Newington Academy, which was now considerably closer.

2 Argyle Park Terrace

From 1868 to 1875 Conan Doyle attended Stonyhurst College in Lancashire. During his final year at Stonyhurst, in 1875, the Doyle family moved to 2 Argyle Park Terrace on the southern fringe of a large public park known as The Meadows. It was from this address that Conan Doyle began his medical studies at the University of Edinburgh in October 1876.

23 George Square

In 1877 the Doyles moved to the northern edge of The Meadows to reside at 23 George Square.

15 Lonsdale Terrace

The Doyle family resided here, on the west side of the Meadows, from 1881 until 1882, until Conan Doyle's mother, brother and sisters moved to a cottage on the Masongill estate in Yorkshire.

Sheffield

Corner of Spital Hill and Hallcar Street

In April 1878 Conan Doyle was hired as an assistant to Dr. Charles Richardson, a post he occupied for just three weeks, parting "by mutual consent." Today the premises are occupied by a cafe.

Ruyton-Xi-Towns

Cliffe House

For the remaining summer of 1878, Conan Doyle was assistant to Dr. Henry Francis Elliot in the village of Ruyton in the Welsh Marches.

Birmingham

63 Aston Road North

During the summer of 1879 Conan Doyle worked as student assistant to Dr. Reginald Ratcliff Hoare in the parish of Aston, now a completely rebuilt inner-city area of the City of Birmingham.

Plymouth

6 Elliot Terrace

In the early summer of 1882, Conan Doyle was invited to join the practice of his friend and university classmate, Dr. George Budd, in Plymouth. Conan Doyle's lodgings were at Elliot Terrace, home of the Budd family.

Southsea

1 Bush Villas

After his partnership with Budd failed, Conan Doyle moved to Southsea on 24 June 1882, and started his own practice at Bush Villas where he lived and worked for the next eight years. The building was destroyed during World War II and a block of flats now stands on the site.

London

23 Montague Place

In March 1891 Conan Doyle set himself up as an ophthalmologist in consulting rooms at 2 Upper Wimpole Street, residing in a flat at Montague Place with his wife Touie and daughter Mary.

12 Tennison Road

In June of 1891, having given up medicine to concentrate on writing, Conan Doyle purchased a house in South Norwood.

15 Buckingham Palace Mansions

While living in Crowborough in 1922, Conan Doyle purchased a flat on Buckingham Palace Road, adjacent to Victoria Station. The area was redeveloped in the 1970s and the office block Belgrave House now occupies the site.

Surrey

Grayswood Beeches

After extensive traveling, the Doyles decided to settle in Surrey; and while their new house was being built, they leased a house called Grayswood Beeches in Haslemere in May 1896.

Undershaw

The Doyles moved into their newly-built home named "Undershaw" on the Portsmouth Road, Hindhead, in the fall of 1897.

East Sussex

Windlesham

Following the death of his wife, Louise, in 1906 and his marriage to Jean Leckie the following year, Conan Doyle and his family settled in Windlesham, a large house at Hurtis Hill, Crowborough, in November 1907. He lived here until his death in 1930.

Hampshire

Bignell Wood

In the autumn of 1925 Conan Doyle purchased a country retreat in the New Forest near Minstead, called Bignell Wood.

Appendix 3.
The Family of Arthur Conan Doyle

Maternal Grandparents

William Foley (1809–40)
Married 24 April 1835 to Catherine Pack (1809–62)

Children
Thomas Scott Foley (1836–?)
Mary Josephine Elizabeth Foley (1837–1920)
Catherine Mary Agnes Mulin Foley (1839–?)

Paternal Grandparents

John Doyle (1797–1868)
Married 13 February 1820 to Marianne Conan (1794/95–1839)

Children
Ann Martha Doyle (1821–99)
James William Edmund Doyle (1822–92)
Richard Doyle (1824–83)
Henry Edward Doyle (1827–92)
Francis Doyle (1828?–43?)
Adelaide Doyle (1830/31–44)
Charles Altamount Doyle (1832–93)

Parents

Charles Altamount Doyle
Married 31 July 1855 to Mary Josephine Elizabeth Foley

Children
Anne Mary Frances Doyle (1856–90)
Catherine Amelia Angela Doyle (1858–58)
Arthur Conan Doyle (1859–1930)
Mary Helena Monica Harriet Doyle (1861–63)
Caroline Mary Burton Doyle (1866–1941)
Constance Amelia Monica Doyle (1868–1924)
John Francis Innes Hay Doyle (1873–1919)
Jane Adelaide Rose Doyle (1875–1937)
Bryan Mary Julia Josephine Doyle (1877–1927)

Arthur Conan Doyle

Married 6 August 1885 to Louise Hawkins (1857–1906)

Children
Mary Louise Conan Doyle (1889–1976)
Arthur Alleyne Kingsley Conan Doyle (1892–1918)

Married 18 September 1907 to Jean Elizabeth Leckie (1874–1940)

Children
Denis Percy Stewart Conan Doyle (1909–55)
Adrian Malcolm Conan Doyle (1910–70)
Lena Jean Annette Conan Doyle (1912–97)

Appendix 4.
Selected Works and Collections of Arthur Conan Doyle

Sherlock Holmes

A Study in Scarlet (1887)
The Sign of Four (1890)
The Adventures of Sherlock Holmes (1892, short story collection)
The Memoirs of Sherlock Holmes (1893, short story collection)
The Hound of the Baskervilles (1902)
The Return of Sherlock Holmes (1905, short story collection)
The Valley of Fear (1915)
His Last Bow (1917, short story collection)
The Casebook of Sherlock Holmes (1927, short story collection)

Novels, Collected Stories, Plays, and Poetry

The Mystery of Cloomber (1888)
Micah Clarke (1889)
Mysteries and Adventures (1889)
The Captain of the Polestar and Other Tales (1890)
The Firm of Girdlestone: A Romance of the Unromantic (1890)
The White Company (1891)
The Doings of Raffles Haw (1892)
The Great Shadow (1892)
The Refugees: A Tale of Two Continents (1893)
Round the Red Lamp: Being Facts and Fancies of a Medical Life (1894)
The Parasite (1894)
The Stark Munro Letters (1895)
The Exploits of Brigadier Gerard (1896)
Rodney Stone (1896)
Uncle Bernac: A Memory of the Empire (1897)
The Tragedy of Korosko (1898)
Songs of Action (1898, poetry)

A Duet, with an Occasional Chorus (1899)
The Green Flag and Other Stories of War and Sport (1900)
The Adventures of Gerard (1903)
Sir Nigel (1906)
The Croxley Master (1907)
The Story of Waterloo (1907, play)
Round the Fire Stories (1908)
Songs of the Road (1911, poetry)
The Last Galley: Impressions and Tales (1911)
The Lost World (1912)
The Poison Belt (1913)
Danger! And Other Stories (1918)
The Guards Came Through and Other Poems (1919)
The Poems of Arthur Conan Doyle—Collected Edition (1922)
The Land of Mist (1926)
The Maracot Deep and Other Stories (1929)

Nonfiction

The Great Boer War (1900)
The War in South Africa—Its Cause and Conduct (1902)
"The Case of Mr. George Edalji" (1907, pamphlet)
Through the Magic Door (1907)
The Crime of the Congo (1909)
"The Case of Oscar Slater" (1912, pamphlet)
"Great Britain and the Next War" (1914, pamphlet)
"In Quest of Truth: Being a Correspondence between Sir Arthur Conan Doyle and Captain (Hubert) Stansbury" (1914, pamphlet)
Western Wanderings (1915)
The British Campaign in France and Flanders (1916)
A Visit to Three Fronts (1916)
The New Revelation: or, What Is Spiritualism? (1918)
The Vital Message (1919)

The Wanderings of a Spiritualist (1921)
The Coming of Fairies (1922)
The Case for Spirit Photography (1922, with others)
Three of Them. A Reminiscence (1923)
Our American Adventure (1923)
Our Second American Adventures (1924)
Memories and Adventures (1924)
The History of Spiritualism (1926)
Pheneas Speaks (1927)
Our African Winter (1929)
The Edge of the Unknown (1930)

University of Minnesota Library: The Sherlock Holmes Collections

The Sherlock Holmes Collections at the University of Minnesota Library constitute the world's largest gathering of material related to Sherlock Holmes and his creator, Sir Arthur Conan Doyle. The Collections consist of over 15,000 items including books, journals, and a wide variety of other forms through which the transformation of the Holmes character from the printed page to a cultural icon can be traced. The Sherlockian materials within the Collections include: artifacts, audio and video recordings, books, journals, license plates, manuscripts, motion pictures and film strips, musical scores, original artwork, periodicals, personal papers and libraries, playbills, posters, radio scripts and original recordings, scrapbooks, statuary, T-shirts, theatrical programs, toys and games.

The Sherlock Holmes Collections began in 1974 with the purchase of James C. Iraldi's small but distinguished library of first editions of the Holmes stories by Sir Arthur Conan Doyle. Thus, the University of Minnesota Library has been building the Sherlock Holmes Collections for more than thirty years. Direct purchases and generous donations have helped the Collections to reach their current size and comprehensiveness.

Two of the more important collections of the many that have been added since 1974 are those of Philip S. Hench and John Bennett Shaw.

Philip S. Hench, MD, was a Mayo Clinic consulting physician and a recipient of the Nobel Prize for medicine (1950), who, with his wife Mary Kahler Hench, built one of the more remarkable Sherlockian libraries ever assembled. The treasures of the Hench library include: unique copies of *Beeton's Christmas Annual* (1887) containing *A Study in Scarlet*, the first Sherlock Holmes adventure; English and American first editions of the stories; plus material related to Sir Arthur Conan Doyle, William Gillette, and Frederic Dorr Steele.

John Bennett Shaw, an entrepreneur from Santa Fe, New Mexico attempted to collect *everything* on or about Sherlock Holmes and nearly succeeded. The Shaw Collection is the most diverse, with items running the gamut from books to stuffed animals.

For more information on the history of the collection, see Timothy J. Johnson, "The Adventure of the Unopened Box: Building the Sherlock Holmes Collections at the University of Minnesota Libraries," *Collection Management* 29, no. 3–4 (2004):121–141.

Using the Collections

The materials in the Sherlock Holmes Collections do not circulate outside of the reading room of the Special Collections and Rare Books Department. Photocopying is available and is subject to applicable copyright laws. Before visiting the Collections in person, please make an appointment with the Collection Specialist for the Sherlock Holmes Collections at the address below.

Sherlock Holmes Collections
111 Elmer L. Andersen Library
222 21st Avenue South
Minneapolis, MN 55455
612-624-3552
www.lib.umn.edu/

Bibliography

Baker, Michael, ed. *The Doyle Diary*. London: Paddington Press, 1978.

Barnes, Julian. *Arthur & George*. London: Vintage, 2006.

Bergem, Phillip G. *The Family and Residences of Arthur Conan Doyle*. St. Paul, MN: Picardy Place Press, 2003.

Booth, Bradford A., and Ernest Mehew. *The Letters of Robert Louis Stevenson*. New Haven: Yale University Press, 1994–1995.

Booth, Martin. *The Doctor, The Detective & Arthur Conan Doyle*. London: Hodder & Stoughton, 1997.

Caesar, Gene. *Incredible Detective*. New York: Prentice-Hall, 1968.

Carr, John Dickson. *The Life of Sir Arthur Conan Doyle*. London: John Murray, 1949.

Chaney, Lisa. *Hide-and-Seek with Angels: A Life of J.M. Barrie*. London: Hutchinson, 2005.

Collin, B.M. *J.P. Hornung: A Family Portrait*. Orpington, Kent: Orpington Press, 1970.

Conan Doyle, Adrian. *The True Conan Doyle*. London: John Murray, 1945.

_____, ed. *Sir Arthur Conan Doyle Centenary, 1859–1959*. London: John Murray, 1959.

Conan Doyle, Arthur, and John Michael Gibson and Richard Lancelyn Green, eds. *Essays on Photography*. London: Secker and Warburg, 1982.

Cooper, Joe. *The Case of the Cottingley Fairies*. London: Robert Hale, 1990.

Costello, Peter. *Conan Doyle, Detective*. London: Constable & Robinson, 2006.

Doyle, Georgina. *Out of the Shadows: The Untold Story of Arthur Conan Doyle's First Family*. Ashcroft, British Columbia: Ash Tree Press, 2004.

Duncan, Alistair. *Close to Holmes*. London: MX, 2009.

Edwards, Owen Dudley. *The Quest for Sherlock Holmes*. Edinburgh: Mainstream, 1983.

Engen, Rodney. *Richard Doyle*. Stroud, Gloucester: Catalpa Press, 1983.

Finkelstein, David. *The House of Blackwood*. University Park: Pennsylvania State University Press, 2002.

Highman, Charles. *The Adventures of Conan Doyle*. London: Hamish Hamilton, 1976.

House, Jack. *Square Mile of Murder*. Edinburgh: Black & White, 2002.

Inglis, Brian. *Roger Casement*. London: Penguin, 2002.

Jackson, Kate. *George Newnes and the New Journalism in Britain 1880–1910 Culture and Profit*. Farnham, Surrey: Ashgate, 2001.

Jones, Kelvin I. *Conan Doyle and the Spirits Aquarian*. Wellingborough, Northamptonshire: Aquarian Press, 1989.

Lamond, John. *Arthur Conan Doyle: A Memoir*. London: John Murray, 1931.

Lancelyn Green, Richard. *The Uncollected Sherlock Holmes*. London: Penguin, 1983.

_____, ed. *Letters to Sherlock Holmes*. London: Penguin, 1985.

_____, and John Michael Gibson. *A Bibliography of A. Conan Doyle*. Oxford: Clarendon Press, 1983.

Lellenberg, Jon, ed. *The Quest for Sir Arthur Conan Doyle*. Carbondale: South Illinois University Press, 1987.

Lellenberg, J., D. Stashower, and C. Foley, eds. *Arthur Conan Doyle: A Life in Letters*. London: Harper Press, 2007.

Liebow, Ely. *Dr. Joe Bell*. Bowling Green, OH: Bowling Green University Popular Press, 1982.

Mackaill, Alan, and Dawn Kemp. *Conan Doyle and Joseph Bell: The Real Sherlock Holmes*. Edinburgh: Royal College of Surgeons of Edinburgh, 2007.

Mackay, James. *Allan Pinkerton: The Eye Who Never Slept*. Edinburgh: Mainstream, 1996.

Nordon, Pierre. *Conan Doyle*. London: John Murray, 1966.

Pearsall, Ronald. *Conan Doyle: A Biographical Solution*. New York: St. Martin's Press, 1977.

Pearson, Hesketh. *Conan Doyle: His Life and Art*. London: Methuen, 1943.

Pound, Reginald. *The Strand Magazine 1891–1950*. London: Heinemann, 1966.

Pugh, Brian. *Buzzin in Sussex: An Investigation into the Connections of Sir Arthur Conan Doyle, His Family and Sherlock Holmes in Crowborough, Lewes, Newhaven, Seaford and Eastbourne*. East Sussex: Conan Doyle (Crowborough) Establishment, 2005.

_____. *A Chronology of the Life of Sir Arthur Conan Doyle.* London: MX, 2009.

Pugh, Brian W., and Paul R. Spiring. *On the Trail of Arthur Conan Doyle: An Illustrated Devon Tour.* Brighton: Book Guild, 2008.

_____ and _____. *Bertram Fletcher Robinson: A Footnote to The Hound of the Baskervilles.* London: MX, 2008.

Redmond, Christopher. *Welcome to America, Mr. Sherlock Holmes.* Toronto: Simon and Pierre, 1987.

Spencer, Frank, ed. *The Piltdown Papers 1908–55.* Oxford: Oxford University Press, 1990.

Stashower, Daniel. *Teller of Tales: The Life of Arthur Conan Doyle.* New York: Holt, 1999.

Stavert, Geoffrey. *A Study in Southsea.* Portsmouth: Milestone Publications, 1987.

Turner, A. Logan. *Story of a Great Hospital: The Royal Infirmary of Edinburgh 1729–1929.* Edinburgh: Oliver and Boyd, 1937.

Wagner, E.J. *The Science of Sherlock Holmes.* New York: John Wiley, 2007.

Waller, Bryan Charles. *The Twilight Land and Other Poems.* London: George Bell, 1875.

Weller, Philip. *The Hound of the Baskervilles: Hunting the Dartmoor Legend.* Tiverton: Devon Books, 2001.

Wynne, Catherine. *The Colonial Conan Doyle.* Westport, CT: Greenwood Press, 2002.

Index